REACHING ACROSS BORDERLINES

REACHING ACROSS BORDERLINES

Collected Essays From
the University of North Carolina Wilmington
and International Islamic University, Islamabad,
Department of State Partnership

EDITED BY

Diana Ashe and Caroline Clements

PUBLISHED BY UNIVERSITY OF NORTH CAROLINA WILMINGTON
WILLIAM MADISON RANDALL LIBRARY

Copyright ©2022 Caroline Clements
All rights reserved

This work is licensed under a Creative Commons CC BY-NC-ND license. To view a copy of the license, visit http://creativecommons.org/licenses.

Suggested citation: Ashe, D., & Clements, C. (Eds.). (2022). *Reaching across borderlines: Collected essays from the UNCW-IIUI Department of State partnership*. University of North Carolina Wilmington William Madison Randall Library.

https://doi.org/10.5149/9781469672854_Ashe

Library of Congress Cataloging-in-Publication Data
Names: Ashe, Diana, editor. | Clements, Caroline, editor. | University of North Carolina, Wilmington, sponsoring body. | International Islamic University (Islāmābād, Pakistan), sponsoring body.
Title: Reaching across borderlines : collected essays from the University of North Carolina Wilmington and International Islamic University, Islamabad, Department of State partnership / edited by Diana Ashe and Caroline Clements.
Other titles: Collected essays from the University of North Carolina Wilmington and International Islamic University, Islamabad, Department of State partnership
Description: [Wilmington, NC] : University of North Carolina Wilmington William Madison Randall Library, [2022] | "These labors bore fruit in the form of two international conferences, one at UNCW and one at IIUI, and in the form of this volume ... The essays in this volume were bright lights at those conferences and serve as artifacts of a scholarly experience"-Page 14. | Includes bibliographical references.
Identifiers: LCCN 2022030804 | ISBN 9781469672847 (paperback) | ISBN 9781469672854 (ebook ; open access)
Subjects: LCSH: International relations—Congresses. | Globalization—Congresses. | English literature—History and criticism—Congresses. | Cultural relations—Congresses. | Education and globalization—Congresses. | South Asia—Colonial influence—Congresses. | LCGFT: Essays.
Classification: LCC JZ1242 .R398 2022 | DDC 327—dc23/eng/20220805
LC record available at https://lccn.loc.gov/2022030804

CONTENTS

viii Acknowledgments

xi Preface From Wilmington: A Transformational Partnership
CAROLINE CLEMENTS AND DIANA ASHE

xix Preface From Islamabad: The IIUI–UNCW Link From Partnership to Friendship
MUHAMMAD SHEERAZ

SECTION I
1 **Literary and Textual Perspectives**

ONE
3 A Moving Empire: François Bernier's Mosques, Mausoleums, and Monuments of 17th-Century Mughal India
PASCALE BARTHE

TWO
19 Colonial Legacy and English Studies
MAHMOOD UL HASSAN

THREE
37 Itinerant Locals and Globals: Hindi Women's Writing in Late 20th-Century Kolkata
RAHUL BJØRN PARSON

FOUR
51 Decentering Religious Traditions: A Deconstructionist Perspective of "Church Going"
IMRAN ADEEL

FIVE
63 A Dialogic Approach to Human Relations in Moshin Hamid's *The Reluctant Fundamentalist*
UBARAJ KATAWAL

SIX

77 Grace of Strategic Silence in Postcolonial Resettlement: A Study of J. M. Coetzee's *Disgrace*
MUHAMMAD SHAHBAZ ARIF AND FAIZA ANUM

SECTION II

89 **Political, International, and Cultural Relations**

SEVEN

91 Evaluating What We Know About Politics, Political Science, and International Relations: A Cross-Cultural Assessment of Political Science and International Relations Education
AARON S. KING, DANIEL S. MASTERS, J. BENJAMIN TAYLOR, MANZOOR AHMAD, SADAF FAROOQ, AND AMNA MAHMOOD

EIGHT

115 The Post-9/11 Politicization of Sufi Islam and the Rise of Barelvi Extremism in Pakistan
MUHAMMAD SULEMAN

NINE

128 Globalization of Islamic Law: A Muslim Perspective on International Law
MUHAMMAD KHALID MASUD

TEN

139 World Cultural Heritage: Does the World Embrace "World Cultural Heritage"? Evidence From the Online Presence of UNESCO National Commissions
DAVID GRABER

ELEVEN

151 Terrorism and Politics: The Strategic Dimension of the Saudi-Led Islamic Military Alliance
NAEEM QURBAN

TWELVE

170 Pakistan's Role in Interregional Connectivity Between South Asia and Central Asia: Opportunities and Challenges in the Age of Globalization
MANZOOR KHAN AFRIDI

THIRTEEN

179 The Role of Family Systems on Couples' Life Satisfaction and Anxiety Levels
ASMA SHAHEEN AND NAZIA IQBAL

SECTION III

195 **Pedagogy and Our International, Intercultural Classrooms**

FOURTEEN

197 Internationalization of Classrooms Through Cultural Hybridity: Pedagogical Design and Challenges
ANIRBAN RAY

FIFTEEN

214 Acculturation, Identity, and Race Relations While Performing Globalization
MICHELE PARKER

SIXTEEN

225 Implications of Urduization in Pakistani English to Comprehend It as a Second Language
HADEEQA SARWAR

SEVENTEEN

237 Rhetorical Listening Across Borders: A Report on Attitudes and Contexts Around English for Academic Purposes at International Islamic University, Islamabad
LANCE CUMMINGS

251 Contributors

ACKNOWLEDGMENTS

The U.S. Department of State created the university partnerships program "to promote increased, long-term, people-to-people ties" through this program and many others. We firmly believe that the partnership between the University of North Carolina Wilmington (UNCW) and the International Islamic University, Islamabad (IIUI) achieved precisely that goal. We will never be able to give enough thanks to the many, many individuals and offices that enabled our international team to reach its goals—and to make this book possible.

First and above all others, we express appreciation to the late Dr. Mumtaz Ahmad, whose support of IIUI, of Pakistan, and of this project resonate even today. He was the initiator and the visionary of the partnership that we celebrate in these pages. We dedicate this volume to his memory and his legacy.

At the Department of State, Richard Boyum, Grachelle Javellana, Afzer Iqbal, and Tanveer Hussan served as our gracious ambassadors and teachers. None of this would have been possible without Nadeem Akbar and Noreen Sher Ali at the American Institute of Pakistan Studies (AIPS). Our friends at the Department of State and AIPS facilitated every aspect of grant-related work. Their contributions to this partnership were incalculable, and we are all better for their advice and guidance.

We are grateful to the countless hours that each institution's steering committee for the partnership contributed. At IIUI, the steering committee included Munawar Iqbal Ahmad (chairman), Manzoor Khan Afridi, Husnul Amin, Ayaz Afsar, Safeer Awan, Noor Fatima, Muhammad Ismail, Muhammad Jamil, Fauzia Janjua, Masood Khatak, Amna Mahmood, Samina Mailk, Shahbaz Malik, and Munazza Yaqoob. We are also grateful to IIUI's highly esteemed rector, Prof. Dr. Masoom Yasinzai, for his generosity and foresight in agreeing to host this partnership and welcome our visiting faculty with so much grace, so many times.

At UNCW, the grant team was led from 2014 to 2016 by Cara Cilano, our initial principal investigator (PI) and founding expert. We are grateful for her guidance, her expertise, and her indomitable spirit. Caroline Clements became our PI after November 2016 and brought extensive experience with large grants to keep us on track. We would like to thank grant team members Florentina Andreescu, Diana Ashe, Jess Boersma, Dan Masters, and Karl Ricanek for, well, everything.

Ensuring that we completed exhaustive assessments and reporting, James DeVita and Bethany Meighen played critical roles in ensuring the success of the project. Graduate students Jeremy Rowley and Victoria Bennett handled innumerable tasks throughout the partnership, becoming valued partners to the grant team. We were lucky to have graduate students Marissa Flanagan, Kaitlyn Patterson, Kate Clauss, Marisa Stickel, and Paul Johnson lending their energies and resources at critical points as well.

At UNCW, we received support for the partnership from every administrator we approached, from the chancellor and the Office of University Relations, to our bookstore and University Learning Center—every door opened to this exciting opportunity to enrich the community.

Within the Wilmington community, we were delighted and appreciative of the work of the Reverend Bob Snell, a Presbyterian minister who provided multiple opportunities for community connections and increased cultural understanding. Wilmington Mayor Bill Saffo and his wife, Renee, were honored guests at a dinner hosted by one of our groups of visiting faculty, and we appreciate his warmth—and their hospitality. We send warm thoughts and gratitude to beloved friend and cricket coach, the late Mark Reilly.

Across the state of North Carolina, faculty developers offered tours, hospitality, and more to our visitors. Some of these partners include Bethany Smith of North Carolina State University; Doug James, then at North Carolina State University (now UNC at Chapel Hill); David Teachout and Laura Pipe of the University of North Carolina Greensboro; Martha Diede, then at Western Carolina University (now Syracuse University); and Eli Collins-Brown, then at Winston-Salem State University (now Western Carolina University).

It is impossible to imagine the partnership working successfully without the support we received from the Office of International Programs, especially from Michael Wilhelm and Jennifer Fernandez-Villa. We are indebted to them both. We are also especially appreciative of Aswani Volety, then dean of the College of Arts and Sciences (now UNCW's chancellor); Martin Posey, then dean of Undergraduate Studies; Denise Battles, provost at the start of the project; Marilyn Sheerer, provost later in the project; and Jose Sartarelli, then chancellor, for their support of the project.

The Sponsored Programs and Research Compliance Office at UNCW helped us at every step as well. We are grateful for their diligence.

Many of our colleagues at UNCW played additional roles that made the partnership better. Sohail Sukhera served as our cultural liaison; we are indebted to him for both his encyclopedic knowledge and his patience. Several colleagues partnered as research mentors for our visitors from IIUI, including Florentina Andreescu, Gao Bei, Herb Berg, Greta Bliss, Susan Catapano, Lance Cummings, James DeVita, David Gilmartin, Paula Kamenish, Remy Kleinberg, Victor Malo-Juvera, and Dan Masters.

Other colleagues were involved in conference planning, visiting IIUI, essay review, and on-campus projects that helped us meet the objectives of the project and ensure a stronger and longer-lasting partnership. Those colleagues include Pascale Barthe, Greta Bliss, Susan Catapano, Lance Cummings, Ben Taylor, Michele Parker, and Anirban Ray. Our IIUI friends and colleagues who assisted in these ways include Manzoor Ahmad, Munawar Ahmad, Saiyma Aslam, Amna Mahmood, Farrukh Nadeem, Nighat Shakur, and Muhammad Sheeraz.

To try to list and thank our Pakistani partners—now friends—would be impossible. We are changed forever by them. Each cohort of visitors was patient and gracious as we learned along the way how to handle the logistics of long- and short-term visits—and each of them became treasured colleagues and friends. We owe a lifetime of gratitude to Manzoor Khan Afridi, Ayaz Afsar, Rizwan Aftab, Manzoor Ahmad, Munawar Ahmad, Husnul Amin, Saiyma Aslam, Muhammad Safeer Awan, Nadia Awan, Akhtar Aziz, Ahsan Bashir, Sadaf Farooq, Noor Fatima, Mahmood ul Hassan, Sofia Hussain, Zulfqar Hyder, Nazia Iqbal, Sonia Irum, Fauzia Janjua, Salma Kalim, Aroosa Kanwal, Masood ur Rehman Khatak, Amna Mahmood, Kashif Suhail Malik, Farrukh Nadeem, Waheeda Rana, Asma Rashid, Nazir Sangi, Tauqeer Sargana, Amal Sayyid, Nighat Shakur, Komal Shazadi, Muhammad Sheeraz, Tanzeela Waqar, and Munazza Yaqoob.

In addition to all of these wonderful people who enriched and strengthened our partnership, all of the grant team members would like to thank the students in both universities for their curiosity and engagement in this project. We feel perhaps the most gratitude of all when we thank our families for helping us make it work and sharing our joy along the way.

PREFACE FROM WILMINGTON | CAROLINE CLEMENTS
AND DIANA ASHE

A Transformational Partnership

The volume in front of you celebrates the work of not only the two dozen scholars whose work is featured on these pages but also the dozens of others who were involved in the important and productive partnership between the University of North Carolina Wilmington (UNCW) and the International Islamic University, Islamabad (IIUI). The partnerships set out to expand faculty teaching expertise at both institutions; to increase individual and departmental research capacities; and to foster and expand student, campus, and regional engagement. The essays in this volume reflect the success of these three objectives and the flourishing of teaching, research, and community connections through this project.

As professors and faculty developers, we were eager to embrace all three objectives from the start. The partnership yielded a tremendous amount of research in its collaborative projects and scholarly conferences, some of which is presented in this volume. What connects each essay is the process through which these essays came to fruition. The process transformed most of its participants, definitely including us. In a sense, this essay is a commentary on the relationships that resulted in the collected essays in this volume.

Our four-year project was underwritten by the U.S. Department of State (DOS), supporting academic partnerships between U.S. and Pakistani universities. The stated purpose of the grant was to invite scholarly exchanges between IIUI professors and UNCW professors in political science and in English as well as to improve pedagogical practice and increase civic engagement in both countries. We also agreed to produce two conferences, one in each country. Our lead grant writer, Dr. Cara Cilano, had extensive expertise in South Asian studies, and, even more fortunately for us, she was the principal investigator as the project began. In 2016, Dr. Caroline Clements became principal investigator when Dr. Cilano accepted a leadership position at Michigan State University.

For each of these objectives, the project brought developments far beyond our initial imaginings over the course of our official partnership. While we would need the space of this entire volume to share all of them, we would like to offer a few highlights in each area that moved the objectives forward powerfully.

Objective 1: Expansion of Faculty Teaching Expertise

Throughout the partnership, we were able to visit one another's classes at both institutions, an especially powerful—and delightful—component of the project. Direct exposure to students and teaching expectations cross-institutionally built our understanding and offered all of us new ideas and ways of thinking. Taking this further, several participants connected students in classes from UNCW and IIUI, offering those students and those faculty a powerful learning experience.

Outside the classroom, deep engagement took place as well. Visitors from IIUI to UNCW participated in workshops given by the Center for Teaching Excellence and the Center for Faculty Leadership, and enhanced our book circles with their expertise and perspective. The grant was able to provide a significant donation of pedagogy-related books for IIUI's library, hoping to build the foundation for a center for teaching and learning on the campus in Islamabad.

An especially exciting element of the teaching component of the partnership was a tour of centers for teaching and learning (CTLs) throughout the state of North Carolina with two of our IIUI colleagues. These explorations of the operations of CTLs of North Carolina State University, University of North Carolina Greensboro, Western Carolina University, and Winston-Salem State University gave us all new ideas and new inspiration. In addition, these visitors were able to attend the Academic Chairpersons Conference in Orlando alongside several of our department heads and learn more about academic leadership training.

Objective 2: Increasing Department and Individual Research Capacities

Our Pakistani colleagues are consummate researchers, and this partnership provided the opportunity for collaborative and innovative research projects to develop. Some of those projects are reflected in this volume, in essays by Lance Cummings (Chapter 17), Aaron King et al. (Chapter 7); and Anirban Ray (Chapter 14). Others are still ongoing and continue to connect our institutions and our nations. Throughout the exchanges, research capacities were expanded by way of panel presentations, invited lectures, shared readings, mentoring, and more. As much as practicable, students were involved in these experiences as well, ensuring the greatest possible reach of the deepest possible ideas. In addition, scholars visiting UNCW were able to work with research librarians and specialists, travel to research libraries, and attend research conferences. The grant project provided mini-grants to support specific projects that would further grant goals, resulting in cross-institutional partnerships and studies.

These labors bore fruit in the form of two international conferences, one at UNCW and one at IIUI, and in the form of this volume. The conferences featured keynote speakers, concurrent sessions, international travel, and tremendous opportunity to connect with thought leaders from across the world. The essays in this volume were bright lights at those conferences and serve as artifacts of a scholarly experience.

Objective 3: Foster or Expand Student, Campus, and Regional Engagement

The third objective was perhaps the most fun, of course, and included everything from museum and aquarium visits to book clubs, movie nights, and our once-in-a-lifetime visit to the Taxila World Heritage Site (for more about UNESCO World Heritage Sites, see Chapter 10, "World Cultural Heritage," by David Graber in this volume).

During each of the peer-reviewed, international conferences, community engagement played a very special role. At UNCW, we hosted an imitation Basant Festival that was open to the community. It was a beautiful spring day, and we were sure to include kites, henna painting, and cricket—at which our Pakistani guests easily and utterly ruled the day. At IIUI we were greeted by so many different opportunities to get to know students, faculty, and community members. We went shopping to get proper shalwar kameez for the conference. We especially loved our interfaith dialogue followed by dinner under the stars with our IIUI colleagues and members of the community. We also got to experience an evening of music and dance with an extremely energetic group of students. This allowed us to get to know areas of Pakistan we had yet to explore and made us want to return many more times. To experience many different gorgeous cultures of Pakistan was life changing.

Reverend Bob Snell, a Presbyterian minister, hosted our visitors for a series of conversations with his congregation in Wilmington, to the edification and delight of all. In Islamabad, visits to mosques and to the Christian neighborhood led to parallel conversations. In panel discussions and over readings, we explored these themes of religion, culture, and understanding together.

Artists, musicians, and even a U.S. presidential election provided opportunities to come together in varying configurations and learn more about our differing ways of being in the world—and our much more significant human commonalities.

Exchanges involved a dizzying array of wonderful food—always a medium of cultural exchange—and we were dazzled by the delicacies our Pakistani colleagues shared with us. Sharing meals or lingering over coffee or tea eased us into conversations that cemented true friendship and cleared up misunderstanding better than almost anything else. While many very special activities were planned for visitors at both institutions, some of the highest quality engagement would often result from our conversations during informal, less choreographed moments.

The justifiable pride our colleagues place in their scholarly and teaching endeavors transforms their students' lives in ways unknown to most U.S. college students. We quickly came to admire our colleagues for these and so many other reasons—and to admire the beauty of Pakistan and its culture, the richness of its literature and history, and the warmth and friendship of its people. We are delighted to share these essays as a remembrance of the journey we took together and in hopes that we will find ways to journey together again someday. We are lucky to have formed fierce friendships along the way. I hope you are informed by the level of scholarship in this volume. It reflects the best of Pakistan and of our partnership, which flourished because of the incredible people involved.

The Resulting Collection of Essays

Section I. Literary and Textual Perspectives

The six essays featured in the section "Literary and Textual Perspectives" consider contrasts and anxieties amid heteroglossia and multivocality. Pascale Barthe takes us back several centuries in "A Moving Empire: François Bernier's Mosques, Mausoleums, and Monuments of 17th-Century Mughal India." Barthe demonstrates nuance in Bernier's writings that evidence early reactions of colonizers to Mughal India—and influences of Indian culture and architecture on Bernier and his thinking as well. In "Colonial Legacy and English Studies," Mahmood ul Hassan performs content analysis on syllabi in

Pakistani university master's courses in English literature and surveys faculty and students to examine the influence of British colonial rule on current curricula. His results enable him to make important recommendations for the expansion of reading lists, methodologies, and curricula to refocus literary study and thought. One example of expanded reading might be the novels in Rahul Bjørn Parson's "Itinerant Locals and Globals: Hindi Women's Writing in Late 20th-Century Kolkata." Parson draws our attention to the novels of Marwari women as "ways in which we can find the local anchors in the moment of global culture," demonstrating the many ways these migrants "challenge the creeping homogenization" of their new homeplace. By contrast, Imran Adeel relies on deconstructionist methods in "Decentering Religious Traditions: A Deconstructionist Perspective of 'Church Going,'" examining Philip Larkin's poem for its tensions and anxieties of a linguistic variety.

Ubaraj Katawal's "Dialogic Approach to Human Relations in Moshin Hamid's *The Reluctant Fundamentalist*" explores the novel's representation of the power of dialogic human relations in creating profound new understanding across divides—even when one half of the dialogue does not speak. Silence is also in focus in Muhammad Shahbaz Arif and Faiza Anum's "Grace of Strategic Silence in Postcolonial Resettlement: A Study of J. M. Coetzee's *Disgrace*." Arif and Anum argue that Coetzee uses silence "as an effective strategy that theorizes the possibility of resettlement, not only in the ethical domain but personal, economic, and political domains as well."

All these essays, when taken together, offer us insight into how difference and distance—both geographic and cultural—can amplify and distort anxieties and tensions; these essays offer us powerful ways of understanding and even overcoming these anxieties as well.

Section II. Political, International, and Cultural Relations

The political science section of the anthology brings together a collection of individual as well as collaborative essays, from authors associated with both UNCW and IIUI. The topics explored are of great relevance for both the United States and Pakistan. They range from comparatively assessing cross-cultural education in political science, understanding the role of Islam in global politics, a political investigation into the concept of "world cultural heritage," and an exploration of terrorism and politics, to finally a discussion of regional integration.

The section commences with an essay titled "Evaluating What We Know About Politics, Political Science, and International Relations: A Cross-Cultural Assessment of Political Science and International Relations

Education," written as a collaborative project involving three scholars, Aaron S. King, Daniel S. Masters, and J. Benjamin Taylor, teaching at UNCW, and three scholars, Manzoor Ahmad, Sadaf Farooq, and Amna Mahmood, associated with IIUI. The essay analyzes the results of a survey aimed at measuring both IIUI and UNCW students' perception of the fields of political science and international relations. Additionally, the authors assess students' awareness of and attitudes toward current events within the United States and Pakistan. This focus on current events evaluates general political knowledge in a domestic and cross-national context. Based on their findings and assessment, the authors offer suggestions on how to improve the quality of classroom instruction, deepen students' understanding of global politics, and encourage cross-cultural dialogue.

The following essay, written by Muhammad Suleman, brings into focus the post-9/11 politicization of Sufi Islam and the rise of Barelvi extremism in Pakistan. Suleman argues that to counterweight religious extremism, the Musharraf regime decided to promote Sufi Islam, as it was perceived to be generally tolerant and pluralistic. For this reason, it established a National Council for the Promotion of Sufism. As pro-Sufi religious groups were encouraged and supported in Pakistan, the generally peaceful school of thought began to be associated with violent elements. In this context, Suleman's essay explores the institutionalization of Sufi Islam as a mechanism to counter religiously radical mindsets and further evaluates the causes and effects of the emergence of violent extremism among its clerics and followers of the Barelvi school of thought. Bringing into focus another aspect of the exploration of Islam in global politics, the essay written by Muhammad Khalid Masud discusses the extent to which international human rights law established global standards against religious, cultural, and gender discrimination. Masud notes that Muslims were singularized for requesting exceptions on behalf of Sharia in international law. Consequently, Masud argues, the globalization of universal human rights, international conventions, and treaties relating to judicialization and legality of women rights, protection, custody of children, marriage, divorce, and inheritance are to be considered and studied as clashes between global and local.

Delving into the intricate connections between politics and culture, David Graber's essay explores the extent to which various governments embrace the concept of "world cultural heritage." Graber pays special attention to the

UNESCO World Heritage Program, created to conserve world sites of outstanding value. His study applies a set of criteria to the websites that each National Commission to UNESCO is encouraged to provide and finds that approximately 75%–80% of the world's countries do not fully embrace the concept of "world cultural heritage." Graber concludes that many countries prioritize national concerns and domestic economic interests over the cosmopolitan ideal of promoting "world cultural heritage."

Moving from a cultural analysis to a discussion of terrorism and politics, Naeem Qurban's essay investigates the establishment, under Saudi Arabia's leadership, of the Islamic alliance to counter terrorism. Qurban notes that the Saudi-led coalition has been criticized for not including Iran. In this context, Qurban engages with the Riyadh summit and its achievements; Saudi Arabia's efforts to counter terrorism and radical Islamists in the Middle East; the various ways in which Iran could influence the Saudi-led coalition; as well as the role played by Pakistan in this coalition.

Transitioning from the discussion of terrorism to an equally important conversation of regional integration, Manzoor Khan Afridi's essay elaborates on Pakistan's role in the interregional connectivity between South Asia and Central Asia. Afridi argues that both South Asia and Central Asia can attain significant profits from regional integration, as Central Asia has massive energy reserves that can be used to fuel South Asian economies. Taking advantage of its unique geographic location and the China Pakistan Economic Corridor program, Pakistan could potentially connect the regions of Central and South Asia. Afridi identifies the Indo–Pak rivalry and their tendency to define national interests through traditional realist perspectives as a major hurdle in linking the two regions.

The following essay moves us from the political to a cultural exploration of Pakistani society, focusing on gender. Asma Shaheen and Nazia Iqbal's essay, focusing on the area of Islamabad and Rawalpindi, investigates the life satisfaction and anxiety levels of couples living in either nuclear or joint family systems. Their research results show that nuclear family systems scored significantly higher regarding life satisfaction, compared to the joint family system. Joint family systems scored significantly higher on anxiety, compared to nuclear family systems. Furthermore, Shaheen and Iqbal find that gender plays an important role in the study, as men and women from joint and nuclear family systems differ in life satisfaction and anxiety levels.

Section III. Pedagogy and Our International, Intercultural Classrooms

The four essays of the pedagogy section address issues that arise when we consider our teaching challenges on a more global stage. In "Internationalization of Classrooms Through Cultural Hybridity: Pedagogical Design and Challenges," for example, Anirban Ray offers two case studies that detail the complexity of relationships and transactions that are necessary for successful international collaborations across classrooms. Ray examines the level of internationalization in each experience and the curricular challenges experienced along the way as he examines both the sustainability and the importance of such projects. Michele Parker asks us to consider the implications of these very same challenges in her essay, "Acculturation, Identity, and Race Relations While Performing Globalization," reminding all of us of the importance of incorporating thoughtful and reflective practices into our work as we grapple with the implications of our own identities and our students' realities. Hadeeqa Sarwar's "Implications of Urduization in Pakistani English to Comprehend It as a Second Language" offers one example of this kind of thoughtful reexamination: Sarwar contends that rethinking our teaching of language serves our students' learning needs more expeditiously than standard practice would have us believe. In other words, a careful reflection on the students' realities makes us better teachers. Likewise, Lance Cummings focuses on a specific type of English in his study, "Rhetorical Listening Across Borders: A Report on Attitudes and Contexts Around English for Academic Purposes at International Islamic University, Islamabad." Cummings's surveys, focus groups, and literature review all reinforce the idea that internationalization thrives by understanding and appreciating local contexts first.

While the essays in this collection reflect many perspectives, sometimes very far from our own, we are honored and delighted to share them—and appreciate the opportunity to learn from them all. Thank you for joining us on this journey!

PREFACE FROM ISLAMABAD | **MUHAMMAD SHEERAZ**

The IIUI–UNCW Link From Partnership to Friendship

Sponsored by the U.S. Department of State, the International Islamic University, Islamabad (IIUI) and University of North Carolina Wilmington (UNCW) Partnership was, without a doubt, the best collaborative project we have ever had at the Departments of English and Politics and International Relations of IIUI. With the unmatched commitment of the UNCW grant team and the IIUI steering committee, the partnership was highly successful. For the IIUI faculty and students, it was useful in numerous ways. It helped us develop our professional skills by learning efficient methods and techniques in teaching and research. It helped us enhance our understanding of the American culture and people and cherish the existence of a global citizenship. Through this partnership, we were able to organize conferences, seminars, and panel discussions for our students and faculty. This brought many of us opportunities to go on a residency at UNCW for different time periods and interact with the able academics there. We also guest-lectured and mentored the very enthusiastic students of UNCW. The partnership allowed many of the IIUI faculty visiting UNCW to travel across the East Coast and visit some of the best museums, monuments, libraries, and other tourist and academic attractions. Some of us were also able to share our thoughts with and present the sounds and colors of Pakistan to the broader community in North Carolina. The most rewarding outcome of this partnership was academic collaborations between two institutions, and their faculty and their students.

The IIUI–UNCW Partnership is one of the many gifts that were conceived, conceptualized, and materialized for IIUI in the late Prof. Mumtaz Ahmad's visionary leadership. No tribute can ever pay back the blessings his presence at IIUI brought us. After his very sad and sudden demise in 2016, Prof. Munawar Iqbal Ahmad shouldered the responsibility as chairman of the steering committee. His democratic approach, practical wisdom, and sincere efforts kept the partnership as productive as before. Supported by a team of senior colleagues on the committee—Prof. Ayaz Afsar, Prof. Nabi Bux Jumani,

Prof. Samina Malik, Prof. Amna Mahmood, Dr. Munaza Yaqoob, Dr. Aziz ur Rehman, Dr. Muhammad Safeer Awan, Dr. Husnul Amin, Dr. Noor Fatima, Dr. Fauzia Janjua, Dr. Manzoor Khan Afridi, Mr. Muhammad Jamil, and Mr. Muhammad Ismail—he was able to successfully arrange visits of 32 IIUI faculty members to UNCW, host UNCW colleagues' study and mentoring visits at IIUI, organize a very successful three-day international conference at IIUI, and many more such activities.

At UNCW, the grant team was led by two of the most talented people on the planet: Prof. Cara Cilano and Prof. Caroline Clements. I have seen them working tirelessly for the success of this project. They had to frequently travel back and forth between Pakistan and the United States to give keynotes and workshops, and to discuss and plan programs and activities with the IIUI steering committee. One of the foremost scholars on Pakistani literature, Prof. Cilano's administrative calculus gave the project a system that was followed throughout the partnership years. Her academic acumen helped me and my students think of novel ways of studying literature. Her questions and feedback on the works of students and faculty brought us clarity of ideas. After Prof. Cilano left UNCW to assume her professorship and headship at the Department of English at Michigan State University (and to reclaim her love for the snowy, stormy weather), Prof. Clements became the director of the grant team. A healer of human minds, Prof. Clements's dealings have been pretty saintly. Her ideals turned the IIUI–UNCW Partnership into an IIUI–UNCW Friendship. Along with Prof. Clements, there were some of the friendliest colleagues on the IIUI–UNCW grant team (Dr. Diana Ashe, Dr. Jess Boersma, Dr. Florentina Andreescu, Dr. Karl Ricanek, and Dr. James DeVita) who can never be thanked enough for all they did for the partnership. Hospitable to the core, the larger UNCW and Wilmington community would always come forward to generously welcome the IIUI visitors. I would like to pay my gratitude to: Dr. Robert Anthony Siegel, Dr. Eleni Pappamihiel, Ms. Lisa Coats, Ms. Jen Fernandez-Villa, and Dr. Pascale Barthe from UNCW, and Bob Snell from the First Presbyterian Church of Wilmington. All my IIUI colleagues who visited Wilmington would agree with me that Sohail Sukhera Sahib's presence in Wilmington was a special gift! His Pakistani mannerisms and American etiquette make him a great ambassador of friendship! Hats off to him for his unconditional support of the partnership! Talking of the people on the project, it would be unfair if I don't acknowledge the active role of the students from both the universities: Jeremy Rowley, Paul Ronald Johnston,

Allison Christine Laajala, Paige Marsicano, Dr. Lance Cummings's Rhetoric class, Dr. David Weber's Intercultural Communication class from UNCW, and Muhammad Noman, Munhib Shah, Fawad Khan, Faheem Javed, Yasir Daud, Shah Salman, Shah Usman, Shah Rukh Khan, and Muhammad Waseem from IIUI. I thank you all.

The partnership gave us three years of constant academic activity. In order to help faculty develop their professional skills in teaching and research, the honorable steering committee came up with a comprehensive plan that was endorsed by the UNCW grant team. This plan included lectures, workshops, and talks by the UNCW scholars at IIUI. Prof. Clements, Prof. Cilano, Dr. Diana Ashe, Dr. Daniel Masters, Dr. Lance Cummings, and Dr. Florentina Andreescu had several academic sessions at different points with the IIUI students and faculty in Islamabad. The plan also included 12 postdoc fellowships, 16 short-term (three-week) study visits, and eight travel grants for the IIUI faculty (and several others for the faculty and students coming from other universities of Pakistan) to present their research at the First IIUI–UNCW Conference in Wilmington. These three travel-based activities made it possible for more than 30 IIUI delegates to conduct, present, and publish their research projects at different academic venues. Additionally, the three-week visitors and the postdoc fellows were able to visit schools, colleges, libraries, churches, monuments, and festivals at different places in North Carolina to engage with the larger community and present a realistic image of Pakistan.

A number of colleagues from IIUI and UNCW collaborated on their research projects. Dr. Lance Cummings and Dr. Ahsan Bashir worked on "Formality/Informality in the English Classroom: Comparisons Between Pakistan and US" and presented their findings at the Second IIUI–UNCW Conference in Islamabad. Dr. Aaron King, Dr. Ben Taylor, Dr. Daniel Masters, Dr. Amna Mahmood, Dr. Manzoor Ahmad, and Dr. Sadaf Farooq collaborated to conduct "A Cross-Cultural Assessment of Political Science Education and Current Events" and presented it at the Second IIUI–UNCW Conference. Ms. Asma Mansoor and Dr. Lance Cummings collaborated to virtually connect their classes so they could engage in an online discussion on various concepts and issues in the courses.

The mega events that brought many people together during these three years were the two conferences. The First IIUI–UNCW Conference, "The New Global City: Presenting and Translating Cultures Within a Worldwide Citizenry," held in Wilmington May 12–14, 2016, was attended by 30 Pakistani presenters and almost an equal number of American presenters, and the Second IIUI–UNCW Conference, "Local Cities, Foreign Capitals: Finding the Local Anchor in Global Cultures," held in Islamabad October 9–11, 2017, was attended by 12 American presenters (Dr. Caroline Clements, Dr. Jess Boersma, Mr. Jeremy Rowley, Dr. Susan Catapano, Dr. Lance Cummings, Dr. Dan Masters, Dr. Michele Parker, Dr. Karl Ricanek, Dr. Ben Taylor, Dr. Florentina Andreescu, Dr. Cara Cilano, Dr. Masood Ashraf Raja, and Dr. Rahul Parson) and about 100 Pakistani presenters. Overall, about 60 papers were presented in the first conference and 90 in the second. Hugely successful, both these conferences echoed the voices burdened and beautified by all that defines our times. Standing on the academic borderlines, the scholars introduced, developed, weighed, and challenged contesting discourses around the aesthetic and the political, the traditional and the modern, and the local and the global.

Apart from the professional development of the IIUI faculty and students, and mutual cultural understanding of both the communities, this partnership's gifts include the establishment of a Center for Teaching Excellence (CTE) at IIUI. Two faculty members from IIUI visited UNCW in January/February 2018 and were given a specialized orientation in running the CTE, including visits to five university centers for teaching and learning in the state of North Carolina. This will help IIUI plan and conduct faculty development programs in the future.

A number of Pakistani scholars have also published journalistic articles and blogs sharing their experiences of traveling to the United States and interacting with the Americans. Ms. Sonia Irum's "Walking the Winds of Wilmington" and my own "Wilmington: Ik Shehr e Tilism" (also translated as "You're a Magic City, Dear Wilmington" by Ms. Komal Shahzadi), "Amreeka min Aala Taleem" (Higher Education in America), "Amreeka ki Librarian" (Libraries in America), are all the result of the partnership.

Now that the three-year partnership has turned into a lifelong friendship, I look forward to staying in touch with UNCW colleagues working in the same academic domains that I work in and continuing productive teaching and research collaborations in the future. I wish IIUI and UNCW a bright future, and hope that all of us will continue such constructive efforts that will further strengthen Pak–America friendship.

I congratulate Prof. Caroline Clements, Prof. Munawar Iqbal Ahmad, and all the members of the grant team and the steering committee for successfully transforming this partnership into a friendship. I also congratulate all the contributors to this volume on the publication of their wonderful work.

SECTION ONE

Literary and Textual Perspectives

CHAPTER ONE | PASCALE BARTHE

A Moving Empire

François Bernier's Mosques, Mausoleums, and Monuments of 17th-Century Mughal India

Serge Gruzinski (2012) and Sanjay Subrahmanyam (1997, 2017) have shown that globalizing trends were very much at work long before the 21st century. In the early modern period, technological advances, changes in diplomatic practices, as well as the rise of confessionalism made travel easier, and sometimes necessary. Better able to journey the world and to extend their stay in far-away lands, European merchants, missionaries, *curieux*, and *literati* saw an increase in the possibilities for observing and reporting on societies and modes of government different from their own. Such opportunities resulted in an unprecedented number of publications, including travel accounts and compilations of earlier works, the subject of which was, in many cases, the East. While in this massive production of the Eastern lore some scholars have identified the genesis of what Edward Said theorized as Orientalism, others prefer to view these encounters as a rather balanced and equitable moment in world history (Longino, 2002; Dew, 2009; Beasley, 2010, 2018). This study examines the writings of François Bernier (1620–1688), a physician and student of the free thinker Pierre Gassendi (1592–1655), and shows the complex views of a Frenchman on Mughal India and, by extension, the difficulty of assessing 17th-century European works on the Orient. It demonstrates that while a *libertin* like Bernier contributed to the creation of "baroque Orientalism" (Dew, 2009) and supported the imperial project of the King of France, he could not help but notice and be moved by the uniqueness and specificities of the Mughal world. Portraying Muslim Asia as tyranny and simultaneously as a place of distinctive estheticism, he described the movement of the Mughal Empire from West to East and hinted at the timeliness of a French empire, all the while questioning the very translatability of empire from Asia to Europe as well as its desirability, ultimately looking beyond empire.

From 1656 to 1669 Bernier lived in Asia where he spent the last 10 years of his prolonged absence from France in India (Tinguely, 2008). There he witnessed the changing political and architectural makeup of the Mughal Empire. When Bernier arrived on the coast of Gujarat in late 1558 or early 1559, he was instantly immersed in the wars of succession that engulfed Shah Jahan's sons, which soon culminated with the ascendancy of Aurangzeb (1618–1707) over his brothers. In his "Histoire de la dernière révolution des états du grand mogol," published by Claude Barbin in 1670 and dedicated to Louis XIV, Bernier gave a detailed account of the internecine war between Dara Shikoh (1615–1659) and Aurangzeb, the last episode of which Bernier watched unfold. While in India, not only did the *libertin* encounter a powerful dynasty of Mughal rulers and a changing political landscape, but he also discovered territory, and particularly an urban architecture punctuating this territory, that had been profoundly shaped and was being transformed by the empire. Focusing on Bernier's description of 17th-century India and specifically on his depiction of its monuments, mausoleums, and mosques, this study questions whether the *libertin* viewed Mughal Indian architecture as a marker of empire.

The early modern Eurasian world saw the construction or the substantial transformation of several major royal or imperial edifices. The Topkapı palace in Istanbul was constructed for Mehmed the Conqueror (1432–1481) in the late 15th century. Between 1590 and 1611 the palace of Ālī Qāpū in Isfahan in Safavid Persia was built for Shah Abbas I (1571–1629). Meanwhile, in India, Akbar (1542–1605) ordered the construction of the Agra Fort (1565–1573), and Shah Jahan (1592–1666) had the Red Fort built in Delhi (1639–1648) (Necipoğlu, 1993). Resolutely last and perhaps least, Versailles was extensively renovated and expanded starting in 1661. Soon after, noticeable changes to the building and its surroundings seem to have attracted *curieux* and foreign visitors (de Scudéry, 1669; La Dantec, 1994). In 1682, Louis XIV moved to what had then become a most royal château at the center of which the Sun King as a new Apollo came to reside and around which nature had been domesticated (Marin, 1991; Himelfarb, 1997). Architecturally speaking then, the French were following and trying to imitate a cluster of extremely successful Muslim empires in the East. In building Versailles, not only did Louis XIV seek to emulate contemporary Eastern rulers, but he also aimed to attract them and compete with them. He was obviously well informed.

When renovations in Versailles started in the early 1660s, Bernier was in India, where he saw and later depicted three major urban centers having undergone recent, major renewal—Lahore, Agra, and Delhi. By detailing Mughal cities and their architectural landmarks, Bernier provided a precious firsthand account of one of the most accomplished and successful imperial systems of the period, one that the French king and his associates were precisely copying in Versailles. Addressed to notables and influential men in the French kingdom, some of whom will be discussed in the following pages, Bernier's accounts would have highly resonated with the architectural transformations that were occurring in 17th-century France.

From Lahore to Agra and Delhi: The Empire on the Move

Traveling with Aurangzeb's court to Kashmir, the French traveler stayed a few days in Lahore, which he depicted, if only briefly, to European readers in a series of letters written in late 1664 and early 1665 and addressed to one of his protectors in France, Monsieur de Merveilles.[1] In addition to the houses in Lahore, which he claims are higher than those in Delhi and Agra but in poor condition, he pays close attention to the fort, which he calls the king's palace. In Lahore, Bernier claims, "Le palais du roi ... est fort élevé et a quelque chose de magnifique; néanmoins, ceux d'Agra et de Delhi le sont bien davantage" (This is a high and noble edifice, though very inferior to the palaces of Delhi and Agra) (Tinguely, 2008, p. 397; Bernier, 1916, p. 384). For Bernier, the Lahore Fort, and by extension the city in which it is located, only ranks third, after Agra and Delhi. This is not an unusual assessment of Lahore, which we find to be absent from most 16th- and 17th-century European travel accounts (Chida-Razvi, 2015). Bernier's short stay in Lahore when his and the Mughal court's destination was Kashmir might explain his brief commentary and rather poor evaluation of the city. The justification the French traveler gives about the city's lack of luster, however, is particularly interesting: whereas Jahangir and his court resided in Lahore for extended periods of time,[2] his son and successor Shah Jahan preferred the imperial cities of Agra and Delhi. Although Shah Jahan, like his predecessors, was the patron of several important architectural projects in Lahore, the imperial aura of the city lost its charm after the death of his father, Jahangir, in 1627. That is at least what Bernier suggests, he who, like his European contemporaries, be they merchants, diplomats, or missionaries, examined the Lahore Fort through the lens of military and political power, one that could only have been diminished with the physical absence of the padshah as head of the empire, despite the vibrant Islamic, Sufi, and economic aspects of the urban center (Chida-Razvi, 2015).

Bernier's unenthusiastic comments on Lahore reflect the political and architectural changes that occurred after Jahangir's death and during the reign of his son, Shah Jahan. They also hint at the political reorganization that was happening in India in the mid-1660s after Shah Jahan's sons had fought to become his successor. By explaining Shah Jahan's marked difference regarding residential preference compared to his ancestors, the chronicler reports on changes that had occurred previously and points to some that might come with the ascension to power of Aurangzeb. What consequences would the new padshah have, architecturally but also politically, on India and the world? Bernier asks. His French readers, as fascinated by all things Oriental as they might have been, also had to wonder what the construction of Versailles and its logical consequence, the ensuing transfer of the court into an entirely new and grand edifice far removed from Paris, might mean for themselves. Bernier's keen remarks on 17th-century India indicate that he is not an antiquarian looking back at a long-lost empire that would wait to be restored and reinvented, as was the case with 16th-century travelers who were discerning traces of Greek and Roman heritage under the Ottoman Empire. Rather, Bernier's thoughts are very much anchored in the present and directed toward the future. He is attentive to recent architectural and political changes affecting Mughal India that could only resonate with the situation of his correspondents in France for whom the *translatio imperii*, as Bernier's writings imply and as the renovations in Versailles would have confirmed, could happen not only with time, as it was traditionally understood, but also with geography.

It is in a letter to Monsieur de La Mothe Le Vayer dated July 1, 1663, and written in Delhi that we find Bernier's most elaborate discussion of the Mughal's imperial cities.[3] There he focuses on both Agra and Delhi, which he calls the capital cities of the Mughal Empire. Bernier quickly covers Agra, underlining its quaint bucolic ("champêtre") aspect. The focus of his description, however, is the newer of the two cities. Delhi, as he sees it, is much larger than Agra and possesses certain characteristics that the French traveler openly favors. Located in the countryside by the Yamuna River, which serves as a natural protective barrier, Delhi, otherwise known as Shahjahanabad—the city of Shah Jahan—is an entirely new city built by the emperor to immortalize his reign: "Il y a environ quarante ans que Shah Jahan, père du Grand Mogol Aurangzeb régnant à présent, pour éterniser sa mémoire, fit bâtir une ville contiguë à l'ancienne Delhi" (It is about forty years ago that *Chah-Jehan*, father of the present *Great Mogol*, *Aureng-Zebe*, conceived the design of immortalizing his name by the erection of a city near the site of the ancient *Delhi*)⁴ (Tinguely, 2008, pp. 236–237; Bernier, 1916, p. 241). Its palace contains the royal apartments, a garden, and a bustling square. It has two large doors leading to the main city streets and is surrounded by red walls, all of which combines to provide a most pleasant view: "Autour du fossé règne un jardin assez large qu'on voit en tout temps plein de fleurs et d'arbrisseaux verts, ce qui fait avec ces grandes murailles toutes rouges un très bel effet à la vue" (Adjoining the ditch is a large garden, filled at all times with flowers and green shrubs, which, contrasted with the stupendous red walls, produce a beautiful effect) (Tinguely, 2008, p. 238; Bernier, 1916, p. 243). Bernier describes the inside of the palace as well as the city at its doors. He emphasizes the architectural layout of both and their integration, mentioning not only the large roads that lead to the palace, but also the surrounding houses of the "omerah," the *seigneurs*, the rich nobles. Mughal architecture is thus intrinsically linked to other men who, along with padshahs, build society: in and out of the Red Fort, merchants and entertainers are active participants in the life of the city and of the palace itself where processions and public justice ceremonials constitute the spectacle of power. Bernier suggests that Delhi is better planned and equipped to demonstrate the political, economic, and symbolic power of Shah Jahan, the Mughal dynasty, and empire. In the 1699 Amsterdam edition of Bernier's works, a sumptuous drawing complements and accentuates the traveler's textual depiction of the Red Fort as the seat of empire. Bearing the title of *La cour du Grand Mogol*, it illustrates the daily audience held by the padshah. A powerful display of justice, the event was also undeniably a grand spectacle, replete with men on horseback, camels, and elephants, as well as silver and gold. At the center of both the reception and the illustration, on his throne, sits the emperor, radiant and resplendent. A second illustration in the same 1699 Amsterdam edition zooms in on the palace and depicts the padshah being weighed in gold, a scene that Bernier also describes in his letter to La Mother Le Vayer. Both images are in black and white. Nevertheless, glittering gold dominates, as it would in Louis XIV's Versailles.

Bernier shares plausible explanations for Delhi's new imperial urban architecture. There were practical as well as ideological reasons for Shah Jahan to turn his back on Lahore and to build a new fort and city, he argues. The River Ravi upon which the Lahore Fort was built is unpredictable; it changes course often, and its floods cause destruction. For some time now, Bernier adds, the river has not been flowing next to the palace, making the life of the inhabitants and, more importantly, of the court difficult. Furthermore, a new imperial city, built purposefully as the capital of the empire, would immortalize Shah Jahan's name and reign. Significantly larger and more open, this new city could accommodate more people, locals as well as foreign dignitaries, and display the power of the ruler in a more grandiose and effective way. Bernier's details of Delhi's layout echo what Versailles was to become and foreshadow its ceremonies with foreign dignitaries such as the Siam embassy of 1686 (Welch, 2017).

In addition to the Red Fort, Bernier comments on several other physical markers of the Mughal Empire, including two monuments that were built under Shah Jahan: the Jama Masjid, constructed between 1650 and 1656, and the Taj Mahal. Both are made of white marble, a stone that became a trademark of Shah Jahan's architectural imprint and that contrasted with the red sandstone used in previous imperial buildings such as the Lahore and the Red forts. Bernier's epistolary account to La Mothe Le Vayer, then, is a refined snapshot of India in the 1660s. Focusing on Mughal palaces and newly built cities, they capture the unmovable physical markers of an empire that are imperial palaces and religious monuments, while recognizing the peripatetic form of government favored by Mughal padshahs, a form constantly redefined by a dynasty of rulers in India—as well as in France. Furthermore, Bernier's texts indicate a spread and, more significantly, a displacement of empire from West to East, from Lahore to Agra and Delhi. Politically speaking, this indication would have meant not so much relief for the French kingdom that was never in direct military contact with Mughal India, but an authorization of sorts: Louis XIV was now free to claim and build his empire without having to worry about a greater and more established one that was "naturally" drifting further to the East.[5]

Empire Decadent

With his concrete and meticulous descriptions of Mughal cities, Bernier encapsulates imperial power in 17th-century India. Located at the center of his golden palace, the padshah is seen as presiding over ceremonials that are designed to display and assert his unique and uncontested position. As Louis Marin (1991) has shown, Versailles was built to emanate the same centrality and omnipotence of the French monarch. Therefore, by further accounting that the Mughal Empire is moving East, Bernier might have given French readers at court a sense that the time had come for the kingdom to develop into an empire. The title of Bernier's report to Jean-Baptiste Colbert (1619–1683), minister of finances, says it plainly: "Lettre à Monseigneur Colbert. De l'étendue de l'Hindoustan, circulation de l'or et l'argent pour venir s'y abîmer, richesses, forces, justice, et *cause principale de la décadence des états d'Asie*" (Letter to Monsieur Colbert Concerning the Extent of Hindoustan, the Currency towards, and final absorption of gold and silver in that country; its Resources, Armies, and the administration of justice, and the principal Cause for the Decline of the States of Asia) (Tinguely, 2008, pp. 197–232; emphasis added). The Mughal Empire is nearing its end, suggests Bernier, and the time has come for the French to move East and to compete with other European powers—the Portuguese, the Dutch, the British. To this very end, Colbert founded the *Compagnie française pour le commerce des Indes orientales* in 1664. Four years later, Bernier penned a *Mémoire… pour l'établissement du commerce dans les Indes* in which he highlighted the strategy that the French should use in India (Subrahmanyam, 2017, pp. 3–8). In this document—which remained unpublished—as in his printed works, the French traveler encouraged some of his readers in France to participate in the taking of Asia. Nevertheless, while assuring Colbert and others of the possibility of competing against Europeans in India and against the Mughals themselves, Bernier is absolutely clear about the danger of empire, which he associates with tyranny as did his predecessors when they observed the Ottomans (Valensi, 1987). Because, as the *libertin* insists, the Mughal Emperor does not allow private property, the "nobles" do not have any incentive, or even means, to build and develop. He laments the fact that with the exception of Shalimar, "*une belle et royale maison*" (a handsome and noble building) (Tinguely, 2008, p. 280; Bernier, 1916, p. 283), there is no equivalent to Fontainebleau, Saint-Germain, or Versailles—which at this point Bernier only knows as a modest hunting lodge—in India. Furthermore, there is nothing built by merchants, bourgeois, and other *gentilhommes* that would resemble Saint-Cloud, Chantilly, Meudon, or Vaux (Tinguely, 2008, p. 280; Bernier, 1916, p. 283). In other words, architecture in Mughal India depends solely on the emperor who shapes and designs cities and palaces for himself and posterity, the same cities and palaces reflecting, in turn, the power of one person and one person only—himself.

A posteriori, the report to Colbert and the letter to La Mothe Le Vayer in which the focus is the mutating and moving Indian capitals underscore an Orientalizing view of the Mughal world. The Orient that transpires from both texts is one that has been commonly and simplistically conceived as despotic in western Europe since at least the 16th century. It is clear, however, that Bernier's criticism is directed at empire rather than at the East. Indeed, while stressing the pomp of the Mughal court and palaces in his texts and illustrations, Bernier underscores the lack of significant construction outside of the imperial cities, which stands in stark contrast with what one finds in France, the "infinité de bourgades et de villages, toutes ces belles maisons des champs et toutes ces campagnes et collines cultivées et entretenues avec tant d'industrie, de soin et de travail" (infinite number of towns and villages; all those beautiful country houses, those fine plains, hills and valleys, cultivated with so much care, art and labor[6]) (Tinguely, 2008, p. 227; Bernier, 1916, p. 233). On the bare "carte de l'empire du Grand Mogol"[7] included in *Histoire de la dernière revolution*, rivers, mountains, and vegetation appear alongside names of cities and provinces (Krusinski, 2011; original in 1728). The contrast between this map and the illustration depicting the lavishness of architecture and the gold-weighing ceremonial that characterize the Red Fort in Delhi could not be starker. There, the center of the imposing urban palace was the focus of the eye and the mind. It illustrated the glorious power of empire, its natural environment being reduced to neatly planted palm trees and artificial rivers and ponds. In contrast, the map of Mughal India displays a physically accurate but crude landscape devoid of population and construction. The land seems consequential but easily conquerable. Furthermore, this illustration shows that, in India, nature outside of the palace has not been cultivated and beautified unlike in France where the countryside and soon the gardens in Versailles show the domestication and the civilization of the entire kingdom. Bernier thus warns Colbert and his readers about the potential abuses inherent in tyranny and empire, in the East and at home.

Bernier's commentaries on early modern India are squarely Francocentric, Parisian even. While providing accurate and detailed descriptions of India's three major cities, Bernier asserts that 17th-century Paris, compared with Agra, Delhi, and even Constantinople, is the most beautiful, the richest, in short, the best city in the world.

> [La vue] de Paris est presque tout artificielle et l'ouvrage des mains des hommes; ce qui la rend sans doute plus considérable en ce qu'elle ressent ainsi davantage le siège d'un grand roi, la capitale d'un grand empire et qu'elle est effectivement, sans nous flatter, et toutes ces beautés de Delhi, d'Agra, et de Constantinople, bien considérées et balancées, la plus belle, la

plus riche, la première ville du monde. (Tinguely, 2008, pp. 236–237)

[I]n Paris, everything, or nearly so, is artificial; which, to my mind, gives more interest to the view of the latter; because the work of man so displayed indicates the capital of a great empire, the seat of a mighty monarch. I may indeed say, without partiality, and after making every allowance for the beauty of Agra, Delhi, and Constantinople, that Paris is the finest, the richest, and altogether the first city of the world. (Bernier, 1916, p. 286)

Like the flourishing villages in the French kingdom, the preeminence of Paris is due, according to Bernier, to industrious men who made the city the seat for a king, a capital for empire. In Delhi on the contrary, Mughal nobles are not able to build, and although craftsmanship is undoubtable, there are no masters under whom painters could learn their trade,[8] a strongly reductive and inaccurate view of a society in which the arts flourished during the Mughal era, as extant illustrated manuscripts and paintings from the 16th and 17th centuries demonstrate.

What is crucial here is Bernier's focus on Paris, not Versailles, for which renovations and expansion had barely begun. Erudite and versatile, Bernier had to be familiar with the rise of urban architecture and architects in France in the late 16th and early 17th centuries. The word "architect" does not appear in Robert Étienne's French–Latin dictionary of 1549, but a first significant work on architecture is published, in French, by Philibert de l'Orme in 1567, and a century later, in 1671, the *Académie royale d'Architecture* is established by Colbert as a fundamental element constitutive of absolute monarchy. Moreover, it is highly plausible that Bernier knew of works by the architect Pierre Le Muet who, in 1645, translated Andrea Palladio's treatise on the five orders of architecture and who had earlier published *Manière de bâtir pour toutes sortes de personnes* (1623), which details different architectural options for urban buildings. As such, Bernier was able to not only communicate factual information about Mughal architecture to his French patrons and to compare it, if not technically at least holistically, to European standards with which his readers were familiar. He also understood that architectural projects, in Asia and France alike, were based on topographical as well as political contexts. Even though Bernier's writings replicate a century of stereotypical views of the Orient, it contains new information that could have been used to support and justify the making of imperial France. Nevertheless, a persistent skepticism toward such a project permeates Bernier's writings. Furthermore, his observations on climate and his sensory response to Indian architecture show that Bernier was sensitive to the local as much as, if not more than, the global.

A Moving Empire

Indeed, the traveler emphasizes the relevance of a Mughal architecture that is perfectly adapted to India, thereby prompting his European readers to suspend their judgment and to consider the possibility of architectural and hence cultural relativism. About the Jama Masjid, Bernier plainly states that although the building does not follow the rules of architecture, it is well proportioned and pleasing to the eye. He states that if there were in Paris a church built on a similar architectural model, people might be a bit surprised but would not disapprove of its looks.

> Je veux bien que cet édifice [Jama Masjid] ne soit pas dans ces règles et ordres d'architecture que nous croyons devoir être suivis indispensablement, néanmoins je n'y remarque rien qui m'y choque la vue; au contraire, tout m'y paraît bien entendu, bien conduit et bien proportionné; et je m'imagine que si nous avions dans Paris une église qui tirât sur cette sorte d'architecture, on ne la trouverait pas laide, quand ce ne serait que pour être à notre égard d'un air extraordinaire et surprenant.... (Tinguely, 2008, p. 276)
>
> I grant that this building is not constructed according to those rules of architecture which we seem to think ought to be implicitly followed; yet I can perceive no fault that offends the taste; every part appears well contrived, properly executed, and correctly proportioned. I am satisfied that even in Paris a church erected after the model of this temple would be admired, were it only for its singular style of architecture, and its extraordinary appearance. (Bernier, 1916, p. 279)

Similarly, the Taj Mahal is a different and peculiar building, and yet it is a lovely edifice that would deserve a place in European treatises on architecture because it is so magnificently conceived and built.

> Ce pavillon [le Taj Mahal] est plus long que large et est bâti d'une pierre qui est comme du marbre rouge, mais elle n'en a pas la dureté. La façade me semble être beaucoup plus magnifique en sa façon, plus longue et autant élevée que celle de Saint-Louis de notre rue Saint-Antoine. Véritablement, on ne voit pas là des colonnes, des architraves et des corniches taillées dans la proportion de ces cinq ordres d'architecture qu'on observe

si religieusement dans nos palais. *C'est une espèce de bâtiment différente et particulière, mais qui ne laisse pas d'avoir de l'agréable dans sa bizarre disposition, et qui, à mon avis, mériterait bien sa place dans nos livres d'architecture.* Ce n'est presque qu'arcades sur arcades, et que galeries ou divans sur galeries disposées et pratiquées de cent façons différentes; et cependant tout paraît magnifique, assez bien entendu et bien conduit, rien n'y choque la vue; au contraire, tout y rit et on ne peut se rassasier de le regarder. (Tinguely, 2008, pp. 288–289; emphasis added).

This pavilion is an oblong square, and built of a stone resembling red marble, but not so hard. The front seems to me longer, and much more grand in its construction, than that of *S. Louis*, in the rue *S. Antoine*, and it is equally lofty. The columns, the architraves and the cornices are, indeed, not formed according to the proportion of the five orders of architecture so strictly observed in *French* edifices. The building I am speaking of is of a different and peculiar kind; but not without something pleasing in its whimsical structure; and in my opinion it well deserves a place in our books of architecture. It consists almost wholly of arches upon arches, and galleries upon galleries, disposed and contrived in a hundred different ways. Nevertheless the edifice has a magnificent appearance, and is conceived and executed effectually. Nothing offends the eye; on the contrary, it is delighted with every part, and never tired of looking. (Bernier, 1916, p. 294)

Relying on reason and observation, using his sense of sight, Bernier is compelled to consider and to acknowledge the beauty, efficiency, and practicality of Indian architecture. There is no reason, here, to detect irony and to doubt the sincerity of the *libertin* who, in these two instances, finds pleasure in gazing at architectural marvels as he enjoyed his "affective relations" (Subrahmanyam, 2017, p. 15) with Daneshmend Khan, his protector in India.[9]

In addition to looking at Mughal India, Bernier listens. Concerts in Delhi can be disconcerting for European ears, claims the Frenchman, who, nevertheless, has grown accustomed to them and admits having come to enjoy them.

C'est un concert bien étrange aux oreilles d'un Européen nouveau venu qui n'y est pas encore accoutumé[….] Jugez de là du tintamarre que cela doit faire. En vérité, cette musique dans le commencement me pénétrait et m'étourdissait tellement qu'elle m'était insupportable; néanmoins, je ne sais ce que fait point l'accoutumance; il y a déjà longtemps que je la trouve agréable, et la nuit principalement que je l'entends de loin dans mon lit de dessus ma terrasse, elle me semble avoir quelque chose de grave, de majestueux et de fort mélodieux. Et il y a bien quelque raison de cette mélodie, car, elle a ses règles et ses mesures et qu'il y a d'excellents maîtres instruits de jeunesse qui la conduisent et lui savent parfaitement modérer et fléchir ces sons forts de hautbois et de timbales, il ne se peut faire qu'ils n'en tirent quelque symphonie qui ne soit pas désagréable à l'oreille, pourvu, comme j'ai dit, qu'on l'entende de loin. (Tinguely, 2008, pp. 254–255)

To the ears of an *European* recently arrived, this music sounds very strangely[....] You may judge, therefore, of the roaring sound which issues from the *Nagar-Kanay*. On my first arrival it stunned me so as to be insupportable: but such is the power of habit that this same noise is now heard by me with pleasure; in the night, particularly, when in bed and afar, on my terrace this music sounds in my ears as solemn, grand, and melodious. This is not altogether to be wondered at, since it is played by persons instructed from infancy in the rules of melody, and possessing the skill of modulating and turning the harsh sounds of the hautboy and cymbal so as to produce a symphony far from disagreeable when heard at a certain distance. (Bernier, 1916, p. 260)

While noting India's shifting imperial cachet, the French epicurean shows signs of being moved by the esthetic beauty of Mughal melody and architecture. Pleasing sensory experiences—the vision of the Taj Mahal, the sound of Indian music—induce and produce a certain degree of cultural relativism in Bernier, thereby counterbalancing an otherwise universalist leaning.[10]

However, when listening to Indian music, keeping "a certain distance" is a must, according to the *libertin*. This indispensable precaution, I would like to argue, does not diminish Bernier's genuine enthusiasm for "diversité."[11] Instead, it must be related to his overall suspicion of empire, be it Mughal or French: music is fine, but loud royal music (with an agenda) is problematic. This admonition must be kept in mind when we analyze the admissions of corruption that Bernier makes. For example, the delightful moment of viewing the Taj Mahal is overshadowed by a fear of being contaminated by Asian habits, a concern regularly shared by many travelers of the early modern period.[12] The *libertin* is so enthralled by the exceptional monument that he wonders if he has not grown accustomed to the Mughal ways. He is seemingly reassured when a French merchant in his company admits the mesmerizing effects of the mausoleum on himself, claiming that he had never seen anything as noble and daring in Europe.

La dernière fois que je l[e] vis fut avec un de nos marchands français qui ne pouvait aussi bien que moi se lasser de le regarder; je n'osais lui en dire mon sentiment, *appréhendant de m'être corrompu le goût et me l'être fait à l'Indienne*, mais comme il revenait fraîchement de France, je fus aise de lui entendre dire qu'il n'avait jamais rien vu de si auguste, ni de si hardi dans l'Europe. (Tinguely, 2008, p. 297; emphasis added)

The last time I visited *Tage Mehale*'s mausoleum I was in the company of a French merchant, who, as well as myself, thought that this extraordinary fabric could not be sufficiently admired. I did not venture to express my opinion, fearing that my taste might have become corrupted by my long residence in the Indies; and as my companion was come recently from *France*, it was quite a relief to my mind to hear him say that he had seen nothing in *Europe* so bold and majestic. (Bernier, 1916, p. 294–295)

Particularly interesting in Bernier's writings are the confessions he makes about himself and the sensory pleasures he experiences while in India. These signs of cultural relativism gesture to self-reflection on the part of the French traveler while pointing to the limits of empires on individuals, free thinkers in particular. As such, they serve as warning against the peril of importing empire.

Bernier was a perceptive traveler who carefully documented the political and urban changes he witnessed in India in the mid-1660s. His commentaries on the architecture of Lahore, Agra, and Delhi are addressed to two French patrons who had direct access to Louis XIV. It is therefore very likely that the French king, who, in 1671, ordered the construction of a new city near Versailles to complement the palace he had begun to grandly renovate a decade earlier, could have read or heard of Bernier's letters. One could argue that just as the textile industry in France was developed in response to Indian cloth (Beasley, 2018, p. 218), absolutist France and the colonial empire it would become were influenced by Mughal India via the *libertin*. By making this claim, however, one would have to dismiss not only India's refined culture but also Bernier's recurrent, open criticism of empire—or interpret it as a criticism of Oriental ways, which, as we hope to have shown, would be simplistic. Furthermore, such an analysis would fail to acknowledge the positive emotions that Mughal India, particularly its architecture, produced on Bernier.

A sophisticated writer as he was, Bernier was aware of the paradoxes present in his writings on India and of the potential failure one could experience in reading them. He concludes his letter to La Mothe Le Vayer by stating: "Pour moi, je ne sais pas bien encore si je n'aurais point le gout un peu trop indien" (As for me, I do not quite know yet whether I might have imbibed too Indian a taste[13]) (Tinguely, 2008, p. 300). Bernier was simply too complex, or perhaps too sensitive, for the court and some of his contemporaries to see.

NOTES

1. We know little about François Boysson, seigneur de Merveilles.

2. Jahangir resided in Lahore and is buried there in a mausoleum. Lahore was at its peak under him (Tinguely, 2008, p. 511).

3. François de La Mothe Le Vayer (1588–1672) was the cofounder, with Gassendi, Gabriel Naudé, and Elie Diodati, of the "Tétrade," a Parisian circle of free thinkers. He was elected to the Académie Française in 1639 and was preceptor to Philippe d'Anjou, the younger brother to the future king of France, Louis XIV.

4. Italics in original. Today, this area is known as Old Delhi.

5. The Ottoman Empire had pressured Europe and France much more directly in the 16th century, but the French had convinced themselves that it was no longer a threat in the 1600s.

6. This quote is from a passage in the letter to Colbert where Bernier insists on the development of the European countryside as a corollary of good kingship.

7. Included in the 1670 editio princeps copy of the Arsenal Library and more systematically in the copies of the 1699 Amsterdam edition according to Tinguely (2008, p. 461, note 2).

8. "On voit qu'il ne leur manque que les bons maîtres et les préceptes de l'art pour leur donner ces justes proportions, et surtout ce vif du visage qu'ils ne peuvent presque jamais arriver" (The *Indian* painters are chiefly deficient in just proportions, and in the expression of the face, but these defects would soon be corrected if they possessed good masters, and were instructed in the rules of art) (Tinguely, 2008, p. 250; Bernier, 1916, p. 255).

9. A cultivated Persian, Mohammad Shafi was a high-ranking personage at the Mughal court. He hired Bernier as a doctor, and both men discussed science and philosophy.

10. Tinguely underlines Bernier's hesitation between universalism and cultural relativism (2008, p. 31).

11. Beasley (2010) underscores the importance of diversity in the salon culture to which Bernier belonged (p. 218).

12. "Turning Turk" is a topos of 16th-century European literature on the Ottoman Empire.

13. I have modified Constable's translation—"It is possible I may have imbibed an Indian taste" (Bernier, 1916, p. 299)—so as to keep the quantifier.

REFERENCES

Beasley, F. E. (2010). Versailles meets the Taj Mahal. In C. McDonald & S. R. Suleiman (Eds.), *French global: A new approach to literary history* (pp. 207–222). Columbia University Press.

Beasley, F. E. (2018). *Versailles meets the Taj Mahal: François Bernier, Marguerite de la Sablière and enlightening conversations in seventeenth-century France*. University of Toronto Press.

Bernier, F. (1916). *Travels in the Mogul Empire* (A. Constable, Trans.; 2nd ed.). Oxford University Press.

Chida-Razvi, M. (2015). Where is the "greatest city in the East"? The Mughal city of Lahore in European travel accounts (1556–1648). In M. Gharipour & N. Özlü (Eds.), *The city in the Muslim World: Depictions by Western travel writers* (pp. 79–100). Routledge.

de Scudéry, M. (1669). *La promenade de Versailles* [Promenade at Versailles]. Claude Barbin.

Dew, N. (2009). *Orientalism in Louis XIV's France*. Oxford University Press.

Gruzinski, S. (2012). *L'aigle et le dragon: Démesure et mondialisation au XVIe siècle* [The eagle and the dragon: Globalization and European dreams of conquest in China and America in the 16th century]. Fayard.

Himelfarb, H. (1997). Versailles, fonctions et legends [Versailles, functions and legends]. In P. Nora (Ed.), *Les lieux de mémoire: Vol. 1* [Sites of memory: Vol. 1] (pp. 1285–1330). Gallimard.

Krusinski, T. J. (2011). *Histoire de la dernière revolution de Perse: Vol. 1* [History of the late revolution of Persia: Vol. 1]. Nabu Press. (Original work published 1728)

La Dantec, D. (1994). Quand le Roi bâtissait Versailles et ses jardins [When the King built Versailles and its gardens]. *Dalhousie French Studies, 29*, 31–54.

Le Muet, P. (1623). *Manière de bâtir pour toutes sortes de personnes* [The art of fair building for all sorts of people]. Marchand Libraire.

Longino, M. (2002). *Orientalism in French classical drama*. Cambridge University Press.

Marin, L. (1991). Classical, Baroque: Versailles, or the architecture of the prince (A. Lehman, Trans.). *Yale French Studies, 80*, 167–182. (Original work published 1989)

Necipoğlu, G. (1993). Framing the gaze in Ottoman, Safavid, and Mughal palaces. *Ars Orientalis, 23*, 303–342.

Subrahmanyam, S. (1997). Connected histories: Notes towards a reconfiguration of early modern Eurasia. *Modern Asian Studies, 31*(3), 735–762.

Subrahmanyam, S. (2017). *Europe's India: Words, people, empire, 1500–1800*. Harvard University Press.

Tinguely, F. (2008). *Un libertin dans l'Inde moghole: Les voyages de François Bernier (1656–1668)* [Travels in the Mughal Empire: The trips of François Bernier (1656–1668)]. Chandeigne.

Valensi, L. (1987). *Venise et la Sublime Porte: La naissance du despote* [Venice and the sublime porte: The birth of the despot]. Hachette.

Welch, H. R. (2017). *A theater of diplomacy: International relations and the performing arts in early modern France*. University of Pennsylvania Press.

CHAPTER TWO | MAHMOOD UL HASSAN

Colonial Legacy and English Studies

The study of the intricate relationship between colonial ideology, education, and curriculum has become important in the postcolonial academy since the publication of *Orientalism* (Said, 1978). It has, therefore, become interesting to study the curricula and pedagogy of former colonies like Pakistan and India in the light of their colonial legacy. Antonio Gramsci, in his theory of cultural hegemony, explains how the ruling elite controls the masses by manipulating the education system and, by this means, inculcates popular discourses with the aim of maintaining the status quo (Gramsci, 2009). Louis Althusser (1971) believes that the education system—the formation and control of a curriculum—is political and often used to serve as an "ideological state apparatus" (p. 143).

Education is not only the channel through which ideas are transmitted, but it is also the apparatus to create ideologies, spread discourses, inculcate values, and thus shape the worldview of a people. The intricate relationship between knowledge and power has long been studied—for instance, Michel Foucault (1980) redefined the relationship between knowledge and power. This study is an attempt to help understand the politics of knowledge/education in the postcolonial context of departments of English at state-owned universities in Pakistan. The basic assumption is that Pakistan, a former colony of Great Britain, in many ways, has not been able to decolonize itself as the legacy of colonialism lives on in different forms, of which education is just one. Blending Antonio Gramsci's (1971) "social hegemony" and Gauri Viswanathan's (1989) "master discourse" into a critical yardstick, the study critiques literary studies in English in the context of "postcolonial" South Asia. Hence, theoretically speaking, the framework is provided by postcolonial theory.

English literature was imported to India by the British colonizers long before it gained acceptance as an academic discipline in the universities of the

United Kingdom (Viswanathan, 1989). The fact remains that literary studies in English (which in the context of Pakistani universities happen to be, predominantly, the study of English literature) are a part, and an extension, of colonialism. The syllabi as well as the teaching methods have not been transformed even after decolonization and the creation of the independent countries of Pakistan and India. In U.S., and even British, universities, departments of English have grown and incorporated literature in English from many nonnative-English–speaking regions like South Asia and Africa. Similarly, the modes of instruction and the methods of literary analysis have also changed. But, interestingly, in former colonies like Pakistan and India, the curricula are still dominated by British writers such as Shakespeare, Milton, Donne, and other canonical writers. The same is true about the methods of literary analysis.

Departments of English in the former colonies of Great Britain have been at the center of debate in many postcolonial societies. Theorists and writers/critics have diverse views about the role of English language and literature in postcolonial societies. Ngugi wa Thiong'o challenges the place and role of English literature in the postcolonial African context. He questions the superior position held by English literature in Africa where most people do not know the English language in the first place (Ngugi, 1972). Ngugi himself abandoned writing in English and chose Gikuyu, his native language, for fiction writing, though adopting the European form of the novel. He suggests that the English department should be abolished and that a department of African languages and literature be established because European literature takes the African far away from their culture and world to the culture and world of Europe (Ngugi, 1972, p. 146). He therefore rejects the idea of resistance literature in the language of the colonizer using appropriation. Bill Ashcroft et al. (1989, 1995) argue the British brought and used English literature with a clear agenda to serve their political interests in India. E. K. Braithwaite (1995) says that the people of Africa were forced to learn things that did not have any relevance to them and that they were seldom told about their heroes; rather, they were changed with the Europeans' heroes. The present study, however, is not an attempt to establish that the department of English has become irrelevant and that it should be abolished. Rather, it is an effort to bring forth the issue and initiate a debate for the formation of a localized canon.

It is important to clarify here that I am not looking at literary studies in Pakistani public sector universities in a nationalistic framework, but rather from a postcolonial transformative perspective, which includes the changed/redefined role of institutions/universities and education in the wake of decolonization. Therefore, I believe that the role of departments of English in the former colonies has also changed. Has it been realized in the context of Pakistan as a postcolonial country? To what extent have revisions been brought into the curricula of departments of English? Have the emerging theories and trends in literary studies been encapsulated? These were the basic questions that challenged me as a student of and a teacher in a department of English in a postcolonial country such as Pakistan.

Research Questions

Research was carried out concentrating on the following questions:

1. What is the relationship between colonial ideology and education in the context of literary studies in English in the public sector universities of postcolonial Pakistan?
2. How lopsided are the curricula/syllabi of literary studies in English in the selected Pakistani universities in favor of the canonical British literature?

Delimitations of the Study

This study, as explained earlier, deals with the examination of the curricula/syllabi of literary studies in English at Pakistani public sector universities with a focus on the practice of teaching/studying English literature. The study, thus, does not include the historical reception of English language and literature in the postindependent Pakistani academy. However, I have linked the study of English literature in the Pakistani context to Gauri Viswanathan's (1989) investigation of English literature in the light of the British Empire's colonization of India. The study is delimited to the state of English literature in public sector universities only; I have not selected any private sector university for the analysis owing to the focus and limitations of this research. The study also concentrates on the curricula/syllabi and teaching practices at the university level alone; it does not consider the curricula of English studies at the college and school levels. Because the research is on a small scale, it focuses mainly on the syllabi of master of arts curricula (English) being taught at present in the English departments of six universities in Pakistan. However, the findings likely reflect the overall situation of the curricula/syllabi and the teaching practice of literary studies in English in other state-sponsored Pakistani universities.

Rationale and Significance

It was considered important to carry out the study because there is a gap in the research regarding the examination of literary studies in English in a larger Pakistani context involving six public sector universities' syllabi and teaching methods. Thus, the study will contribute to bridging the gap between what exists in the present situation and what is desirable regarding the contents of syllabi and the teaching practice of English literature in English departments at Pakistani public sector universities. Moreover, it will pave the way for researching literary studies in English in the Pakistani context. The rationale of the research, thus, lies in the very fact that it is aimed at benefiting departments of English at Pakistani universities in formulating and developing their curricula and syllabi for various degree programs as well as bringing a shift in the teaching/studying practices of literary studies in English based on genuine local research. It will, I believe, set the standard for the design and development of research-based curricula/syllabi in English departments at Pakistani universities. It is meant to change and/or reform the curricula/syllabi as well as the teaching practices of English departments in Pakistan, which, as underscored in the study, is of paramount importance for postcolonial Pakistan.

Moreover, the research will enable departments of English in these and other Pakistani universities to coordinate and work toward the development of balanced curricula/syllabi and a diversified practice of teaching literary studies in English. The results and recommendations of the study will prove beneficial for committees/boards on curriculum development. At the same time, I hope, it will provide departments, faculty, and researchers a level playing field for future research into curriculum and the related issues in English departments of Pakistani and other universities in the postcolonial world.

Review of Literature

There have been many studies conducted in Pakistan, India, Bangladesh, and elsewhere that have examined colonial education concerning English literature. These studies have, indeed, provided tremendous help in carrying out this research.

Reviewing English literary studies in colonized India, Gauri Viswanathan critiques Lord Macaulay's Model of Indian Education that was adopted by the British government in 1835 introducing English language and literature in India, which, according to her, was to inculcate the Western values and thus transform Indians into "[W]esternized [O]riental gentlemen" who would act as agents to accomplish the colonial agenda of the British Empire. It was also aimed at, according to Viswanathan, introducing European and British values and culture without converting the native Indians. She argues that colonial education with the introduction of English language and canonical English literature, following Macaulay's model, proved to be an ideological apparatus designed and deployed to enhance the process of colonization. Thus, according to Viswanathan, literature was brought to India to make it work as a tool of colonialism without violating the noninterference policy toward the indigenous religions (i.e., Hinduism and Islam). To explain this, she gives the example of funds allocated to promote Western literature, particularly English literature. Lord Macaulay made it clear that Western literature should be promoted in India at the expense of Oriental languages and literature so that English language and literature would replace the privileged position occupied by the local languages and literature such as Hindi and Persian. This approach served the purpose of detaching Indians from their culture and civilization. She further argues that if the British did not abolish the seminaries of Hindus and Muslims at the beginning of their regime, it was not out of respect for the native culture and religions; rather, it was a pacifying gesture. However, in 1835 Lord Macaulay's Model of Indian Education was fully implemented. Thus, education was brought out of the religious seminaries and confined to the education institutions totally devoted to conducting education in the Western style with the English language as the medium of instruction (Viswanathan, 1989).

Terry Eagleton (1996) criticizes the liberal humanist approach to literature and says that literature has never been detached from ideology because it is an ideology that constructs it. He analyzes the rise of English literature in English and briefly explains its role as a vehicle of cultural imperialism in colonized nations such as India. He discusses the early rise of English literature and the way it substituted for religion in Victorian England, explaining the role played by Matthew Arnold, F. R. Leavis, T. S. Eliot, and others in that regard.

Thus, according to Eagleton, the purpose of studying English literature was to develop conformist sensibilities among the individuals to establish British intellectual hegemony and thus to accomplish the agenda of cultural imperialism (p. 16). He also censures the canonicity of English literature advocated by Harold Bloom (1994)—the canonical writers popularized and introduced in the curricula were conservative. They did not make the readers challenge the norms; rather, they made them conformists (Eagleton, 1996, p. 28).

Building on Viswanathan's critique of English studies in India, Rita Raley traces the politics of English studies for literary and literacy purposes in British India. She opines that English studies were incorporated in the curricula of Indian universities in order to achieve two purposes: first to "civilize" the natives through English literary studies, and second to enable some Indians to work as agents of the colonizers—to help them establish the hegemony of the empire (Raley, 2000).

Alastair Pennycook (2002) tries to establish a link between English-language teaching (ELT) through literary texts and colonialism, unveiling the British Empire's hidden agenda of "linguistic colonization." The English language played a very important role in creating the discourse of British colonial hegemony. Departments of English language and literature became and are still operating as "civilizing centres" (Pennycook, 2002). According to Pennycook, the English department was established, and teaching practices and theories were designed by English colonizers, with the goal of enhancing their imperialist plan (2002, p. 19).

Dewi Candraningrum Soekirno (2006) studies the relationship between colonialism and the curricula of English language and literature. He underscores the role of canonical literature in the propagation of British colonial values and its intellectual hegemony. He says that the canonical texts that formed the curricula of English departments of the colonized countries produced and maintained a "fixed discourse" to determine the power relation between the colonizer and the colonized (pp. 71–72).

Golam Gaus Al-Quaderi and Abdullah Al Mahmud (2010) explore the state of English-language pedagogy in the English medium schools of Bangladesh. The findings of their study emphasize reshaping and localizing the curricula and the practices of teaching English to Bangladeshi students. They also emphasize the need for teachers' training to devise a suitable methodology to teach English literature.

Fizla Waseem (2014) reviews the historical background of the English language in Pakistan from a postcolonial perspective. She argues that the propagation of the English language has marginalized the local languages like Persian and Urdu. She explains how linguistic imperialism has led to the failure of what she calls the indigenous system of education.

Monazza Makhdoom and S. M. Awan (2014) also study the ramifications of neocolonialism on the curriculum of literature in the context of the University of Punjab. Looking into the history of curriculum development, they try to establish that the department of English at the University of Panjab has not evolved in line with the current trends.

Framework and Methodology

As explained earlier, the basic idea that laid the foundation for this study was taken from the Gramscian (1971) theory of hegemony; however, the writings of Edward Said (1978, 1994) and Viswanathan (1989) about English literature and its relationship with colonial ideologies have been helpful in devising the critical framework. Therefore, I have adopted postcolonial theory as it provides the perspective to study canonical English literature vis-à-vis other literature in English, offering an appropriate theoretical framework to study colonial ideology of curricula of literary studies in English.

To carry out the study, it was considered appropriate to devise an integrated methodology that combines the content analysis of the curricula of literary studies in English in the selected public sector universities of Pakistan with survey research. For content analysis, the syllabi of master of arts (English literature) curricula being taught in the departments of English at the selected universities at present were collected and analyzed. Most of the universities' contents of the scheme of studies for master of arts (English literature) curricula were obtained from their official websites. However, in some cases, the material was obtained by requests to the universities' English departments and the faculty members through email and personal contacts. The choice of the contents of the syllabi of master of arts (English literature) curricula from the selected universities was made based on the following criteria:

1. A master of arts (English literature) degree is the oldest and the main degree program of all the universities selected, since their inception.

2. It was among the first programs initiated at all the universities.
3. It usually attracts more students than any other program related to English literature at all the universities.
4. The degree program is offered not only in annual but also in semester systems of examination in some of the selected universities.
5. It attracts students who are hardworking, ambitious, and competent; hence, it has been a more competitive program than any other program in the humanities and social sciences.

The universities selected for the content analysis as well as for the questionnaire-based survey of teachers and students included:

- University of Karachi
- University of the Punjab, Lahore
- Bahauddin Zakariya University, Multan
- University of Peshawar
- National University of Modern Languages, Islamabad
- International Islamic University, Islamabad

The sampling of universities was done with the following criteria in mind:

1. The university must have taught English literature at the graduate/undergraduate level for at least 15 years.
2. The universities must be sponsored by the state of the Islamic Republic of Pakistan.
3. Classical/canonical English literary texts must have been an essential part of the syllabi since the inception of these universities, and they must be taught religiously.
4. The selected universities are spread all over Pakistan; hence, they attract students from around the country.
5. All the universities have students from lower- and middle-class Pakistani society.

The content of courses offered in the syllabi of master of arts (English literature) curricula was qualitatively analyzed. The findings of the content analysis were critically discussed in the light of the hypothesis, aims, and objectives of the study. The findings/results and recommendations/suggestions based on the analysis of the contents of the syllabi and the survey research were put forward in the conclusion. To authenticate the assumptions drawn from the contents' analysis and to verify them further, a survey consisting of two versions of a questionnaire were conducted. For this purpose, two versions of a questionnaire (i.e., one each for the teachers and the students) were designed and sent to the teachers and the students of English literature in the selected departments following certain criteria outlined below. While designing the questionnaires, the rules of the qualitative–quantitative survey were addressed. In designing the questionnaires, some important considerations taken into account included:

1. Respondent's views about the curricula and the practice of teaching English literature at the master of arts degree level,
2. Teaching methodologies and approaches in practice at present,
3. Prevalent techniques of interpreting an English literary text,
4. Popular notions about English literature such as the universality of the British canon, and
5. The legacy of departments of English in the Pakistani context.

Analysis and Discussion

The study was aimed at researching the present state of affairs of the curricula as well as the modes of teaching literary studies in English in the selected universities of Pakistan. I believe that the analysis and findings of the study will help revolutionize the curricula of these departments in the light of recent developments in literary studies and postcolonial pedagogy. This leads us to the analysis of the contents of the syllabi that will be followed by a discussion on the outcome of the survey. It is a general critique of the syllabi with specific examples.

Table 1 shows the ratio of British literary texts vis-à-vis the non-British ones. It verifies the basic postulation/hypothesis of the study—the syllabi are clearly lopsided in favor of canonical British literature. In almost all these departments of English, canonical British literature holds the central position while American, South Asian, and other literatures in English are either marginalized or are altogether ignored. For instance, Pakistani literature in English was not included in the syllabus of a master of arts degree in English in many departments of English at the selected universities. The same is true of South Asian literature. Moreover, the courses are often not structured with multiple perspectives/interpretations, objectives, and modes of instruction in mind; hence, in most cases it boils down to an indirect study of British political history. For example, while studying Shakespeare the students are led to believe

Table 1. Syllabi of MA (English) of the Selected Departments of Pakistani Public-Sector Universities

University		British	Non-British	% (British vs. Non-British)
University of Karachi		8	1 (Optional on American literature)	88.88 vs. 11.11
University of the Punjab	Semester system	13	6 (None include South Asian and Pakistani)	68.82 vs. 31.57
	Annual system	8	1 (Optional on literatures around the world)	88.88 vs. 11.11
Bahuddin Zakariya University, Multan		6	1 (American or South Asian literature in English)	85.71 vs. 14.28
University of Peshawar		8	0	100 vs. 0
National University of Modern Languages		10	1 (American and Canadian literature)	90.9 vs. 9.09
International Islamic University, Islamabad		10	7	58.82 vs. 41.17

that English literature is superior to all other literatures in all the languages of the world. It is then connected to the Renaissance spirit that is universalized as if the values of the Renaissance and Elizabethan eras are relevant to the students living in former colonies like Pakistan. The very fact that there is an exclusive course on Shakespeare is indicative of that fixed mindset. At the same time, there is only one course on, for instance, South Asian literature in English, and that is only in a few departments. This explains the problem I am trying to underline here. It is, however, important to mention, once again, that I do not mean to purge the syllabi of British literature and writers like Shakespeare who are very important, indeed. It is rather to create a balance and make the syllabi diverse as per the needs of a department of English in the postcolonial setting. The syllabi should also serve as a guide on how to study and teach the courses that have been missing until now.

In all the universities under study, there is at least one course on the history of English literature that is invariably the history of the British Empire, usually starting in the Anglo-Saxon period and proceeding to the Enlightenment. For example, the objectives of the course on the history of English literature at the University of Peshawar clearly state that the course is meant to help the students understand English literature in the light of British and European history starting from the Middle Ages to the 20th century. Similarly, several other courses of canonical English literature in the syllabi of these departments, such as Classical Drama, Classical Fiction, English Prose, and more, covertly aim to enhance students' understanding of British culture and its sociopolitical history. Thus, students of literary studies in English spend most of their time studying the British Empire and its sociopolitical history. I am not saying that they must not study British culture and politics. What I am trying to contend is that studying other literature and narratives in English coming from other regions of the world is equally important, particularly the ones from South Asia and other former colonies. The syllabi, nonetheless, do include, in some cases, important courses such as Literary Theory, Postcolonial Literature, and Literature From Around the World, but some of these courses are optional and most of them are missing important writers and critics as the core writers—for example, writers like Edward Said and Terry Eagleton, who are critical of English literature, have not been included as the core writers/critics. Edward Said is being taught as an essayist rather than a theorist/critic.

The selected departments, therefore, by design, have been propagating the colonial ideology even after decolonization. Even though we are 70 years down the road of independence, the curriculum has not changed much. Elsewhere, especially in the United States and South Africa, after decolonization, the canonical British literature has been reviewed thoroughly, and as a result, new literatures in English from the United States and South Africa as well as from around the world have been made part of the universities' syllabi. The teaching practices and methodologies have also been revised and restructured accordingly. It seems that there is a method in that because the study of the canonical English literature gives a certain power, a privileged position. Alok K. Mukherjee (2009) explains this in his idea of the localization of colonialism in what he calls "minimal hegemony" achieved through the tool of English language and literature. He explains the way English is being used by the Indian elites (which is true about Pakistan as well) to create and maintain hegemony following the colonial models, which he calls "alternative hegemony." The dominant elites, according to Mukherjee, internalized the superiority of European knowledge and English language to act as the replacement for colonizers (Mukherjee, 2009). That is why there has been very little or no reformation of the syllabi or the teaching practices in these departments. This proves the postulation of the study that the lack of diversity in the curricula of literary studies in English and the absence of a predefined methodology of literary analysis for teaching literature have a lot to do with the colonial legacy that these departments continue to carry. Hence, the status of canonical English literature did not change, even after the process of decolonization; in fact, it may have become more entrenched. Postcolonialism and literatures in English produced in the former colonies (which are termed as postcolonial or resistance literature) are creating ripples in the literary world and are behind numerous major changes in the curricula and the teaching practices in departments of English globally.

The survey questions were asked about the existing syllabi as well as the methods of reading and teaching the texts in the context of postcolonial Pakistan. The data obtained from the survey based on the questionnaires was then organized, tabulated, and analyzed following a critical framework derived mainly from postcolonial literary theory and pedagogy. A short review of the results of the survey and its analysis shows that the teachers, as well as the students, of master of arts level English at the selected universities seem to have appropriated the colonial ideology propagated in English literature. It shows that English literature incorporates the history of the British Empire. For instance, when asked about the methods of literary analysis and interpretation of the texts, the majority of the teachers (i.e., 72%) said that they followed traditional and practical critical approaches derived from liberal humanism. The same was reiterated by the students in their response to a similar question. This indicates, as discussed earlier, that the study of English literature follows traditional and practical critical approaches and lexical analysis of the texts. Therefore, we can say that the modes of instruction and methods of interpretation are fundamentally based on liberal humanism, which does not take into account the colonial politics of the texts in the context of the postcolonial Pakistani setting.

Similarly, when asked whether the respondents think that the ideas and values presented in English literature were universal and not provincial, most of the respondents—both the faculty and students—said that that was true. The basic argument for this inquiry lies in the observation that in most of the universities, English literature is still being taught and studied with the view that the ideas and values presented in English literature are universal. I think the notion that English literature and whatever it presents is relevant to every society, irrespective of cultural and historical differences, is based on the colonial myth that universalized the British values—which in my view is a colonial construction that has not changed over the decades.

Another question was whether it was important to understand British sociopolitical history to understand English literature. The results suggest that most of the teachers, as well as the students (i.e., 67.5% and 65%, respectively), think that the study of British sociopolitical history is important to understand English literature. When asked whether the critical insight that English literary criticism (including Sidney, Arnold, Wordsworth, Eliot, and others) offered was inevitable to understand any literature, most of the respondents were either unsure or agreed. Questions were also asked about English writers such as Shakespeare, Milton, Donne, Hardy, Dickens, Austen, and others. The responses indicate that the faculty, as well as the students, consider those writers as universal in their approach. They said that they were "timeless and townless." The impression that English writers transcend the boundaries of time and space is based on the Enlightenment program that justified imperialism of colonies like India and Nigeria.

While responding to the question of whether or not the syllabi of master of arts English programs (offered in the English departments of the selected universities) included an adequate number of literary texts from the nonnative-English–speaking world like South Asia, the majority of the respondents (i.e., 80% teachers and 53% students) responded that the syllabi did not have a satisfactory representation of the literary texts in English, or the translation works from the nonnative-English–speaking world like Pakistan, India, and other countries. Similarly, the respondents were asked if the study of English literature made them socially and culturally alien to their societies. A majority of the respondents were not sure about that. In the same way, when asked whether the respondents felt while teaching or studying English literature that it had nothing or little to do with the indigenous cultures and traditions of their students, the majority of the respondents were not sure about that either.

These results prove the hypothesis of the study that English literature is not a mere study of the English literary texts on linguistic and lexical levels, but also a study of British values, culture, philosophy, and thought. It thus proves the basic content of the study—that the study of English literature has been political and ideological, and that it cannot be studied in isolation. Hence, there is a need for a broader theoretical framework that is missing in the universities at present.

To sum up, I will say that the departments of English in Pakistani public sector universities have played the role of merely perpetuating the colonial ideologies because they have not been reformed in the wake of decolonization. Much of canonical English literature and the world-famous writers such as Shakespeare, Milton, and others have consciously or unconsciously been taught and studied as a part of colonial discourse and ideology. English literature, thus, is still being used as a tool to colonize the minds and hearts of the students in the universities included in the study. I feel the need to explain here that the purpose of this study has never been to suggest abandoning English literature or to "abolish the English department." I also affirm that I do not look at that in a nationalist framework, but from a broader postcolonial transformative perspective; therefore, it is meant to identify the problems in the curricula of literary studies in English in these universities and to consider the necessary revisions in the light of the findings of this study. Viswanathan, too, does not suggest shunning the study of English literature in Indian universities for the fact that it is a colonial legacy; she, however, does expose the way English literature was influential in furthering the process of colonialism (Viswanathan, 1989, p. 41).

Findings

No Transformation/Lack of Diversity

The valorization of British canonical texts in the curricula of the state-run universities of Pakistan has not changed with what is called decolonization. Canonical English literature and the political history of the British Empire continue to remain the cornerstone of the syllabi. Most of the departments have not been able to give sufficient representation to the literature in English produced in the nonnative-English–speaking countries such as Pakistan, India, Bangladesh, Nigeria, Kenya, South Africa, and the Caribbean Isles.

Valorization of the British Canon and the Denigration of Local/South Asian and Other Literature

There was a time when today's established writers like Achebe were struggling to find publishers, and often their fiction was called anthropology, not literature. The study shows that the attitude of people in the departments of English in these universities regarding South Asian and Pakistani writers as opposed to the British canon is no different. Most of the students in the departments of English in numerous Pakistani universities often do not know or have not read writers of Pakistan or South Asia.

The survey reveals that many teachers (unequipped with novel methods of critical literary analysis) are themselves very much convinced that the highest aesthetics lie only in canonical British literature. However, there are some who believe otherwise—that the contents of the syllabi have strong ideological and political implications, that there is a need to include South Asian and other writings in the syllabi, and that there is need to reform teaching methods.

The Absence of a Predefined Methodology of Literary Analysis

The prevalent practices of teaching English literature disregard the political and ideological dimensions of the texts as they focus, mainly, on the traditional historical-biographical approaches and practical criticism—which, indeed, do not and cannot offer a critical reading of the texts. The traditional methodologies and practices focus mainly on characterization, story, plot construction, writer's style, writer's points of view, themes of the story, historical and autobiographical aspects of the text, and more. A majority of teachers continue to remain committed to the tradition that validates and valorizes British literary texts (classical and modern—that constitute the major portion of canonical English literature). The teachers mostly follow liberal humanist approaches that emphasize textual, formal, and lexical analysis of the text rather than contextual methods of literary analysis. After learning of the Saidian theory of Orientalism, studying a literary text is no longer an innocent activity of appreciating its aesthetic values and plot construction. Rather, the text is taken as the interplay of politics, culture, and history.

Commitment to the Traditional/Stereotypical Views

Most if not all students have stereotypical views about British writers—for instance, that they are universal in their appeal and themes and that their genius is unmatched. Either the students have not studied critical/literary theory, such as postcolonial theory, deconstruction, and counter-discourse, or they are not able to connect those ideas to the study of literature. Hence, their views about English literature are based on the ideals of the Enlightenment and Modernism. The canonical texts that formed the curricula of English departments of the colonized countries produced and maintained a "fixed discourse" to create and maintain the power relation between the colonizer and the colonized. Unfortunately, the local elites have coopted the same agenda for their hold on power and privileges.

Recommendations

Two-Pronged Policy: Expansion of the Canon While Following an Integrationist Approach

We need to expand the canon—including writers from other parts of the world where literature in English has been produced. I recommend an in-depth revision, or, if I dare to say, a decolonization of the curricula of literary studies in English from undergraduate to postgraduate levels. In this regard, I believe an open-minded approach is required while drafting the curricula. We must not be swayed by the nationalistic, patriotic, and anti-West slogans, however. We need to deconstruct the colonial constructs and ideologies. This, however, does not mean that we should abolish English literature; its study is helpful, but it should be studied and taught in a way that highlights the context of colonialism and the formation of South Asian society. The inclusion of South Asian texts should not marginalize other literature.

Launching New Programs

We need to launch undergraduate and graduate programs in other literature in English as well, which is already being adopted by many universities, particularly in the United States and in some European universities. Similarly, we can also offer bachelor of science, master of arts, and master of science degrees in South Asian literature in English alongside a master of arts degree in British English literature, a master of art degree in the literature of North America (i.e., the United States and Canada) in English, and probably a master of arts degree in the literature of Africa, the Caribbean, and Australia in English as well. I am sure that it will help the departments of English keep pace with the international universities in meeting the challenges posed by the 21st-century globalized world.

Revising the Teaching Methodology

Alongside changing literary texts, the methods of literary analysis need drastic revision in the light of the globalized world and regional needs. Displacing Eurocentric narratives, we must move from textual to contextual approaches of studying and teaching literary texts (i.e., liberal humanism to theory). But that does not mean we should abandon the textual approaches altogether; rather, a diverse approach of studying and teaching literary texts, based on literary theory and postcolonial pedagogy, will enable students to critically evaluate different literary texts from around the world as well as local texts as expected from a student of English literature. Thus the purpose should be to make students think critically about different ideologies, colonial and others, that the texts carry within. How can students be critical of the British canon if the syllabus, as well as the teaching practices, are the same as prescribed by the colonizers themselves for colonized Indians? At the same time, it is important to make students think critically about their societies. Therefore, I think it is essential to enable students studying English literature to expose and neutralize the hegemonic agendas of the texts so that they may think about themselves and their society objectively, critically, and in a broader postcolonial and historical context.

REFERENCES

Al-Quaderi, G. G., & Al Mahmud, A. (2010). English literature in English medium schools in Bangladesh: The question of post-colonial pedagogy. *Asiatic: IIUM Journal of English Language & Literature, 4*(2), 121–154.

Althusser, L. (1971). Ideology and ideological state apparatuses. In *Lenin and philosophy, and other essays* (B. Brewster, Trans.) (pp. 127–188). New Left Books.

Apple, W. M. (2004). *Ideology and curriculum*. Routledge Flamer.

Ashcroft, B., Griffiths, G., & Tiffin. H. (1989). *The Empire writes back: Theory and practice in post-colonial literatures*. Routledge.

Ashcroft, B., Griffiths, G., & Tiffin. H. (1995). *The post-colonial studies reader*. Routledge.

Bloom, H. (1994). *The Western canon: The books and school of the ages*. Riverhead.

Braithwaite, E. K. (1995). Nation language. In B. Ashcroft, G. Griffiths, & H. Tiffin (Eds.), *The post-colonial studies reader* (pp. 309–313). Routledge.

Eagleton, T. (1996). *Literary theory: An introduction*. Blackwell Publishing.

Foucault, M. (1980). *Power/knowledge: Selected interviews and other writings, 1972–1977*. Pantheon.

Gramsci, A. (1971). *Prison notebooks*. International Publishers.

Gramsci, A. (2009). Hegemony, intellectuals and the state. In J. Storey (Ed.), *Cultural theory and popular culture: A reader* (4th ed., pp. 210–216). Routledge.

Makhdoom, M., & Awam, S. M. (2014). Education and neo-colonization: A critique of English literature curriculum in Pakistan. *A Research Journal of South Asian Studies, 29*(2), 411–421.

Mukherjee, A. K. (2009). *This gift of English: English education and the formation of alternative hegemonies in India.* Orient Blackswan.

Ngugi, T. W. (1986). *Decolonizing the mind: The politics of language in African literature.* James Currey.

Pennycook, A. D. (1998). *English and the discourses of colonialism.* Routledge.

Said, E. W. (1978). *Orientalism.* Vintage Books.

Said, E. W. (1994). *Culture and imperialism.* Vintage Books.

Soekiro, D. C. (2006). Inquiring the neo-imperial ideology in the English department curriculum: Teaching for reading against the grain using reader-response. *Teflin Journal, 17*(1), 69–80.

Viswanathan, G. (1989). *Masks of conquest: Literary study and British rule in India.* Columbia University Press.

Waseem, F. (2014). The legacy of the colonial project of English education in Pakistan. *International Journal of Business and Social Science, 11*(1), 138–146.

CHAPTER THREE | RAHUL BJØRN PARSON

Itinerant Locals and Globals
Hindi Women's Writing in Late 20th-Century Kolkata

The title of the conference, "Local Cities, Foreign Capitals: Finding the Local Anchor in the Global Cultures," suggests that local anchors must indeed be *found* and that they are not always evident and in the open. Or that if they are in the open, they may not be immediately visible. To this end, local literary techniques may suggest ways of seeing and being that make the local visible, namely, narrative strategies that reveal the lenses of the local and translocal, seeing past or through discourses of global homogeny. This study considers the writing of migrant communities in Kolkata—specifically the communities who write in Hindi, as most scholarship considers Bengal squarely as a Bengali literary field. I want to draw a connection between neoliberal political and economic reforms and the critique that emerges from the literary sphere. The sustained meditation on meanings of the local, especially in an era in which multiple erasures and homogenizations appear to be taking place, is where we see a critique and resistance in migrant literature. Recent Hindi writing from women in Kolkata is instructive in this regard, as it offers us a way to *read* the plurality of the city and the streets, also mining history for threads of diversity and identity that have not managed to consistently inform the present.

Hindi and Urdu once flourished in Calcutta; however, toward the end of the 20th century, Calcutta's Hindi legacy was by most accounts moribund (Miśra, 1983). But then, along with other upheavals and ruptures that attended the liberalization of the Indian economy beginning in 1991, a spate of Hindi novels emerged on the scene; they came from an unexpected portion of Calcutta's demographic—Marwari women. Marwaris are merchant-traders hailing from Rajasthan, who migrated to nearly every part of the subcontinent. It had been, in fact, a previous stage of economic and material globalization that brought the Marwaris to Bengal: "The Marwar area ... encompasses ancient trade routes across northern India, the economic impact of British rule impoverished that area ... forcing emigration, since the nineteenth century" (Mansingh, 2006, p. 389). I will briefly discuss works from Alka Saraogi (b. 1960), Prabha Khetan (1942–2008), and Madhu Kankaria (b. 1957), three Calcutta-based Marwari women writers. This spate of Hindi prose literature coincides with neoliberal economic reforms in the Indian state, compelling writers to reflect on the consequences of globalization and late capitalism in Calcutta at the close of the 20th century. The writing acknowledges a shared cultural space with Bengali and English, while presenting a sensibility of Hindi-speaking migrants. These novels circumvent the mainstream and majoritarian narrative of Calcutta and its history, yet they are nourished in the cultural richness of this literary city.

In the last two decades of the 20th century, a succession of Hindi writing emerged in Calcutta, once again claiming a literary place for Hindi in the predominantly Bengali literary milieu. As Meenakshi Mukherjee has noted, the phenomena of relocated communities have seldom been examined closely regarding literary representations: "It is surprising that [Marwaris] have rarely figured in Bangla fiction or film—except as caricatures. Even in the three Calcutta-centered films by Satyajit Ray ... the occasional Marwari character enters only to fulfill a completely predictable role of a crude moneymaker" (Mukherjee, 2008, p. 50). From this predicament of always being represented as threatening stereotypes and comic figures arises a collective need for a self-representation that writes the community into a dynamic cultural and imaginative existence. While this literature maintains a dialogic engagement with popular constructions of the Marwaris as an undifferentiated mass, it seeks to also go beyond corrective or apologetic positions toward a closer examination of identity as it relates to writing.

I shall illustrate with a couple of examples some central motifs and commonalities of this literature, namely deterritorialization and itinerancy, as a way of seeing local diversity, buried histories, and the virtue of plural perspectives. This last one is key—it is a rejection and critique of homogenizing hegemonies such as globalization. These themes, among others, endeavor to reinsert and rediscover diversity in Calcutta's history and literature, and to recover its plurality and militate against the homogenization of narratives and perspective. Every literary act is embedded in networks of material practices; literary and nonliterary "texts" interact and are dialogic. The physical city and the personal anecdote function as prominent literary devices in Calcutta

Hindi fiction, and they represent forms of knowledge available in the bazaar and the home; they are the loci of minor histories, minor literature.

The first of these writers to come on the literary scene was Prabha Khetan (1942–2008). Her novel *Pīlī Āndhī* (1996) was the first to explicitly deal with Marwaris as a migrant community. *Pīlī Āndhī* is a story that spans three generations of a Marwari family as they acquire identities in the diaspora as modern Marwaris, capitalists, citizens, and residents of British Bengal and independent India. Khetan traces a communitas and liminality of the Marwaris, as they are at the threshold of a transition and are "simultaneously blending into the ethos of their adopted region at work while retaining their separate identity within the domestic space" (Mukherjee, 2008, p. 48). As in all of Khetan's work, the story is a retelling of events and anecdotes from her experiences and family. Writing this type of *historical* novel calls for an act of critical fabulation in which the author has to invent a people who are at once real but not actual. Khetan thereby confronts the negative associations of her community by generously exposing the degree to which they confirmed, but also to disabuse the public of any essentialist conclusions.

It should be mentioned that Khetan was keenly interested in issues of plurality and the questions of local and global forces. A glance at her nonfiction writing offers insights into what these issues meant to her and how they manifest in her fiction: *Within the Market—Against the Market: Globalization and the Question of Women* (*Bāzāra Ke Bīca: Bāzāra Ke Khilāpha: Bhūmaṇḍalīkaraṇa Aura Strī Ke Praśna*, 2004) and *Globalization: Brand Culture and the Nation* (*Bhūmaṇḍalīkaraṇa: Brāṇḍa Saṃskṛti Aura Rāshtra*, 2007).

The novel *Pīlī Āndhī* examines the deterritorialization of the Marwaris from Rajasthan and their reterritorialization in Bengal. This requires an immense canvas: the spatial and temporal expanse of the novel moves across North India and from the end of the 19th century to the end of the 20th. The scope makes it impossible to have one protagonist or central character. Rather, the novel is about a collective of several individuals and their individuated freedom struggles. While these struggles in the novel are often of a community, they are staged as personal histories and relationships.

Pīlī Āndhī is about storms of sand and history, the violent forces that move territories and their inhabitants. The displaced must create new stories, both historical and fictional, for the home they lost and the home they seek. Below, I will examine the storm of history and sand that propels the Rūṅgṭā family into the predicament shared by all Marwaris in Calcutta—the paradox of adapting while staying the same, the homesickness of migrants. György Lukács writes of this *Heimweh* as a component of all great novels: "The novel's normative incompleteness is a true-born form in the historico-philosophical sense and proves its legitimacy by attaining its substratum, the true condition of the contemporary spirit. The idea of becoming becomes a state, and hence its form" (Lukács, 1971, p. 73). This homelessness, anxiety of belonging, and state of becoming manifest in *Pīlī Āndhī* as a need to create fictions and metafictions, as a way to ground a people to a literary past and inscribe their story into the terrain. The metafictions in the novel, the account books, and the memoirs of Marwaris are an analogy for artistic creation and the function of fiction—literally accounting for merchants. The home is a dissonant trope in the novel, simultaneously sought and fled in a state of perpetual incompleteness. The trope appears variously as a homeland (Heimat, *deś*), domesticity, land-*zamīn* (property), and belonging. The home also contains a type of history, namely in the way the novel invites other forms of private discourse (gossip, anecdote, and memoir) to push back against hegemonies.

Thus, in *Pīlī Āndhī*, as in much minor literature, the "'familial' and 'conjugal' situations appear unnaturally large, as if seen through the distorted focus of a microscope, and with only an isolated or mere 'local color' significance" (Renza, 1985, p. 32). This type of author can write as a communal or nonindividual figure, which enables her to produce literature "positively charged with the role and function of collective and even revolutionary utterance" (Deleuze, 1986, p. 17). Khetan's utterance, collective or not, was unprecedented for Marwaris living in such a literary city. Such a pioneering work as *Pīlī Āndhī* made the Hindi novel an available avenue for others in the community to consider their past and present.

Khetan spent a large portion of her life ostracized from the community and its functions and weddings, and yet this may have helped her write about the community:

> It is literature that produces an active solidarity in spite of skepticism; and if the writer is in the margins or completely outside her fragile community, this situation allows the writer all the more possibility to express another possible community and forge a means of another consciousness and another sensibility. (Deleuze, 1986, p. 17)

Khetan's writing brings out the fact that in Bengal a ghettoization of Marwaris occurred, and this isolation was most profoundly visited upon the women in the community, but not only. The remembrance of the deś (homeland) is a strong theme for immigrants, but while this is not necessarily a desire to return, it is an acknowledgment of something lost, and reinvestment in the value of the local and translocal. Further, in the effort to recover or conserve something, a stifling conservatism can emerge, taking the shape of the "apolitical." The first protagonist, Mādho, while still a child, is not particularly interested in the historical and discursive reasons for why Bengalis may see Marwaris as exploiters; the complexity of historiography escapes him. Rather, he is defensive and threatens that his people can quit Bengal if no convenient and amicable commercial conditions present themselves.

> Yes, Shīl Bābū, my uncle stays clear of politics. He simply says, "what's it to us?" We've come here to earn our bread, and we are earning our bread. If we don't meet with favorable conditions we go settle elsewhere. We've abandoned our homeland, so what's the big deal leaving Bengal? It's not as if there is nowhere else in the world for us to go. (Khetān, 1996, p. 54)

Their deterritorialization has become an asset and liberation. Having no roots affords the Marwaris great mobility as fluid, "apolitical" agents of capital. Remaining aloof of politics is a subject that comes up at every turn in the novel. But, ironically, the very solidarity of the Marwari polity consistently brings their actions into the political. Mādho feels that politics is a regional concern. Collectively unmoored, they are attached only to the market, yet the market and Marwaris become politicized by nationalist forces. The concept of private property gains purchase among Marwaris of Mādho's generation precisely because of this insecurity and nonbelonging. For the men, belonging with regard to private property and the national utility will eventually lessen the weight of local, regional issues. The women, alternatively, experience the weight of the local and the anxiety of belonging more severely because of the insulated sphere of the Marwari home in Bengal.

This sense of belonging through ownership and economic nationalism is not available to women. Mādho's aunt, Rādhā Bāī, laments about her loneliness in Bengal—a condition she feels is acute for both men and women. When Rādhā Bāī asks about women in Calcutta, Mādho tells her that they are completely different from women back home: "They play instruments, sing, and read books as they like. They don't do anything else. In the evenings they get in buggies and go see plays" (p. 62). Rādhā Bāī pines for the homeland; she finds life here is very lonely for men and women, and even Madho is so busy he can't be a child. Rādhā Bāī's account runs counter to what one might assume about Bengal because it was to be the home of India's most emancipated women, the *bhadramahila*.

> At first, Rādhā Bāī liked this frantic unbridled flow of water. Now, however, she has begun to recall those dry winds. She gets annoyed now when she sees that the morbid rains don't even consider the word "pause" for weeks. If the sun emerges it doesn't dry the earth, rather it increases the stuffiness, then the dense black clouds return, swirling, dancing and roaring, the leaves on the trees rustle, the frogs croak, and with it a deluge of serpents and scorpions. Millet is nowhere to be seen. Ker–Sāngar must be carefully saved to make anything. A few Marwari families have settled nearby. They recall the summertime swing, but where shall I go here? On what swing may I swing? In the village, even in purdah, there was no restriction on movement. At least we women went to the well morning and evening. At the well there was always a little festival going on, someone showing off a veil or piece of jewelry, etc. . . . But in this land there are grave restrictions. Both man and wife live in misery. (Khetan, 1996, p. 52)

Rādhā Bāī is the first woman in this family to live in Bengal. She had very little contact with the region, which she looks on with suspicion. She makes some interesting inversions: linking the rains with morbidity, purdah (seclusion) as mobility, and Bengal as more restricted for a woman than Rajasthan. Rādhā Bāī longs for the grain and millet from the land she knows to be in a severe drought. Mādho's impression of Bengal's rain and lush vegetation are of wonder and plentiful resources. The climate of "Bengal" seems to push Rādhā Bāī indoors. She finds nowhere to belong, no communal well at which to socialize, and no swing for amusement. The Rūngtā women stay indoors for the next three generations.

Khetan's novels were the first rumblings of dissatisfaction after which other Marwari women began to write. Khetan's last novel appeared in 1997, one year before Alka Saraogi's award-winning *Kali-Katha: Via Bypass* took similar themes into the mainstream of Hindi letters.

The multiple entendre titles of Alka Saraogi's *Kali-Kathā: Via Bypass* (1998) suggests a story, or *kathā*, that is simultaneously about the metropolis of Calcutta and the *kaliyuga* (the end-time), but also, as the subtitle suggests, about perspectives that bypass dominant and official versions of history and the present. The narrative interrogates differing layers of history and uses of the past by juxtaposing the representation of time and space on the street and in the home, and the historical tensions and incongruities between the 1940s and the 1990s. By holding these moments (and spaces) side by side, the narrative highlights the plurality of people and ideas in the early part of the 20th century that have become homogenized in the 1990s, though the threads of this former diversity remain defiantly available to the urban flaneur. *Kali-Kathā,* via its narrative structure of bypasses, shows that history and progress are nonlinear and that these sea changes and reforms often contain as many regressive positions as they propose to undo. The narratives place a high premium on texts and streets as dialogical spaces of plurality and sites of resistance against the homogenizing juggernaut of late-capitalist consumer culture. As a flaneur, Kishore Babu (the protagonist) is the chronicler of the city's history and political economy. Walter Benjamin suggests that this is a function of the flaneur in literature: "The flâneur is the observer of the marketplace. His knowledge is akin to the occult science of industrial fluctuations" (2002, p. 427). As Kishore strolls around the city, he can see a material matrix with its invisible ideology and power structures operating in different historical contexts. In this way, the "experiential horizons" of the minor subjects of history enter into the narrative, placing their defiance and conformity in context. It is not correct to think of Kishore as simply a flaneur. It is perhaps inappropriate to assume he fits 19th-century European bourgeois categories so neatly. In the novel, he is referred to as a fakir, perhaps a different type of flaneur, befitting a non-European context. Below we will explore what this difference may represent.

> Exactly in the middle of the speeding cars, the smoke of the buses and mini-buses, and the screeching sound of the horns and brakes of Calcutta's Lansdowne Road, in front of the city's newest and most expensive restaurant "Golden Harvest," Kishore Babu was seen crossing the street without looking. (Saraogi, 2002, p. 5)

Kishore at this moment can *see* things that had remained invisible to him, especially as he has stopped looking in the more conventional ways (i.e., at the traffic or the expensive restaurant where people from his social class would be dining). He is presumably visible to his social peers in and around the restaurant as he jaywalks to investigate what he thinks is a group of men urinating in an unorthodox manner. As a fakir, he is not visible, and that is the whole point of the fakir, distinguishing this figure from a flaneur.

This episode of jaywalking continues in the following chapter in the form of a note that Kishore has written. Kishore's wife, Saroj, finds the note and conceals it because she considers the note deeply embarrassing. His "visibility" appears, then, most likely only in the written form, and that is quickly suppressed. This is the first indication of tension between the "street" and the "home." The home, in a sense, attempts to suppress the vulgarity of the street, here in its written form. Kishore narrates that the line of squatting men turns out to be diners, who are eating a cheap lunch with a plank for a table. In this space of heterogeneous convergence, Kishore can see life outside his upper-class milieu. From the vantage point of the *street*, Kishor sees one of his employees eating with the others sitting at the plank. He writes in his note that he was very surprised to see his employee, Shiv Babu, sitting there. Kishor wonders if Shiv Babu's wife is sick and therefore unable to prepare tiffin for him to take to work. Then he realizes that he doesn't know whether or not Shiv Babu has a wife. He reflects on the fact that one of his workers is so removed from him socially that he has no idea whether or not he is married. His thoughts then return to urination. He wonders where women can relieve themselves while walking in Calcutta. Though these ideas seem banal, for Kishore they are radical regarding class and gender consciousness, and they represent a break with the former Kishore who could never conceive of these concerns. Kishore stands between the cheapest and most expensive places to dine in Calcutta, forcing him to confront the social realities he has hitherto failed to notice—at least not since he was a teenager in the 1940s.

Another way social discourse enters novelist discourse is the through the anecdote. As Catherine Gallagher and Stephen Greenblatt show,

> the anecdote satisfied the desire for something outside the literary, something that would challenge the boundaries of the literary … the sphere of practice that even in its more awkward and inept articulations makes a claim on the truth that is denied to the most eloquent of literary texts. Or rather the anecdote was a way into the "contact zone," the charmed space where the genius literarius could be conjured into existence. (2000, p. 48)

Kali-Kathā's exploration of memory and anecdote excavates histories of identity, diversity, and the perpetually dying city of Calcutta. Thus, *Kali-Kathā* does something much more than recover history; the novel "conjures" the "genius literarius" in its very contact with Calcutta. The streets of Calcutta become the text into which all of these histories are inscribed: "The Bengalis, the British, the Marwaris, the Armenians, Jews, Parsees, Greeks all left traceable marks on the city like Armenian Street, The Greek Orthodox Church, and Jewish Girls' School, etc." (Saraogi, 2004, p. 19). Thus the streets are also an archive of numerous cultures and histories. Muslims are not on this list, because unlike these other communities, they are still a major part of the city's demographic, in fact, 20% in Kolkata (27% statewide), but they are also not adequately represented in film or literature of the city.

The road or street in the history of the novel is an important space of encounter and plurality, particularly regarding the local exotic. Mikhail Bakhtin asserts that the road is "profoundly, intensely etched by the flow of historical time, by traces and signs of time's passage, by markers of the era" (1998, p. 244). Bakhtin describes the street in terms typically associated with text (etched, traces, signs, and markers), implying that the street is itself legible. Kishore is said to repeatedly map and measure the street, amounting to the cartography of memory: "In this world, nothing from the past is ever lost. How could it be lost when we still remain? At most, like old ruined cities, it gets buried under many layers deep within us" (Saraogi, 2002, pp. 13–14). *Kali-Kathā*'s narrative structure seeks to avoid retrospective, teleological histories that Sudipta Kaviraj identifies as *anachronistic* history, for "anachronism distorts our historical judgment" by giving the impression that "earlier periods and cultures were structured like our own in their institutions, practices, discourses, meanings, and significations of concepts, etc." (Kaviraj, 2010, p. 173). Kaviraj maintains that this type of anachronistic historiography is the result of a degree of arrogance with which the present views the past:

> The conceit of the present, the precarious ontological privilege that it enjoys over the other times, is expressed often in another, subtler and more fundamental fault of historical vision. This is the temptation to believe that the only function of the past, its only conceivable justification, was to produce the present. (Kaviraj, 2010, p. 6)

The historical vision and structure of *Kali-Kathā* reverse the concept of the present, a type of anachronistic historiography. The novel explores the ideological plurality of the past, ranging from figures like Gandhi to Subhash Chandra Bose, which cannot be reconciled to the mainstream homogenized present. The interstices in the dominant narrative (the narrative this story is *bypassing*) leave space for some minor stories that make claims on history but are not contiguous or consistent with the official version of the present.

The conclusion of the novel demonstrates that marginal social formations and historical trajectories may remain below history and society until the material conditions for their reassertion mature. The reversal of class hierarchy in the postapocalyptic conclusion reveals the presence of invisible social formations and narratives. The disjuncture among ideologies and trajectories between the 1940s and 1990s represents a failure to locate and include social formations and ideologies that fall below history's gaze. Here we see the rise of the subaltern:

> Now the happiest man was the poorest one, who had just been living on the land and used to going by foot. The most important task in order to eat became the production of grains, fruit, and vegetables and people acquainted with this work became the highest paid. (Saraogi, 2002, p. 214)

In Madhu Kankariya's novel, *Khule Gagan ke Lal Sitare [Red Stars from the Open Sky]*, a story of love and revolution, the poles of Bengaliness and Marwariness, Naxalism and Jainism, begin to dissolve in the first-person narrator: a move toward a synthesis of Calcutta's heterogeneity. Thereby a highly plural voice of the Calcuttan emerges that seems to have been previously drowned out. The consciousness of the novel becomes an analog of ancient Jain epistemology known as *anekāntavāda*—multiple perspectives. *Khule Gagan*, then, not only tells a marginal story of Calcutta, a *Via Bypass* story, as it were, but it attempts to offer another way of seeing. Thus, *anekāntavāda* is recovered, from 2,000 years ago, to help one understand that everyone has some claim to truth. *Khule Gagan* privileges the many voices of Calcutta's streets; they appear as public texts where the flaneur or fakir may read forgotten histories. As the novel shows, the walls along every road in Calcutta bear highly stylized political graffiti that is an unending political conversation writ large (Kāṅkariyā, 2000, p. 162). Yet to see these histories and texts, the protagonist frequently seizes the "telling" of the story, becoming at those moments the narrator. This is a feature of Calcutta Marwari writing that insists on interventions (*hastakṣep*) in the narrative as a comment on the politics of representation. For in Bengal, the treatment of Marwaris in literature and film has been static and demonstrates the durability of a stereotype. The act of writing itself develops as a liberation struggle from a painful past and as an *aide à penser* for a complicated present. Through her encounters on the streets around Presidency College, Maṇi begins to see her home life through different eyes, a process which at first reproduces the stigmatization of popular attitudes toward Marwaris. However, through the process of writing and thinking, she develops a nuanced understanding of her Marwari identity and of differing ways of being in the world.

Madhu Kankariya uses several types of discourse and speech genres in her novels, even more so after *Khule Gagan*. The protagonist-cum-narrator appears to be conducting very personal research, and the voices and languages surrounding the objects of her research penetrate her consciousness throughout the novel. Kankariya's style has an element of reportage that is akin to Gonzo journalism in that it does not make claims to objectivity and interjects (*hastakśep*) the "fiction writer's" opinions and experiences throughout the narrative. The narrative style moves among various discourses—from journalistic, ethnographic, historical, diaristic, political, and propagandistic, to novelistic. This cacophony is the novel's heteroglossia, as Bakhtin notes:

> The novel can be defined as a diversity of social speech types (sometimes even diversity of languages) and a diversity of individual voices, artistically organized. The internal stratification of any single national language into social dialects, characteristic group behavior … languages of the authorities, of various circles and of passing fashions, languages that serve the specific sociopolitical purposes of the day. (1998, pp. 262–263)

The speech genres operating in the novel place it historically and geographically in Calcutta of the Naxalite era—it is what develops the novel's space–time, or chronotope. It is also the basis of the dialogism that is the characteristic "epistemological mode of a world dominated by heteroglossia" (Bakhtin, 1998, p. 426). While the novel is focalized through Maṇi, the character zones of the other main characters are voiced in her mind.

Maṇi is a 45-year-old Marwari Jain woman who teaches in a school and is single. Twenty-six years after the fact (the mid-1990s), she is trying to piece together and write the story of the Naxalite movement and the disappearance of her lover Indra. The basic frame is a series of interviews with a former Bengali Naxalite (Gobind Da) that are punctuated with flashbacks to the late 1960s and early 1970s. Gobind Da had been a central figure in the movement; he operated a printing press where the party published its ideological writings and propaganda pamphlets. The fictionalized printing press, *Yugvrati* (renunciant, or vow-taker of the age), became the nerve center connecting the various ideologues in the movement, making for Gobind's privileged position in the organization. Gobind's account of the movement and the violence that accompanies it cause Maṇi to recall her days at Presidency College and her home life during the period. The narrative reconstructs the love story of Maṇi and Indra through her diaries and memories, against the backdrop of rapidly intensifying political violence in West Bengal. Maṇi recalls that in those *red-hot* days her family was intensely insulated, steeped as it was in Jain tradition. As she reconsiders those years, Maṇi cannot avoid juxtaposing the seeming opposites of Naxalism and Jainism. On the level of narrative, however, the opposite poles look more like two extremes of disillusionment, rejection, and the opting-out of mundane hypocrisies. Gradually, the speech genres and heteroglossia of the worlds of the Naxalite and the Jain begin to merge, describe, and critique one another. This process complicates the construction and location of identity—everything Maṇi voices is populated with her encounter with Bengal, its streets, and her Marwari heritage. The vocabularies and utterances of the Bengali Naxal-Violent-Political and the Marwari Jain-Nonviolent-Apolitical fill and cross-pollinate Maṇi's experience of both worlds.

The first chapter is called *A Meeting Consigned to Death/Time (Kāl)*. Speaking to Maṇi in a mixture of Bengali and Hindi (*bangālī miśrit hindī*), Babul Da, her Naxal contact, leads her through "a little historical alley emerging from Calcutta's Hathibagan District ... Sikdar Bagān Street ... whose history lives only in the memory of its inhabitants. In those hot days, 1970–1972 the Naxalites called this street *Lāl Galī* (Red Alley)" (Kankariya, 2000, p. 9). Across the street from the house is a neglected old memorial of the revolutionary Jatin Das (1904–1929)—small, dusty, and covered in pigeon droppings. To quote Bakhtin again, the Calcutta streets are "profoundly, intensely etched by the flow of historical time, by traces and signs of time's passage, by markers of the era" (1998, p. 244). The road or street in the history of the novel is an important space of encounter and plurality, particularly regarding the local exotic, as opposed to the foreign exotic. As Bakhtin has shown, the "road is always one that passes through *familiar territory* ... it is the *sociohistorical heterogeneity* of one's own country that is revealed and depicted" (1998, p. 245). The "Red Alley" is the site of layered history that Maṇi has come to uncover. It is a history that only lives in the inhabitants (*bāśindā*) of the alley. The desire to know and to uncover mysteries and lost narratives becomes existentially significant to Maṇi; she cannot continue her own story until she completes the story of her lover Indra, who was murdered during the paramilitary repression of the Naxalite movement. Again, the narrative strategies use the figure of a person, moving through the streets and various textual archives, to locate forms of resistance and former struggles that have been silenced, and now more than ever must be found in the local.

Like Kishore Babu of *Kali-Kathā*, Maṇi decries the India of the late 1990s as an increasingly homogenizing entity, which offers no resistance to globalization or Westernization, or to the hegemonic rule of the Communist Party of India (Marxist), which has no Indra to cry "Yankee Culture *nipāt jāk* (down with)." In other words, she rejects the one-sided (*ekāntavāda*) half-truth of the present and strives for a comprehensive view of the present reality and history.

Implications

This new literature then gives Calcutta Marwaris a literary past in Hindi—one in which their collective history and identity can be imaginatively explored. Khetan, Saraogi, and Kankariya expand the Hindi tradition to include the subjectivities and domesticities of Calcutta's migrants. The novels share several intriguing qualities, which make their comparison rich and productive. The tropes of writing, memory, identity, and history loom large in all the work, the street and market as layered texts, and finally, narrative interventions, or seizing the telling. The similarities and patterns in the works show that something radically collective is operating in the literature. Each novel discusses the act of writing as a trope and writing what is patently fictional, in a quest for truth. Along these lines, the novels also suggest multiple versions of truth and history—*anekāntavāda*. Hindi literature in Bengal offers alternative ways of reading the city and its multiplicity, grafting minor narratives onto Bengali and world literary traditions, with an upcountry accent.

The discovery and exploration of such literature offer ways in which we can find the local anchors in the moment of global culture. Additionally, the novels perform practices of seeing and reading that render visible a matrix of power as well as the buried plurality and defiance that can challenge the creeping homogenization. It is the task of the reader and the scholar to give attention to minor acts of cultural production to gain a broader view of our present and the way forward.

REFERENCES

Bakhtin, M. M. (1998). *The dialogic imagination: Four essays* (11th ed.). University of Texas Press.

Benjamin, W. (2002). *The arcades project* (H. Eiland & K. McLaughlin, Trans.; R. Tiedemann, Ed.). Belknap Press of Harvard University Press.

Deleuze, G. (1986). *Kafka: Toward a minor literature*. University of Minnesota Press.

Gallagher, C., & Greenblatt, S. (2000). *Practicing new historicism*. University of Chicago Press.

Kāṅkariyā, M. (2000). *Khule gagan ke lāl sitāre [Red stars from the open sky]*. (1. saṃskaraṇa. ed.). Rājakamala Prakāśana.

Kaviraj, S. (2010). *The imaginary institution of India: Politics and ideas*. Columbia University Press.

Khetān, P. (1996). *Pīlī āndhī* (1. saṃskaraṇa ed.). Lokabhāratī Prakāśana.

Lukács, G. (1971). *The theory of the novel: A historico-philosophical essay on the forms of great epic literature*. M. I. T. Press.

Mansingh, S. (2006). *Historical dictionary of India* (2nd ed.). Scarecrow Press, Inc.

Miśra, K. (1983). *Hindī sāhitya: Baṅgīya bhūmikā* [Preface in Bengali on Hindi Literature]. (1. saṃskaraṇa. ed.). Maṇimaya.

Mukherjee, M. (2008). *Elusive terrain: Culture and literary memory*. Oxford University Press.

Renza, L. A. (1985). *A white heron and the question of minor literature*. University of Wisconsin Press.

Saraogi, A. (2002). *Kali-Katha: Via bypass* [*The Story of Kali: Via bypass*]. Rupa and Company.

Saraogi, A. (2004). *Streaming up memory in-between past and present: A river of words—Meeting the Indian writers Alka Saraogi and Anita Nair*. L'Harmattan Italia.

CHAPTER FOUR | IMRAN ADEEL

Decentering Religious Traditions
A Deconstructionist Perspective of "Church Going"

The notion of a multiplicity of meanings in literary works got its spark in literary criticism incorporating the theory of deconstruction. To grasp a comprehensive picture of an artistic piece, considerable significance has been given to poststructural approaches to deconstruct the meanings, symbols, and interpretations. In the case of interpretations of the text, poststructuralism seems to rebel against structuralism because it accuses the latter of being too conventional in deducing the meanings by putting the text in the context of broader structures. Moreover, poststructuralists accuse structuralists of being too limited in their intellectual system, on which they have no other means to approach reality. It also leads to the questioning of one of the basic assumptions about language, set by structuralism: that language constitutes and shapes reality. So in this way, the only medium left to approach reality is language. But as poststructuralism claims that there is no inherent connection between the sign and signifier, they become "unmotivated signs," leaving no fixed interlink between the word and the real object or the mental concept of that object to which that particular word refers. Additionally, by leaving no fixed intellectual reference, poststructuralism leads us to a gravity-free universe, with no clear identification of direction. This gravity-free universe is free of any center on which it can be referenced to a fixed landmark beyond perception—a "decentered universe" (Barry, 2002).

"Deconstruction" aims to reveal the conflict between the word and the object that it signifies. This conflict leads us to doubt any certainty about the meaning and reality created by the language in the text. But here the doubt arises about how deconstructive study would be considered systematic and methodological. The answer lies in the close reading of significant recurrent items that are the key factors in the development of conflict. In this regard, Barbara Johnson suggests, "The deconstruction of a text does not proceed by random doubt or arbitrary subversion, but by the careful teasing out of warring forces of signification within the text itself" (1980, p. 5). So it deals with skeptical attitudes toward poetic language and poetic realities focusing on "decentering" meaning and interpretation. All centers of meanings, references, and foundations of identities are brought under skepticism, resulting in the establishment of radical uncertainty. This skeptical attitude toward foundations leads us to the unreliability of language (i.e., "linguistic skepticism"), which constitutes the world. This notion of decentering has its roots in historical events destroying some established centers, which resulted in disillusionment about the hegemony of these centers. For example, the First World War and Holocaust tarnished the illusion of Europe as the center of civilization and its uniform economic prosperity, along with scientific discoveries (i.e., the theory of relativity) and the influence of modernism in the fields of creative arts, which led the world to the disillusionment of already established centers (Barry, 2002).

By assuming this phenomenon as the key factor of the study, this essay attempts to analyze the phenomenon of the "decentering" of the church in modern times depicted in "Church Going," one of the excellent poems by a leading modern English poet, Philip Larkin. This poem perpetuates the notion of decentralizing the church in contemporary modern societies of England. The poem primarily deals with the religious skepticism regarding the outdatedness of churches in modern society with a description of a narrator who has an unintended visit to the church, where he performs some norms not inspired by his reason or institution but by the dysfunctional dogmatic tradition. Second, it also attempts to explore the "linguistic anxiety" created by paradoxes, disunities, and gaps in the language of the poem. As it is obvious that Philip Larkin is a postwar and modern poet, significantly captivated by the notions of modernity in poetry, he excessively provides his readers with the multiplicity of meanings and multifold interpretations with the incorporation of deep-rooted metaphors, linguistic ironies, and implicit ideas. These features of his poetry are a powerful stimulus for a researcher to analyze his work from a deconstructionist perspective. Moreover, it focuses on the notion of how a postwar poet treats the object of the church regarding modernity. The influence of modernity has tarnished the authority of the church and also distorted the religious traditions into the disintegration of faith and its beholders, resulting in a decentralized and uncertain society with no defined aspirations related to traditional religion.

Literature Review

A brief overview of deconstructionism is necessary to understand the interventions of this essay. In this respect, it is difficult to define "deconstruction" because, as Gregory Jay points out, "deconstruction has now become an indeterminate nominative" (1990, p. xi). By saying this, Jay signifies the importance of reference in defining the theory of deconstruction. He furthermore holds that it is considered that the element of uncertainty always lies with the concept of deconstruction. Although it is hard to narrow down the deconstructionist framework, a clear analysis of the problem can lead to the appropriate meaning (Jay, 1990).

Although it is hard to narrow the concept of deconstruction to a single definition, it is extremely useful here to operationalize the theory of deconstruction to its beneficial elements after scrutiny. In this regard, Jacques Derrida (1982) argues that deconstruction is more than a method of investigating the recurrent and contrasting patterns. It is usually assumed to be an attitude of mind toward the text rather than critical theory. In the same context, J. Hillis Miller (1976) argues in favor of the implementation of theory while defining deconstruction. He signifies the particular context created by the specific examples on which the theory is supposed to be applied. As he says,

> [T]he sentences of the form "Deconstruction is so and so" are a contradiction in terms. Deconstruction cannot be defined, since it presupposes the definability or, more properly, "undecidability" of all conceptual or generalizing terms. Deconstruction, like any method of interpretation, can only be exemplified, and the examples will, of course, all differ. (Miller, 1976, p. 231)

Moreover, Chung Chin-Yi (2016) also signifies the contextualization of Derrida's theory. She is of the view that the determination of any discourse is influenced by its own shadow, or broadly speaking its ghost, because, in excluding or distinguishing the represented constituent elements, the process of the opposition of relational terms and a defining axis is meant to be considered.

To operationalize the theory of deconstruction on any piece of text, Peter Barry's three-stage analysis method has been a distinctive critical approach that intends to show the intrinsic disunities in texts that seem to be united. In his method, Barry (2002) points out that contradictions or paradoxes may help critically invoke the recurrent patterns in the literary language that ultimately result in the disunity of thought proceeding into an exploration of "linguistic anxiety." Thus, in the process of analyzing a poem with the deconstructive approach, Bhagyashree (2016) says that the analysis of the poem, by putting it under a deconstructive reading, can lead the reader to a multiplicity of meanings and a diversity of linguistic dimensions. Furthermore, as she signifies the multiplicity regarding meanings and interpretations by analyzing the poem in "syntagmatic" and "paradigmatic" chains of lexical choices, she incorporates the metaphoric and metonymic expression of language in her analysis. She also focuses on the objectivity of interpretation regarding its authenticity, the appropriateness of analyzing the syntactic structure, and the role of semantic meanings in the analysis. Meanwhile, Bassel Almasalmeh (2014) identifies the instability of poetic language regarding binary opposition. He perpetuates the notion that binary opposition collapses into a decentering of meanings and blurring of realities when they are put into the context of broader structures, as in structuralism. Moreover, he signifies the process of scrutinizing deconstruction theory into its representative elements and exploring linguistic anxiety and language instability regarding its meanings and interpretation, resulting in not only the better understanding of the piece of art, but also the theory itself.

To implement the theory of deconstruction, it is important to scrutinize its representative elements that would be analyzed in the poem. The most basic and important element is "linguistic anxiety." Carmen Chaves Tesser (1991) has implied some key defining features while analyzing the novel, with linguistic anxiety as the key factor regarding the decentering of meanings and identities. In this due course, he aims to determine linguistic anxiety, paradox, tension in the novel, and the decentering of meanings and identities. So, in his attempt, he tries to interpret the novel regarding "absence of meaning" in a way that searches for the meanings that are missing or unuttered by the novelist. What is said in the novel is interpreted as against itself. Additionally, the betrayal of binary opposition is highlighted. According to him, meanings that are defined regarding the binary opposition are unreliable and incomplete. They seem blurred in a foggy image. The only way to approach the clear picture is the prior knowledge and the shared context of the meanings.

In the same fashion, the poem "Church Going" will be analyzed from the deconstructionist approach by focusing on the representative elements of this theory including decentering, linguistic anxiety, and paradoxes. By exploring these elements, the place of churches in modern societies, the poet's treatise with the church, and the multiplicity of meanings would be easy to understand. In this respect, Pericles Lewis (2004) puts considerable significance on the issue of religious rituals and their appropriateness in modernity regarding the quest for understanding their meanings. He further argues in favor of giving attention to secularization rather than disenchantment, which provokes the shift in emphasis on private experiences contrary to the public sphere. Additionally, he puts considerable emphasis on the place of this poem, "Church Going," in the triumph of modern literature regarding secularization. With the above views on modernity, it is clear that there is room for a deconstructionist reading of the poem.

Research Framework

To meet the objectives, this essay incorporates a research framework that includes a three-stage analysis of the deconstructive process consisting of verbal, textual, and linguistic stages (Barry, 2002). The verbal stage attempts to analyze the poem in a more conventional way, holding a close reading of the poem. Moreover, it attempts to invoke the recurrent patterns in the poem, including paradoxes, contradictions, and ambiguities, which result in linguistic anxiety. The exploration of linguistic anxiety will further lead to the "decentering" at upcoming stages.

The next stage, the textual stage, takes the poem beyond the separate words and phrases and analyzes the shifts, breaks, and disunities in the overall continuity of the poem. The poem is investigated regarding the instability of language by attending to its shift in focus, time, or tone. Additionally, it holds the approach regarding the change in narration (i.e., from the first person to third, or a change in tense). Moreover, these shifts and changes in narration result in the identification of the instability of language and the unreliability of realities created by that language.

The third stage, the linguistic stage, looks for the instances in the poem when the proficiency and adequacy of poetic language itself are brought into question. The linguistic stage also questions the poetic language as a medium of communication regarding instabilities and unreliability. Additionally, it attempts to unearth the intrinsic and implicit references to the untrustworthiness of the linguistic medium. For instance, it may involve the moments when the poem says something or acts in such a way that is described as beyond saying or opposite to the overall tone of the poem. This stage also signifies the hidden or implicit ideology that has not been said by the poet, leading readers to the point of reference at which explicit and overt linguistic signals help explore the implicit and overt or unconscious of the poem.

These three-stage analyses will lead to the exploration of linguistic anxiety pertaining to paradoxes, ambiguities in meanings, and disunities in the continuity of tone in the poem. Additionally, it will help us dive deeply into the unconscious of the poem to have a comprehensive understanding of the work. Moreover, this process will lead us to the identification of instabilities of linguistic medium and unreliability of reality created by poetic language, resulting in the decentering of conventional reality constituted by the language of the poem.

Analysis

This part starts with a summary of the poem and proceeds to the three-stage analysis of verbal, textual, and linguistic components, respectively. The poem starts with the description of an uninspired visit by a 20th-century bored cyclist to an empty and disenchanted church, where he experiences the church rituals in an unintended fashion. He steps inside the church after confirming that nothing is going on there with an onomatopoeic sound of the church door "thud[ding] shut" behind him. Inside, he seems unimpressed by the environment of the church with its seats, matting, and brass along with the architecture of the church building. He also witnesses the tense and unignorable silence that causes him to act awkwardly. Furthermore, he touches the holy font scribed at a place and reads some verses from the holy book in an unusual way. His unintended observance of religious rituals seems clear with his dropping of sixpenny in the drop box. Moreover, he wonders about the future of churches when people stop visiting them. He addresses them as "unlucky places," thinking their end a mere dummy for modern religious beliefs or the superstitious cure for cancer or other diseases. Additionally, he wonders who will be the last man visiting these places that supposedly deal with a limited number of affairs, such as marriage, birth, and death. Surprisingly, all these events and descriptions of rituals lead the reader toward religious skepticism and modern secular beliefs in the 20th century. The boredom in spirit and disengagement with traditional religious rituals also signify the outdatedness of dysfunctional churches.

As discussed in the research framework, the verbal stage of analysis attempts to invoke paradoxes, ironies, and ambiguities that constitute the contradictions in meanings as in the opening lines of the first stanza: "Once I am sure there's nothing going on / I step inside, letting the door thud shut." The reader is left understanding that no action was performed in the first line, but then the poet steps inside the church, which suggests that an action of "stepping in" has occurred. So a paradox is observed, which creates a complexity of meaning. Additionally, the poet at first intends his reader to imagine the church with no proceedings, no visitors, and no clear objective, but in the very next moment he visits the church and breaks the notion of "nothing is going on" by stepping into the church. Second, in the seventh line of the same stanza, he describes a kind of dense silence inside the church, but the "thud[ding] shut" of the door with his entrance creates a contrary effect to his statement when he says, "And a tense, musty, unignorable silence." Moreover, in the second-to-last and last lines of the stanza, the poet offers rituals of respect, albeit ironically. Being "hatless," he removes his "cycle-clips" to observe the respect for church tradition. His words, "Hatless, I take off / My cycle-clips in awkward reverence," clearly suggest mockery and satire of the outdated tradition of the church in modern life. Additionally, his use of the paradoxical expression of "awkward reverence" also vitalizes his satirical intentions because reverence, a reference to something respected, in an "awkward" fashion arouses linguistic anxiety. Through all these notions of decentralization, the poem signals that churches in modern times are dysfunctional and the worshippers are just the hollow followers of religious traditions.

The poet sets the stage for the rhetorical question in which he first addresses the roof of the church, and then he poses a question in the following lines: "From where I stand, the roof looks almost new – / Cleaned, or restored? Someone would know: I don't." He first describes the roof as new, and then he transforms his observance into a question; he disowns by saying, "I don't." The poet's two statements in the second stanza seem in conflict with each other because he describes what he sees and poses a question about that, but at the very next moment, he denies having a knowledge of that which results in a paradoxical statement. Furthermore, he says, "I peruse a few Hectoring large-scale verses," in the same stanza, intending to read a few lines from the holy book. Here, too, his action ironically suggests his mockery of the tradition of reciting verses.

His expression of "peruse" and his use of the adjective "hectoring" create an ambiguity of meaning and lead to his paradoxical use of two ideas, because to peruse is to read something carefully, which draws a curtain over the exploration of meaning when it is combined with the notion of "hectoring," which means aggressively. So reading carefully but also aggressively creates a paradox resulting in linguistic anxiety. Additionally, his depiction of reading the verses is another instance of a paradoxical statement, saying, "and pronounce 'Here endeth' much more loudly than I'd meant." Here he means to pronounce a word loudly, which he does not mean. So it draws a contrary effect in the meaning when the poet intends an action that he does not intend to be performed. This same paradoxical sentiment can be observed in the last line of this stanza where the poet thinks about the visit as having no worth, while on the contrary, his interest in performing the traditional norms of the church (i.e., donating money to the church box, signing the book at the back door, or "mounting the lectern") opposes his thoughts. So a contrast can be seen in what he thinks and what he does, which results in a state of disbelief in religious traditions.

The poet's concerns about functionalities of churches in upcoming modern times become increasingly clearer in the third and fourth stanzas. Here the poem goes beyond the poet's superficial physical actions into his deeper thinking about the future of churches in modern societies. In both these stanzas, he is observed wondering, posing the questions, and then himself answering those questions, resulting in a complex form of rhetorical questions. It sounds like he is in dialogue with himself because the church is unvisited by most of the community. Thus, it has lost its core purpose of communication and connection with its people. He wonders about the future of unused, dysfunctional, and unvisited churches in upcoming modern times. He supports his intention from the ironic and satirical expression to draw dense ironies in terms of modern attitudes toward the churches, for instance, putting churches "chronically on show" or placing the "parchment," "plate," and "pyx" in the cases in order to have a memorial to their past association or letting the churches be destroyed by rain and grazing animals. These ironic expressions and rhetorical questions lead to the more complex and ambiguous meanings of the poet's intention. Additionally, another paradoxical expression leads to ambiguity and contradiction in the meanings of the poem, when the poet says, "or on some / Advised night see walking a dead one?" in the fourth line of the same stanza. His use of the qualitative expression "walking" with "dead" creates an ambiguity regarding how those walking can be dead or the dead can be walking.

Another instance of paradoxical expression can be observed in the fifth stanza when the poet uses phrases like "a shape less recognizable" and "a purpose more obscure." He intends to dissolve the notion of a physical object into what it is not regarding its shape in the first phrase. The description of a particular shape that goes unrecognized is a paradoxical statement, too. A particular shape is what we can recognize, in a sense what it seems to be, but saying that it is "less recognizable" increases the ambiguity in meaning. The same is the case with the second phrase, in which a purpose is depicted in contradiction with its notion of being obscure.

The poet takes support from ironic and paradoxical statements in the sixth and seventh stanzas to make his reader dive deeply into the vast sea of his modern treatise with the church. In the last lines of the sixth stanza, the poet's exploration of his mind toward his intention of visiting the church becomes more ambiguous and complex when he says, "For, though I've no idea / What this accoutered frowsty barn is worth, / It pleases me to stand in silence here." The poet declares that he has no idea about the worth of this place, but he feels pleased to stand before it. This declaration also signifies the irony in what he thinks and what he does. Additionally, the linguistic anxiety in the medium of language arises with the incorporation of the paradoxical expression of "accoutered frowsty" applied to the barn place like a said church. The term "accoutered" refers to something that is properly organized, dressed up, but its depiction with "frowsted," smelling bad, intends to highlight the linguistic anxiety with the incorporation of paradox.

Moreover, in the last stanza, the poet ironically declares the church as "A serious house on serious earth," intending to relate this notion of "seriousness" with the act of "robed as destinies." In this due course, his previous actions performed in the church and his thinking about the future of the church also illuminate the ironic expression to the churches. It is significant to note that the ironic use of the poem's title, "Church Going," also illuminates the ironic visit to the church regarding his intention to portray that fulfillment of traditional religious rituals is no longer a choice for a modern man. This idea seems clear when he expresses his feelings of disenchantment with church traditions in the last line of the third stanza, "Reflect the place was not worth stopping for," resulting in the realization of his visit to the church as a "loss" in the first two lines of the fourth stanza.

The textual stage accounts for more broad contradictions, disunities, and shifts regarding the time, focus, and tone of the poem. The poem undergoes a process of shift in time as the first and second stanzas deal primarily with actual events in present time, for instance, stepping inside, taking off cycle-clips, running a hand on the font, reading verses from the book, signing the book, and dropping money into the box. Alternatively, the third and fourth stanzas cause a shift in time and focus of the poem into the future and an exploration of the poet's mind, respectively. The poet is observed being mainly captivated by expressing his thoughts in an ironic treatise with the church in future times by modern man. Here his tone becomes more ironic and rhetorical. The sixth and last stanzas seem to result in a shift in time and focus again. Here the poet shifts his viewpoint to the more sacred functions of a church in the life of a man instead of superstitions, traditional observance of rituals, and purposeless visits. Additionally, his tone becomes more purposeful and didactic.

The linguistic stage attempts to invoke the instances in the poem when the adequacy of the poetic medium itself is brought into an account of skepticism. The questioning attitude toward the language of the poem results in an unreliability and a decentered reality constituted by language. For instance, the poem is observed with a description of action that it does not intend to do as in the case of a visit to the church. The poet negates the traditional fulfillment of rituals, but he is observed actually doing them. The overall, surpassing idea of the poem leads the reader to be prejudiced against the church, but in the last stanza, the poem draws attention to the core objectives and sacred purposes of the church. Additionally, the visitor professes a worthlessness of his visit to the church by saying, "Reflect the place was not worth stopping for," but the poem negates this idea itself and constitutes a counter-argument of the worthiness of church, which seems especially clear in the last stanza when the poet says, "In whose blent air all our compulsions meet." The poem concludes this idea with an argument that although modernity has tarnished the traditions of the church, it still possesses a pull concerned with the organizing and robing of our compulsions as destinies by saying, "Are recognized, and robed as destinies." Someone will always feel an urge to be wise by returning to it, as he says in the next lines of the last stanza.

In a broad sense, the actions and thoughts of the poet—for instance, the unintended visit, the lack of inspiration from the rituals, and the ironic respect of the church in modern life—are obvious clues to one of the vital facets of modernity called "secularization." The visit to the church in the poem can be taken as the "modern attitude" toward religion by most of the population. The "churchgoers" seem to be visitors rather than worshippers, resulting in an alienation by the traditional rituals they observe in churches. Also, these instances suggest searching for new ways to deal with the understanding and interpretation of religious traditions, which will provide them with an authentic practice of religion. Moreover, the inculcation of secular and rational thinking in the traditional dealings of the church results in the rise of the spirit of modernity.

Conclusion

In conclusion, the three-staged analysis of the poem has explored linguistic anxiety by identifying paradoxes, contradictions, ironies, and shifts in time, focus, and tone in the poem. It has also explored the decentering of religious traditions with the help of invoking the instabilities and unreliability of poetic language, which mainly constitutes the reality. Additionally, it has exposed the rational and secular thinking imparted by modern man to get rid of the mere following of traditional dogmas and the disenchanted observance of rituals. Moreover, this analysis has depicted the poet's treatise with the outdated, dysfunctional, and obsolete notion of a church that has lost its spiritual enchantment and inspired fascination with the rational inculcation of modernity. Furthermore, the analysis has shown that although modern societies have avoided the church in their daily conduct of life, the church still possesses the sacred position in the daily lives of their followers, though they no longer visit and worship in them.

REFERENCES

Almasalmeh, B. (2014). A deconstructive reading of W. B. Yeats' "Sailing to Byzantium" and William Blake's "London." *Damascus University Journal, 30*(3), 95–108.

Barry, P. (2002). *Beginning theory: An introduction to literary and cultural theory.* Manchester University Press.

Bhagyashree, S. (2016). Reaching out to merge the emerging borders: Poetry as a bridging discourse. *LangLit: An International Peer-Reviewed Open Access Journal, 2*(4), 245-251.

Chin-Yi, C. (2016). On Derrida's method. *International Journal of Research, 3*(1), 30–42.

Derrida, J. (1982). *Margins of philosophy.* University of Chicago Press.

Jay, G. S. (1990). *America the scrivener: Deconstruction and the subject of literary history.* Cornell University Press.

Johnson, B. (1980). *The critical difference: Essays in the contemporary rhetoric of reading.* Johns Hopkins University Press.

Larkin, P., & Thwaite, A. (1993). *Collected poems*. Noonday Press.
Lewis, P. (2004). Churchgoing in the modern novel. *Modernism/Modernity, 11*(4), 669–694.
Miller, J. H. (1976). Stevens' rock and criticism as cure. *Georgia Review, 30,* 34.
Tesser, C. C. (1991). Post-structuralist theory mirrored in Helena Parente Cunha's *Woman Between Mirrors*. *Hispania, 74*(3), 594.
Varma. B. (2016). Reading a poem with post-structuralist glasses: A creative interpretation of *Stopping by Woods on a Snowy Evening*. *LangLit: An International Peer-Reviewed Open Access Journal, 2*(3), 36–39.

CHAPTER FIVE | UBARAJ KATAWAL

A Dialogic Approach to Human Relations in Moshin Hamid's *The Reluctant Fundamentalist*

Critic Peter Morey (2011) argues that Moshin Hamid's novel *The Reluctant Fundamentalist* (2007) helps us rethink the notion of world literature within the framework of interconnectedness (Morey, 2011, p. 142). This rethinking has become even more important in a world steeped in anti-Muslim and anti-immigrant rhetoric. It is crucial to understand that Hamid's *The Reluctant Fundamentalist* challenges any simplistic approach to intercultural relations that ignores the level of complexity underlying such relations. As Anna Hartnell (2010) cogently argues, the figure of the immigrant is a typically American experience, and that in this experience the European past "only partially captures the nation's roots, and the make-up of contemporary America" (p. 343). As I will argue in this essay, Hamid's Changez challenges us to reconsider our position in the way we participate in or give tacit consent to the othering of peoples and cultures.

Few critics have argued that even though Hamid employs dramatic monologue to depict Changez's identification as Other, such a literary technique undermines his anticolonialist message as he resorts to the colonizer's typical method of one-sided discourse. If looked at from this angle, *The Reluctant Fundamentalist* is "*falsely polyphonic*" (Morey, 2011, p. 139; italics in the original). Morey further argues that because other voices are "ventriloquized by Changez, who may well be an unreliable narrator and whose story has its political rationale," the novel cannot be considered dialogic (2011, p. 139). It seems to me, however, that Hamid's novel shows a genuine attempt to initiate a dialogic relation. What is more, the dialogue is presented through "Others'" perspective, or, in Edward Said's (1993) term, a literary "voyage in" (p. 244). As the open-endedness of the novel indicates, the novel demands that we hear both sides of the story in an event when a situation of conflict is involved. More importantly, despite a clear explanation of what happens in the end, the novel indicates a possibility of peace as the parties involved have shown some willingness to engage in a conversation. It is true that Changez is the sole speaker in the novel. However, I contend that his narrative is conditioned by the presence of his narratee, his unnamed American interlocutor, whose slight movement or change in gestures forces Changez to modify his narrative accordingly. Hamid, as I will show later, successfully utilizes the form of a dramatic monologue in a new and inclusive manner, not least because throughout his narrative Changez is self-reflective.

Michael Holquist, the editor of Mikhail Bakhtin's *The Dialogic Imagination* (1981), defines dialogism as a "characteristic epistemological mode of a world dominated by heteroglossia. What everything means is understood, as a part of a greater whole—there is a constant interaction between meanings, all of which have the potential of conditioning others" (p. 426). Heteroglossia, as opposed to monoglossia, is a situation in which different languages and dialects coexist within a national language, thereby rendering them indispensable for the existence of a national language. Similarly, interactions with other languages, which result in a situation within a language that Bakhtin calls "other-languagedness" (1981, p. 63), provide a language with its life force. As Bakhtin writes,

> Where languages and cultures interanimated each other, language became something entirely different, its very nature changed: in place of a single, unitary sealed-off Ptolemaic world of language, there appeared the open Galilean world of many languages, mutually animating each other. (1981, p. 65)

The novelist is, according to Bakhtin, equipped with a "polyglot consciousness," meaning that the novelist makes room for a polyphony of opposing voices within a work (1981, p. 65). The point that I would like to emphasize throughout my essay is that the interlocutors in *The Reluctant Fundamentalist*, viz. Changez and his American addressee interanimate and mutually condition each other, if not through their speech, then by their very presence and physical gestures. This interanimation gives the novel its dialogic character, rendering it a truly polyphonic work.

A dialogic relation begins with one's willingness to listen to others, especially those perspectives that we may not share. This is precisely because, as Hartnell (2010) suggests in her examination of the novel, we share the reality, even if partially, no matter the differences that separate us as Black or Asian or Muslim (p. 341). It is this openness to different identities that allows for the others to make their presence felt. In a dialogic relation, all the parties involved let a conversation take place, an opportunity that is mutually conditioned. This kind of conversation rarely happens in what Bakhtin (1981) calls a "monoglotic world" (p. 64), which is marked by mistrust and antagonism. As Frantz Fanon (1952) uncovers in *Black Skin, White Masks*, in a colonial model of human relations, the parties involved suffer from either a superiority or an inferiority complex because such relations do not allow for any middle ground. It is a relation of alienation (Fanon, 1952, p. 29). Similarly, Mahmood Mamdani (2001) makes it clear through his astute analysis of Rwandan genocide in *When Victims Become Killers: Colonialism, Nativism, and the Genocide in Rwanda* that the one-time victims inculcate techniques of violence they have been put through to replicate them on their victims. Both Fanon and Mamdani remind us of the dangers of replicating colonial forms of human relations, hinting at a more democratic relation marked by dialogism or polyphony. Hamid's novel suggests that only through entering a dialogic relation can we ameliorate the violence facing the world today.

As I have mentioned earlier, it might seem at first as if the whole conversation that takes place in the novel is a reversed form of colonial relations, in which now only the "Other" speaks. One could equally argue that Changez's dramatic monologue replicates the Othering he experienced as a Muslim immigrant in America. As Morey (2011) implies in his examination of the novel, an "imperial stand-off between neo-colonizer and neo-colonized" toward the end of the novel rather than "re-inscrib[ing] the old colonialist binary opposition," introduces readers to new forms of once-colonial habits, which are, alas, available globally, regardless of a person's or country's socioeconomic status (p. 143).

There is, however, more to the novel than meets the eye. It is true that the novel as a whole is presented to the readers through Changez's perspective, who is the narrator. However, I argue that this perspective is inclusive. An inclusive perspective is open to change and exists only in connection with others' perspectives. This is evident in the novel because any changes in the addressee's general disposition will influence the narrative orientation, as shown in the opening paragraph of the novel:

> Excuse me, sir, but may I be of assistance? Ah, I see I have alarmed you. Do not be frightened by my beard: I am a lover of America. I noticed that you were looking for something; more than looking, in fact you seemed to

> be on a *mission*, and since I am both a native of this city and a speaker of your language, I thought I might offer you my services. (Hamid, 2007, p. 1; emphasis in the original)

Here the speaker, Changez, is conscious of the effect his appearance has on his addressee, who is an American, and he quickly adjusts himself to the situation by revealing his feeling, even if cockily, toward the American so that the addressee feels more at home. Changez does this after addressing the source of the addressee's fear directly: "Do not be frightened by my beard: I am a lover of America." It is true that after 9/11, the media at large have instilled in the American public fear of brown men as a trope of death and destruction by repeatedly showing images, often depicting bearded brown men next to violent scenes. No matter the complex network of power relations and discourse that engender violence in the first place, the media magnify any violent act by a man of color, while brushing under the rug the death and devastation as a result of the supposed counter-terrorism missions initiated by the West. This method of dehumanizing the Others has become a rule, rather than an exception, in Pax Americana. It would be a mistake, as Bruce Robbins (2012) reminds us, to blame any single news outlet since the practice of "othering" runs deep in both the pre- and the post-9/11 Western thought (p. 8).

Changez has his fear about the addressee that the American might be on a mission. Once it is made evident that they both have their fears against each other, the speaker launches into what some might call a rant. Again, I call this encounter between Changez and his American interlocutor a conversation precisely because the speaker and the listener are mutually conditioned, not only because any change of attitude in one will necessarily affect the way the other behaves, but also because neither of them is obligated to abide and listen to the other if he prefers not to. Take the following moment, for example:

> But why do you recoil? Ah yes, this beggar is a particularly unfortunate fellow. One can only wonder what series of *accidents* could have left him so thoroughly disfigured. He draws close to you because you are a foreigner. Will you give him something? No? Very wise; one ought not to encourage beggars, and yes, you are right, it is far better to donate to charities that address the causes of poverty rather than to him, a creature who is merely its symptom. (Hamid, 2007, p. 40; emphasis in the original)

When his interlocutor gets distracted, Changez cannot continue with the conversation before tackling the concern first. In this particular example, a beggar approaches them, and while the American flinches, Changez empathizes with and offers him some money.

Changez, as Hartnell (2010) suggests, is first the product of the American-led globalization that he rebels against later (p. 341). He learns about the American Protestant and capitalist work ethics throughout his stay in the United States. After having graduated from an elite institution, he has worked for a top American company. What is more, he has excelled in his job to such an extent that he wins favor from his superiors. His short stay in the United States is nothing short of achieving an exemplary form of the American Dream. Then 9/11 happens, and things quickly take a downward turn for Muslim Americans, especially to those from Middle Eastern and South Asian backgrounds. After the terrorist event in New York City, where Changez's company's headquarters are located, Muslim Americans are subjected to random public and police harassment.

It is not without some remorse that he resigns from his job and returns home to Lahore, Pakistan, where his family struggles economically and depends on him for financial support. Changez's situation reflects the dilemma of many postcolonial scholars and professionals living and working in the West. On one side, the West offers them opportunities for upward mobility, which is something one finds hard to resist. On the other side, the West also dehumanizes non-Western cultures and identities either directly invading their native countries or through cultural dehumanization, shown so well in Said's (1993) *Culture and Imperialism*, or in the media spectacle of a bearded brown man in the inset of a graphic scene. As Matthew Hart and Jim Hansen (2008) cogently put it, the novel is about, among other things, "limits of cosmopolitan space" (p. 507). Faced with these attacks and coupled with daily public stares and random police harassment, Changez feels that he has no room in New York City to function independently and professionally. Whereas at one point, Changez had eagerly adopted rugged capitalist practices of hiring and firing people based solely on financial necessities, he now realizes his mistakes after meeting Juan-Bautista, the chief of a publishing company in Valparaiso, Chile. Juan-Bautista believed in the publication of literary works, even though such publication could be a financial drag for the whole company. What Juan-Bautista awakens in Changez is the sense of interconnections among peoples and cultures, despite capitalism's imperial separations and classifications.

It is no accident that Juan-Bautista recommends Changez to visit the house of Pablo Neruda, the Chilean poet and Nobel laureate for literature. Neruda's house dredges up in Changez something that his profit-oriented business practices never recognized, namely the celebration of small things. Later, Juan-Bautista tells Changez of the janissaries, who, like Changez, lost their way and ended up helping the Ottoman Empire to launch a war against their people.

It seems to me that the main question that *The Reluctant Fundamentalist* raises is the cycle of violence as a result of a lack of self-reflection and respect for other cultures and people. Changez believes that the existing divides between nations and cultures are detrimental and engender a cycle of violence. For example, when the United States declared its war on terror soon after 9/11, many people, including Changez in the novel, took it to be more of a war against Islamic civilization than anything else. Moreover, the war made more people homeless, impoverished, and more vulnerable to fundamentalist groups such as the ISIS (Islamic State of Iraq and Syria) and the Taliban.

For this reason, the novel showcases a situation in which two opposing sides make their points, a situation which empowers both sides by creating a condition of possibility. And while it is true that Changez's American interlocutor has not said much as compared with Changez, that is only because this is the beginning of something "eventual," which could easily develop into something that is "offered to all, or addressed to everyone, without a condition of belonging being able to limit this offer, or this address" (Badiou, 2003, p. 14). As the novel is left open-ended, one could make a point that when they sit together the next time, it will be the American who will relate everything about himself in the manner that Changez has done in the novel.

However, the nagging question remains as to how the dialogic relation presented in *The Reluctant Fundamentalist* could be taken as a model, and not just as an aberration. The two main interlocutors presented in the novel do not even fully expose the degree of animosity that is often displayed between any two cultures: whether it is between Islam and Christianity, or between Hinduism and Islam. And after all, it is not people like Changez, the "lover of America" (Hamid, 2007, p. 1), who constitute the majority of the fundamentalist Islamic groups. As Hart and Hansen argue, "as a secular Muslim, [Changez] is no religious fundamentalist" (2008, p. 509). In the least, one could argue that Changez is a fundamentalist in the making if the American posture on the world stage does not change.

It might come as a surprise to some that more often than not, we humans create our enemies. To put it differently, people become enemies once they know each other closely, and find out that they could not get closer. Violent acts are often committed to avenge a real or perceived loss of self-respect from someone people already know. In *Habitations of Modernity: Essays in the Wake of Subaltern Studies* (2002), Dipesh Chakrabarty relates to us the story of a Bengali Hindu family who takes sympathy on a poor but promising Muslim poet when the latter is still young and takes care of him as a family member. The young poet, Jasimuddin, is happy as an adopted son until he finds out that the family has accepted him only as a promising future poet, but not as a Muslim (Chakrabarty, 2002, pp. 147–148). He expresses his displeasure for not being accepted into the household in the way that everyone in the family is. He asks the mother in the family, "Mother, if it is true that I am one of your sons, why do you feed me seating me outside? Why is it that you never let me sit with your sons to eat from the same plate?" (Chakrabarty, 2002, p. 146). Chakrabarty's discussion of the significance of Jasimuddin's questions aside, I think the problem here is not about distance, but of proximity that is not close enough. To put it differently, Jasimuddin's frustration stems from the fact that the family insulted his self-respect by not accepting him as he is, a frustration that has the potentiality to fester into bitterness, and eventually into violence.

We can draw a more familiar literary example from Shakespeare's *The Tempest* in which Caliban feels slighted and wronged after he realizes that he has been disinherited of his island by his mentor, Prospero. As a result, he attempts to do something "villainous" to Miranda. In a telling response to Miranda's accusation that his whole race is wild, Caliban responds, "You taught me language, and my profit on't / Is I know how to curse. The red plague rid you / For learning me your tongue!" (Shakespeare, 1997, p. 3066). Caliban does not do anything to Miranda or Prospero when they are still his guests on the island; it is only after the latter colonize him while teaching him the English language that he begins to feel wronged and thinks of revolting. These examples show that there is a clear link between loss of self-esteem from someone one already knows and the accompanying violence.

How do these examples help us better interpret Changez's situation? More importantly, how do these examples help us understand the relationship between the United States and the so-called "terrorist" individuals, groups, and nations around the world? As the story from Chakrabarty shows, people both at individual and group levels become disgruntled only when they feel that they are humiliated, or that they have lost their self-respect because of the actions of someone, be it a group or nation, whom they know. If we bring this situation to bear on the international scenario, the United States has played a major role in supporting or dismantling governments. At the same time, as Robbins (2012) reminds us, the United States continues to support hereditary rulers such as in Saudi Arabia even though their records on human rights are less than stellar (p. 5). Of course, it is a known fact that the United States continues to support Israel despite the latter's harsh treatment of the Palestinians. All in all, the United States has created resentments in many people around the world, especially Muslims, who feel that the West under the aegis of the United States denigrates their culture and religion.

Examined through this wider historical context, Changez's schadenfreude at seeing the Twin Towers collapse on 9/11 makes a lot more sense. As he confesses to his interlocutor, he could not explain at first how he could take pleasure at seeing the deaths of thousands of innocent people: "So when I tell you I was pleased at the slaughter of thousands of innocents, I do so with a profound sense of perplexity" (Hamid, 2007, p. 73). Changez tells his audience (both the narratee and the actual readers) that he is no sociopath, who takes pleasure at other people's misery, but a man who feels sympathy at others' sufferings (p. 72). In other words, he would not have been pleased with seeing an individual suffer, no matter the individual's identifying predicates. That would be evil, for which there is no justification.

The real reason that Changez smiles at the burning of the Twin Towers in New York City is that he sees in it the United States as that power that cannot accept him completely for who he is. Just like Jasimuddin in Chakrabarty's story, Changez is allowed into the United States, and it is here that he gains the skills necessary to land a coveted job at Underwood Samson. For all this he is grateful. However, the United States does not accept his other attributes such as being a Pakistani Muslim. Even before 9/11, Changez felt like an outsider in the company of his American coworkers, who put on airs and showed disrespect toward elderly people when they were vacationing in Greece. He wonders,

> [B]y what quirk of human history my companions—many of whom I would have regarded as upstarts in my own country, so devoid of refinement were they—were in a position to conduct themselves in the world as though they were its ruling class. (Hamid, 2007, p. 21)

Notice that Changez uses the term "upstarts" to refer to his American friends, but also indirectly to his aristocratic family background; however, this could be allegorically meaningful to examine the United States as a nation that has acted as the ruler of the world, which the Islamic civilization finds hard to chew and digest.

It would be naïve to think that the world is seamlessly divided between Christian and Islamic cultures and civilizations. As Said strived to emphasize throughout his oeuvre, the world is a much more nuanced place than it might appear to an uncritical eye. "Too much attention paid to managing and clarifying the clash of cultures," Said (2000) argues, "obliterates the fact of a great, often silent exchange and dialogue between them" (p. 583). This has been demonstrated in Hamid's novel through the figure of Juan-Bautista. For one thing, Juan-Bautista clearly opposes capitalist greed and instrumental approach in the publication industry, a situation that forces us to reexamine more closely the notion that capitalist worldview and Christianity are the same things, even though, as Max Weber has convincingly argued in *The Protestant Ethic and the Spirit of Capitalism* (2002), the Protestant Christian worldview fostered the profit-driven, no-nonsense world order in which people like Juan-Bautista have no place. As said earlier, work is a fundamental aspect of the Protestant and capitalist ideology, and because literature may motivate one toward "idling" time away, capitalist ideology views literary imagination as detrimental (Weber, 2002, pp. 106–107). Against this capitalist/Protestant philosophy, Juan-Bautista promotes the publication of literary works. In Juan-Bautista's polyglot consciousness, non–profit-bearing literary works have equal, if not more, value as profit-bearing educational publications, simply because literary imagination not only makes possible the coexistence of polyphonic voices, but it also encourages such practices.

As I have elaborated the point in a slightly different context in my article "Becoming a 'British Hindoo': Errant Subjectivities in Bharati Mukherjee's Fiction" (2011), Hamid's novel demonstrates possibilities opened up by a dialogic form of human relation. Now I would like to explore this by examining instances in the novel in which communication takes place between characters despite their obvious differences. The most conspicuous instance is the one between Changez and Wainwright. Being coemployees of the company that promotes business fundamentals, such as efficiency, attention to financial details, and competition, Changez and Wainwright compete against each other to be at the top of the tops. Moreover, they do not share the same ethnic and cultural backgrounds. Wainwright has ancestral links to Barbados, but like many other African Americans, he comes with a Christian religious background. Despite all this, they become friends; they discuss cricket, quote lines from the movies that they both have watched, and go out to dinner at a Pak-Punjab deli (Hamid, 2007, p. 39). As Changez relates to us:

> Although we [Changez and the man at the restaurant, who would not accept an American Express card] were speaking in Urdu, Wainwright seemed to understand. "I have cash," he said. "This stuff looks delicious." I was pleased he thought so; our food, as you have surely gathered in your time here, is something we Lahoris take great pride in. Moreover, it is a mark of friendship when someone treats you to a meal—ushering you thereby into a relationship of mutual generosity—and by the time fifteen minutes later that I saw Wainwright licking his fingers, having dispatched the last crumb on his plate, I knew I had found a kindred spirit at the office. (Hamid, 2007, pp. 39–40)

I quoted this episode at length because it best captures what it takes to reach out to others and find a bond in spite of existing differences. The obvious difference between the two friends is the fact that they do not have the same linguistic and cultural roots. That does not, however, stop them from understanding what the other person is experiencing. Wainwright knows that Changez needs cash to pay for their dinner, and it appears that he does not have it. Also, Wainwright enjoys the food they buy, giving Changez a reason to believe that his gesture of friendship toward another human being has not gone unreciprocated. Small though the moment may be in Hamid's novel, it is a significant moment in demonstrating alternatives to colonial forms of human relation.

The second instance takes place not only between Changez and Juan-Bautista, but also—in a way—between Changez and Pablo Neruda. Coincidentally, food becomes once again a means of connection when Juan-Bautista invites Changez for lunch at a restaurant for a local special, sea bass cooked in salt (Hamid, 2007, p. 150). It is during this meeting that Juan-Bautista tells Changez the stories of the Janissaries. Why would Juan-Bautista, a Christian, remind a Pakistani man about this story? I would argue that Juan-Bautista can see people as they are, not based on some generalized identitarian predicates but as another human being in need of help. For this reason, earlier in the story he recommends Changez visit Neruda's house. When Changez arrives at Neruda's place, he feels as if he is back home in Lahore, Pakistan. Neruda's neighborhood did not look much different from his own when he noticed "children racing by on wooden carts that appeared to be shipping crates to which wheels had been attached" (Hamid, 2007, p. 147). More importantly, he hears someone playing the guitar; the sound "was a delicate melody, a song with no words" (Hamid, 2007, p. 148). The reason I call this moment Changez's intimate communication with Neruda is that he visits the poet's place to learn and listen, not to observe and judge. Only when one approaches other cultures and peoples with a readiness to learn something new, rather than just to know and judge them, can one establish a dialogic human relation. For this reason, a dialogic relation is more about an approach than anything else. Granted, Neruda himself was long dead and could not speak with Changez. That, however, is not the point. The more important thing is that Changez goes there with an open mind and ear, and easily connects with the place and the music coming from a distance. Changez can connect with Neruda's surroundings and ultimately with how Neruda must have felt living in that house.

Finally, a better example of a dialogic relation shows itself in Changez's relationship with his unnamed American audience, and with his actual readers. As I have pointed out this fact briefly at the beginning of this essay, Changez and his interlocutor are mutually interdependent for their existence. Any changes in the behavior of either party will have an impact on the other. But how does this relation become dialogic? Why would only one person do the talking if it is a dialogic relation? To me, effective communication happens only when the concerned parties are ready to listen and learn from each other. There has to be not only a readiness to hear out the other's position but also a readiness to adjust one's worldview if and when necessary. It is true that Changez does all the talking in the novel, which makes it a dramatic monologue; however, he adjusts to changes that occur in the course of his story. In other words, he knows or strives to understand how his interlocutor, or his ideal reader, is feeling at a particular moment. For instance, when Changez confesses his schadenfreude moment at seeing the World Trade Center collapse on September 11, 2001, he notices the effect the confession has on his interlocutor. Changez then allows his audience to know that he knows their reaction to his sociopathic feeling about the tragic deaths of so many innocent people. He says, "Your disgust is evident; indeed, your large hand has, perhaps without your noticing, clenched into a fist" (Hamid, 2007, p. 72). Indeed, there is a hint of Poesque vindictiveness in Changez's voice when he relates his feelings about the event.

But it seems to me that Changez knows exactly what kind of impact his storytelling is having on his listener. In the movie adaptation, director Mira

Nair lets the interlocutor express his emotions in words. However, it does not change the dynamic much because we as readers already know that Changez's audience is not pleased to hear Changez's initial reaction to the 9/11 event. After listening to Changez, the American does not terminate the conversation both in the novel and in the movie version, rendering the speech unnecessary.

When nationalist rhetoric takes precedence over everything else, how many of us will ever have the time and willingness to read a novel like *The Reluctant Fundamentalist*, which I think is an opposing voice par excellence? Moreover, looking back on the past few decades, as the world has become more polarized, it is not an individual, no matter how powerful they may be, but corporations and lobbyists that determine who qualifies to be considered an "ally" and who belongs with evil. Insomuch as corporations find it fit, the government carries out aggression against other countries that do not cooperate with its interests, which usually means capitalist grabbing of their wealth and natural resources. And the aggression does not begin and end with direct military invasions; direct military invasions take place only after the "enemy" side is first either completely disarmed or is considered too weak to defend itself. The military invasion follows a nonmilitary assessment and disarmament of a nation; equally important to a military invasion is the cultural and economic invasion through which the capitalist empire gobbles up its reluctant prey.

The same is true on a smaller scale when it comes to relationships between the nation-state and its Others. As Partha Chatterjee argues in *The Nation and Its Fragments* (1993), the nation-state carries out many wars outside the nation and developmental projects within not necessarily to create jobs or to make people's everyday life easier, so much as to fulfill corporate demands. Chatterjee contends, for example, that "an underlying current of thinking about the sociological bases of Indian politics continues to run along channels excavated by colonial discourse" (1993, p. 224). Chatterjee's point is that classification and objectification of every human relation has been the colonial legacy of postcolonial nations such as India.

Literary works such as Hamid's novel provide us with much-needed guidance to charting a peaceful course in a historical conjuncture. The final line of the novel gives us reasons to hope that a polyglot consciousness will prevail over violence if some initiatives are taken. As Changez tells his interlocutor regarding the glint of the metal in the latter's hand: "Given that you and I are now bound by a certain shared intimacy, I trust it is from the holder of your business cards" (Hamid, 2007, p. 184). In the course of the novel, Changez has told his American visitor that "no country inflicts death so readily upon the inhabitants of other countries, frightens so many people so far away, as America" (Hamid, 2007, p. 182). This is what I call the other side of the story to American exceptionalist narrative, and Changez's American audience has heard it out. Through this long dramatic monologue, Changez has reminded his American "friend" that they have had enough of the American war on terror. Readers do not know what impact Changez's story has had on his American interlocutor. However, the fact that he is there until the end of the novel suggests he has listened to it at the very least. Telling and listening to ideas and perspectives necessarily make the participants open up to each other's worldview. Hamid's novel demonstrates what it takes to begin a dialogic human relation. A dialogic relation does not bring all conflicts to a peaceful end. However, it provides an opportunity for people to be in a more intimate relation, and to examine the world from alternative angles. As the open-endedness of the novel suggests, anything could happen after the dialogue, including mutual destruction. However, the very fact that the concerned parties have sat and dined together and have spent time adjusting to each other's reactions to the story told are indications for something natal.

REFERENCES

Badiou, A. (2003). *Saint Paul: The foundation of universalism*. Stanford University Press.

Bakhtin, M. M. (1981). *The dialogic imagination* (Michael Holquist, Ed.; Caryl Emerson and Michael Holquist, Trans.). University of Texas Press.

Chakrabarty, D. (2002). *Habitations of modernity: Essays in the wake of subaltern studies*. University of Chicago Press.

Chatterjee, P. (1993). *The nation and its fragments: Colonial and postcolonial histories*. Princeton University Press.

Fanon, F. (1952). *Black skin, white masks*. Grove Press, 1967.

Hamid, M. (2007). *The reluctant fundamentalist*. Harcourt, Inc.

Hart, M., & Hansen, J. (2008). Introduction: Contemporary literature and the state. *Contemporary Literature, 49*(4), 491–513.

Hartnell, A. (2010). Moving through America: Race, place and resistance in Mohsin Hamid's The Reluctant Fundamentalist. *Journal of Postcolonial Writing, 46*(3/4), 336–348.

Katawal, U. (2011). Becoming a "British Hindoo" Errant subjectivities in Bharati Mukherjee's fiction. *Postcolonial Text, 6*(3), 1–15.

Mamdani, M. (2001). *When victims become killers: Colonialism, nativism, and the genocide in Rwanda*. Princeton University Press.

Morey, P. (2011). "The rules of the game have changed": Mohsin Hamid's *The Reluctant Fundamentalist* and post-9/11 fiction. *Journal of Postcolonial Writing*, 47(2), 135–146.

Robbins, B. (2012). *Perpetual war: Consmopolitanism from the viewpoint of violence*. Duke University Press.

Said, E. (1993). *Culture and imperialism*. Vintage Books.

Said, E. (2000). The class of definitions: On Samuel Huntington. In E. Said (Ed.), *Reflections on exile and other essays* (pp. 569–590). Harvard University Press.

Shakespeare. (1997). *The tempest*. In S. Greenblatt (Ed.), *The Norton Shakespeare* (pp. 3047–3107). W. W. Norton.

Weber, M. (2002). *The Protestant ethic and the "spirit" of capitalism and other writings* (P. Baehr & G. C. Wells, Trans.). Penguin Books.

CHAPTER SIX | MUHAMMAD SHAHBAZ
ARIF AND FAIZA ANUM

Grace of Strategic Silence in Postcolonial Resettlement

A Study of J. M. Coetzee's *Disgrace*

Speech is no mere verbalization of conflicts and systems
of domination, but that it is the very object of man's conflict.
(Foucault, 1967/1972, p. 216)
Petrus has the right to come and go as he wishes; he has exercised that
right; he is entitled to his silence. (Coetzee, 1999, p. 116)

This essay is an attempt to examine the grace of strategic silence in postcolonial resettlement concerning J. M. Coetzee's Booker Prize–winning novel *Disgrace* (1999). Coetzee's novel *Disgrace* is set in newly postcolonial South Africa. *Disgrace*, therefore, illustrates the rather dramatic phase of postcolonial role reversal of both the colonizer and the colonized. We argue that *Disgrace* corroborates the viewpoint that silence is one strategy that facilitates postcolonial subjects in settling with the rapid and abrupt shifts and changes of roles during the immediate postcolonial phase. Almost all the characters, major and minor, in *Disgrace* employ silence as a strategic tool to preserve their grace during the disgraced postcolonial phase. For example, David Lurie, a White colonizer, prefers to leave his job as a professor of English but refuses to confess his violation of Melanie Isaacs before the tribunal. Likewise, Lurie's daughter, Lucy, opts for silence, which is why she does not report her rape to the police and also warns her father to abstain from the same. Petrus, a colonized Black South African, is yet another character in *Disgrace* who chooses silence and does not reveal the identity of Lucy's rapist to Lurie and the police.

Disgrace, thus, narrates the journey of reconciliation and resettlement of its various characters, all of them surviving as postcolonial subjects in the newly postcolonial South Africa. As Stuart Hall (1996) suggests that the postcolonial phase witnessed "new relations and dispositions of power" (p. 246), the postapartheid or postcolonial South Africa, too, witnessed a major tilt of power dynamics between the colonizer and the colonized. Coetzee's *Disgrace* fully captures this reconfiguration of the power shift in postcolonial South Africa, as the privileged White colonizer, Lurie, is shown as:

> A dog-man, Petrus once called himself. Well, now he has become a dog-man: a dog undertaker; a dog psychopomp; a harijan. Curious that a man as selfish as he should be offering himself to the service of dead dogs. There must be other, more productive ways of giving oneself to the world, or to an idea of the world. (Coetzee, 1999, p. 118)

During the postcolonial phase, the identities of both the colonized and the colonizer are redefined; therefore, Lurie also undergoes a process of change. His hubris as a privileged colonizer is leveled down when his daughter chooses Petrus, colonized and Black, as her protector while rejecting Lurie's suggestion of leaving Cape Town and moving with her mother. Lurie is the only postcolonial subject in the novel who is blind to the strategic grace of silence during the disgraced postcolonial phase. *Disgrace*, therefore, encompasses Lurie's initial ignorance of the grace of silence as a colonizer to the transformation when he begins to empathize with the silent death of the dogs in Bev Shaw's clinic, thus the silent death of his colonialist hubris, too.

Lurie's daughter, Lucy, also accommodates the changed social, political, and economic setup of postcolonial South Africa. In postcolonial South Africa, Lucy, a White woman, recreates and relives the image of the colonized Black woman:

> She had fallen in love with the place, she said; she wanted to farm it properly. He helped her buy it. Now here she is, flowered dress, bare feet and all, in a house full of the smell of baking, no longer a child playing at farming but a solid countrywoman, a boervrou. (Coetzee, 1999, p. 50)

Thus, clearly, during the postcolonial phase both the colonizer and the colonized are required to reconstitute their personal, political, social, and economic relations. The colonized subjects have to rebuild themselves out of the disgraced phase of colonialism, as does Petrus in *Disgrace*. At the same time, the colonizer must readjust to the new postcolonial setting—where "the clear-cut distinctions between colonizers and colonized" are blurred (Hall, 1996, p. 242).

Therefore, it is essential to address the larger question of how to negotiate with the legacies of bygone colonialism. Is postcolonial resettlement a possibility or not? And what are the possible strategies to procure postcolonial reconciliation and resettlement? Could postcolonial literature only question, deconstruct, and condemn colonial operations and relations? Or is postcolonial literature powerful and visionary enough to imagine alternatives to contemporary social and political conditions? For Fanon (1961/1990), "[N]o conciliation is possible, for of the two terms ['conciliation' and 'possible'], one is superfluous" (p. 39).

The pertinent question, therefore, is about the possible strategies that both the colonizer and the colonized could employ to accomplish "interracial negotiations," and a comparatively peaceful future (McGonegal, 2009, p. 3). Thus, at this point, it is interesting to probe Julie McGonegal's (2009) theorization of the possibility of forgiveness and reconciliation based on "the fragile horizon of ethical relations" (p. 149) in *Disgrace*.

Julie McGonegal's Theorization of the Possibility of Postcolonial Reconciliation

Julie McGonegal (2009) claims that "academic postcolonialism has generally neglected to address the politics of reconciliation, despite the recent emergence of reconciliation political programs and movements in a wide range of national and international contexts" (p. 8). McGonegal argues that not unlike the "postcolonial," "reconciliation" is a "theoretically and politically ambiguous term" (2009, p. 32). In its English usage, the term "reconciliation" generally signifies "an attitude of resignation, surrender or submission that precludes the possibility of struggle, antagonism or opposition" (McGonegal, 2009, p. 32). McGonegal further suggests:

> Perhaps this explains the reluctance on the part of many postcolonial critics to concede the possibilities of a politics of reconciliation, since what the term conjures almost immediately is the image of oppressed, marginalized communities capitulating to the violent and unjust conditions of contemporary life. (2009, p. 32)

McGonegal, thus, proposes an alternative definition of reconciliation "as the establishment of new conditions of interactions-conditions centered on the ideals of negotiation, collaboration, and reciprocity" (2009, p. 33). She perfectly realizes that "no compensation can ever adequately redress wrongs, and that the losses suffered by victims can never be fully recovered" (2009, p. 36). Yet, McGonegal proposes that "to subscribe to a politics of reconciliation—to opt not to endorse principles of punishment or retribution—is perhaps to place one's wager on the future, to take up the challenge of beginning anew without denying an ongoing sense of loss" (2009, p. 36).

Therefore, to procure "postcoloniality," practically "to place one's wager on the future," the postcolonial subjects must subscribe to the politics of reconciliation (McGonegal, 2009, p. 36). It is thus an essential task of the postcolonial critic and the postcolonial writer to consider and propose some practical ways of postcolonial reconciliation, resettlement, and negotiation.

J. M. Coetzee as a Political and Postcolonial Writer

J. M. Coetzee (born in 1940 in South Africa), the recipient of the Nobel Prize in Literature in 2003, is one such political and postcolonial novelist, whose works predominantly imagine the possibilities of postcolonial reconciliation, resettlement, and negotiation. In an interview, Coetzee contends that he is often

> taken as a political novelist, it may be because I take it as a given that people must be treated as fully responsible beings: psychology is no excuse. Politics, in its wise stupidity, is at one with religion here: one man, one soul: no half-measures. What saves me from a merely stupid stupidity, I would hope, is a measure of charity, which is, I suppose, the way in which grace allegorizes itself in the world. (1992, p. 246)

McGonegal (2009) also explicates that Coetzee repeatedly invokes the term "grace" in his critical and fictional writings (p. 128).

In *Oxford Advanced Learner's Dictionary* (Wehmeier et al., 2005), "grace" is defined as "a quality of behavior that is polite and pleasant and deserves respect." Johanna Manley (1992) evaluates the term "grace" within the religious framework of Christianity and claims that grace is the demonstration of the inherent goodness of the spirit for the sake of grace itself (p. 151). However, in the Derridean understanding of the term, "the right to grace" (Derrida, 1997/2001, p. 59) exhibits "forgiveness." Moreover, Derrida (1997/2001) says: "What I dream of, what I try to think of as the 'purity' of forgiveness worthy of its name, would be forgiveness without power: unconditional but without sovereignty" (p. 39). Derrida (1997/2001) demarcates that the "right to grace" or "the right to forgiveness" "should never amount to a therapy of reconciliation." On the contrary, "there is always a strategic or political calculation in the generous gesture of one who offers reconciliation or amnesty" (p. 8). Hence, for Derrida, the graceful act of forgiveness, in particular in postcolonial situations, always has strategic calculations to its end.

Rationale of the Study

Therefore, adhering to McGonegal's optimistic deliberations on the possibility of forgiveness and reconciliation during the postcolonial phase, the present study examines the strategic relevance of the grace of silence in postcolonial reconciliation, resettlement, and negotiation. For this purpose, this research analyzes Coetzee's *Disgrace* (1999) as a text that intends to imagine the possibility of postcolonial reconciliation, resettlement, and negotiation in South Africa by preserving the silence of various postcolonial subjects in the novel. Thus, we argue that by adopting strategic silence during the postcolonial phase, both the colonizer and the colonized could resettle their political, social, economic, and personal terrains. Moreover, this research aims to demonstrate the political potential of novels like *Disgrace* in envisioning solutions to complex political problems, such as "postcolonial reconciliation." We, therefore, argue that Coetzee's *Disgrace* projects silence as an effective strategy that theorizes the possibility of postcolonial resettlement, not only in ethical domains but also in personal, economic, and political domains.

Review of Related Literature

Since its publication in 1999, Coetzee's novel *Disgrace* has perplexed researchers about the uncanny, "uncomfortable and unanswerable questions" that it leaves to readers, claims Rita Barnard (2003) in her article "J. M. Coetzee's *Disgrace* and the South African Pastoral" (p. 199). That is why most research that is being attempted on *Disgrace* endeavors to examine, one way or another, some "uncomfortable and unanswerable questions" in the novel (Barnard, 2003, p. 199).

Michael S. Kochin (2004), in his "Postmetaphysical Literature: Reflections on J. M. Coetzee's *Disgrace*," argues that *Disgrace* seemingly is a novel "about endings": the end of romance, the end of humanity, the end of grace, and more (p. 4). Kochin, however, claims that *Disgrace* in reality is "a novel of beginnings and not just endings," and has a postmetaphysical tilt to it, because the novel proposes "an indefinable hope, a hope that something is coming up in the postcolonial world of South Africa" (2004, pp. 5–8). Kochin, though, is unable to decode the "indefinable" force of hope that *Disgrace* instills in its reader.

Suzie Gibson (2009), in her article "Being Irresponsible in J. M. Coetzee's *Disgrace*," highlights the point that the sense of ethics that *Disgrace* projects is the ethics of irresponsibility (p. 287). Moreover, the ethics of irresponsibility in the novel cannot be "absorbed, reconciled and appeased" (Gibson, 2009, p. 285) because the characters in the novel consider ethics to be a purely personal problem. That is why the characters in *Disgrace* do not care about demonstrating ethics in a public forum. Therefore, "*Disgrace* may not deliver or 'give' the reader ethics, as a letter, package, or object is given or delivered, but it awakens the desire for such a thing" (Gibson, 2009, p. 301).

David Atwell's (2015) "Migrations: Irreconcilable Lives—*Elizabeth Costello, Disgrace*," in his book *J. M. Coetzee and the Life of Writing*, examines Coetzee's *Disgrace* as a text that uses "debates on animals" as "touchstones for debates about cruelty in general" (p. 219). Therefore, a quest of inquiry into the relationship between animals and humans is yet another uncanny question that *Disgrace* probes.

This essay, thus, too, is an endeavor to answer yet another unanswerable question in *Disgrace*, which is about the possibility of imagining resettlement, reconciliation, and negotiation between the colonizer and the colonized during the postcolonial phase in South Africa. Moreover, this research explores the almost uncanny potential of strategic silence in forging the ground of graceful forgiveness during the disgraced postcolonial phase.

Discussion

Pointing to the ways of resettlement in the newly independent South Africa, *Disgrace* is a novel that preserves the silence of various survivors in the postindependence period while lending ambiguity and indeterminacy to the narrative. Therefore, "on the issue that so resoundingly defines South Africa, its politics and its people, the issue of color, Coetzee chooses to be silent, and this silence creates a space which begs to be filled" (Hewson, 1988, p. 64). The space that silence harbors, therefore, begs to be filled with the hope of interracial negotiations and postcolonial resettlement. This explains that the silence of both Coetzee and his characters in *Disgrace* on the colonial and the postcolonial wrongdoings is an attempt to imagine grace, thus forgiveness, with the hope to attain resettlement and reconciliation during the postcolonial phase in South Africa.

In *Disgrace*, Lurie is one such character who considers the strategy of silence to preserve personal grace during the disgraced postcolonial phase. It is due to his concern for his grace that Lurie refuses to submit an official confession to the university tribunal for the charges of sexual harassment filed against him by Melanie. Lurie is not concerned about his image in public but his conviction. That is why Lurie rescues his grace by not voicing an official confession. Before the tribunal, Lurie explains his concern for his grace in the following words: "'I have no challenge in a legal sense,' he replies. 'I have reservations of a philosophical [thus personal] kind, but I suppose they are out of bounds'" (Coetzee, 1999, p. 41).

Lurie resigns from his old self-conviction that "he is too old to learn lessons" (Coetzee, 1999, p. 141). The changed setting of postcolonial South Africa has enlightened Lurie over the fact that

> [i]t is a new world they live in, he and Lucy and Petrus. Petrus knows it, and he knows it, and Petrus knows that he knows it. In spite of which he feels at home with Petrus, is even prepared, however guardedly, to like him. Petrus is a man of his generation. Doubtless Petrus has been through a lot, doubtless he has a story to tell. He would not mind hearing Petrus' story one day. (Coetzee, 1999, p. 97)

Therefore, while struggling for survival in the postcolonial phase, Lurie carves a new self that recognizes the ethics of compromise, tolerance, and sacrifice. Following the same desire of postcolonial reconciliation, Lurie visits Melanie's family—the Isaacs—with the intention to express his guilt over his mistreatment of their daughter. However, once again, he picks on the strategy of silence and does not express that "something else..." on his "heart," thus protecting his grace (Coetzee, 1999, p. 137).

Jane Poyner (2009), in her book *J. M. Coetzee and the Paradox of Postcolonial Authorship*, contends that "a number of Coetzee's protagonists are only minimal, symbolic authors of their texts"; their "identity is reconstituted in the silences they weave around themselves as authors of their lives" (p. 12). About Poyner's proposition, the case of Lucy's rape and her decision to keep it hushed offers an interesting reading. The silence of Lucy about her rape and the silent patronization of Lucy's rapist by Petrus are the most debatable cases of silence in the novel. However, Lucy, the new settler, a postcolonial subject, decides to employ the strategic grace of silence to avoid further tussles with the colonized, with the intent to initiate the postcolonial "interracial negotiations" in South Africa (McGonegal, 2009, p. 3).

Lucy's father, Lurie, strongly criticizes his daughter's decision of not reporting the event of her rape to the police. Lurie fears that his daughter's decision would be misread as a cowardly reaction by the culprits—colonized Black boys. Lurie explains to Lucy:

> They will read that they are being sought for robbery and assault and nothing else. It will dawn on them that over the body of the woman silence is being drawn like a blanket. Too ashamed, they will say to each other, too ashamed to tell, and they will chuckle luxuriously, recollecting their exploit. Is Lucy prepared to concede them that victory? (Coetzee, 1999, p. 92)

Lurie evaluates Lucy's silence in the sense that it will invigorate the history of women being silenced and suppressed under the tag of the vulnerability of their gender. However, Lucy's side of the story is in stark contrast to Lurie's. She says:

> You want to know why I have not laid a particular charge with the police. I will tell you, as long as you agree not to raise the subject again. The reason is that, as far as I am concerned, what happened to me is a purely private matter. In another time, in another place it might be held to be a public matter. But in this place, at this time, it is not. It is my business, mine alone. (Coetzee, 1999, p. 93)

Therefore, Lucy as the "author" of her "life," by employing silence, weaves an identity for herself—which is a "private"/"personal" identity. Hence, silence helps the disgraced postcolonial subjects in securing their grace.

Moreover, Petrus's clandestine patronization of Lucy's rapist is yet another case that manifests the role of silence in preserving personal grace. Lucy's rapist is one of the relatives of Petrus, therefore Petrus's protection of Lucy's rapist can find justifications in the idea of silence as one of the tools to preserve personal grace. Petrus, with the intent to preserve his grace, hides the fact that he has given shelter to Lucy's rapist—who is a son of one of his relatives. Lurie also realizes that:

> As yet Petrus has offered no explanation for his absence. Petrus has the right to come and go as he wishes; he has exercised that right; he is entitled

> to his silence. But questions remain. Does Petrus know who the strangers were? ... In the old days one could have had it out with Petrus. In the old days one could have had it out to the extent of losing one's temper and sending him packing and hiring someone in his place. But though Petrus is paid a wage, Petrus is no longer, strictly speaking, hired help. (Coetzee, 1999, p. 97)

Therefore, Lurie precisely knows that Petrus, the colonized Black man in postcolonial South Africa, is no longer powerless. Lurie realizes that Petrus "is entitled to his silence" to preserve his grace (Coetzee, 1999, p. 97). Lurie's pertinently aggressive response on seeing Lucy's rapist in Petrus's party, thus, can be deduced as the response of a father, not a postcolonial subject.

Moreover, interracial negotiations and collaborations within the economic structure between the colonizer and the colonized during the phase of postcolonial resettlement are essential to imagine the grace of forgiveness. Furthermore, political stability in postcolonial nations is guaranteed only if their economic structures are built and managed on fortified grounds. In this regard, despite her father's disagreement, Lucy's contractual marriage with Petrus purely on economic terms is a productive blueprint for the hope of resettlement between the colonizer and the colonized in the newly decolonized South Africa.

Coetzee's narratological strategy of inserting the performance of the parabolic play *Sunset at the Global Salon* within *Disgrace* is suggestive of Coetzee's hope of the postcolonial resettlement, reconciliation, and negotiation in South Africa. *Sunset at the Global Salon*, the play within the novel, is described as "a comedy of the new South Africa set in a hairdressing salon in Hillbrow, Johannesburg." The play shows:

> On stage a hairdresser, flamboyantly gay, attends to two clients, one black, one white. Patter passes among the three of them: jokes, insults. Catharsis seems to be the presiding principle: all the coarse old prejudices brought into the light of day and washed away in gales of laughter. (Coetzee, 1999, p. 21)

Therefore, by juxtaposing the auditory image of "gales of laughter" with "silence," it can be implied that a graceful reconciliation between Blacks and White South Africans is possible only if the colonial wounds are kept concealed either under the sheet of silence or the gales of laughter.

The theatrical enactment of the play *Sunset at the Global Salon* is repeated twice in the novel: first in the beginning of the novel and then toward the end in Chapter 21. This repetition stresses the need for resolution between Black and White people in the backdrop of newly postapartheid South Africa. Therefore, like the comedy *Sunset at the Global Salon*, which enacts the resolution between Black and White South Africans amid the roars of laughter, Coetzee's *Disgrace* is a tragedy that attempts to devise a strategy of resettlement between the White colonizer and the Black colonized in South Africa. This strategy is the voluntary silence by the postcolonial subject on the colonial and the postcolonial wrongs.

Therefore, the acts of personal sacrifices, collaboration, and negotiation by the postcolonial subjects, in the long run, could bring about considerable positive changes within the political outlook of the nation's surviving the challenging postcolonial phase. Personal and political life are not divorced from each other; rather, there is a confluence of private and public life. This marriage of personal and political life is also suggested by Lucy when she says that "in another time, in another place, it [the private matter of her rape] might be held to be a public matter" (Coetzee, 1999, p. 93).

This suggests that Lurie's, Lucy's, and Petrus's preservation of their grace, by employing strategic silence, yields ground for a graceful settlement in the political space of South Africa by deliberately avoiding further tussles, and thus to forge a forum of negotiation between the colonizer and the colonized. McGonegal (2009) also suggests the same, that "the conditions of inequality that structure postcolonial societies cannot be altered unless we venture to seriously engage ethics of reconciliation, unless we strive to realize time and space beyond violence (p. 31). Moreover, it is obvious that silence as a strategy of postcolonial reconciliation by no means could compensate for the colonial and postcolonial wrongs. The strategy of employing silence as a tool of postcolonial resettlement indeed is "an ongoing sense of loss," however, "to place one's wager on the future, to take up the challenge of beginning anew," this loss can be tolerated and would end in reward (McGonegal, 2009, p. 36).

Conclusion and Recommendations

Therefore, it is argued that silence within the postcolonial context not only signifies suppression and subjugation of postcolonial subjects at the hands of the colonizer. On the contrary, like the visible rerouting of personal, political, social, and economic structures during the postcolonial phase, the hermeneutics of silence are also redesigned. In this way, silence becomes a strategy on the part of the postcolonial subjects to reimagine grace during the rather disgraced phase of postcolonial resettlement. Therefore, silence enunciates a "third" space of "negotiation, collaboration, and reciprocity" between the colonizer and the colonized while harboring the desire for postcolonial resettlement (McGonegal, 2009, p. 18).

In the end, it is suggested that Lucy's decision of not aborting her child—who is a product of silence because it is an outcome of her rape, which is described as "a blanket [that] has drawn silence on her body"—brings a conspicuous ray of hope of a graceful resettlement in postapartheid South Africa (Coetzee, 1999, p. 92). The survival of her multiracial child gives vent to a new course of history that endorses racial assimilation and hybridization of identities.

The research, therefore, will bring into focus the need to demonstrate the political potential of novels, like *Disgrace*, in envisioning solutions to complex political problems, such as "postcolonial reconciliation." Moreover, this study would invariably pave the way for further research ventures into generating alternative hermeneutics of "silence" in literature. Further, the study could help mobilize research in the domain of postcolonial reconciliation. Moreover, the study would redound in engendering the ethics of compromise, tolerance, and sacrifice essential for human survival in the contemporary world of globalization.

REFERENCES

Atwell, D. (2015). *J. M. Coetzee and the life of writing: Face to face with time*. Oxford University Press.

Barnard, R. (2003). J. M. Coetzee's *Disgrace* and the South African pastoral. *Contemporary Literature, 44*(2), 199–224.

Coetzee, J. M. (1992). Autobiography and confession. In D. Atwell (Ed.), *Doubling the point: Essays and interviews: J. M. Coetzee* (pp. 243–250). Harvard University Press.

Coetzee, J. M. (1999). *Disgrace*. Penguin.

Derrida, J. (2001). *On cosmopolitanism and forgiveness* (M. Dooley & M. Hughes, Trans.). Routledge.

Fanon, F. (1990). *Wretched of the earth* (C. Farrington, Trans.). Penguin.

Foucault, M. (1972). *The archaeology of knowledge* (A. M. S. Smith, Trans.). Pantheon. (Original work published 1969)

Gibson, S. (2009). Being irresponsible in J. M. Coetzee's novel *Disgrace*. In T. Wagner (Ed.), *Literature and ethics: Questions of responsibility in literary studies* (pp. 285–303). Cambria.

Hall, S. (1996). When was "the post-colonial"? Thinking at the limit. In L. Chambers & L. Curti (Eds.), *The post-colonial question: Common skies, divided horizons* (pp. 242–260). Routledge.

Hewson, K. (1988). Making the "revolutionary gesture": Nadine Gordimer, M. Coetzee and some variations on the writer's responsibility. *Ariel: A Review of International English Literature, 19*(4), 55–72.

Kochin, M. S. (2004). Postmetaphysical literature: Reflections on J. M. Coetzee's Disgrace. *Perspectives on Political Science, 33*(1), 4–9.

Manley, J. (1992). *Grace for grace: The psalter and the holy fathers: Patristic Christian commentary, meditations, and liturgical extracts relating to the Psalms and Odes*. St. Vladimir's Seminary Press.

McGonegal, J. (2009). *Imagining justice: The politics of postcolonial forgiveness and reconciliation*. McGill-Queen's University Press.

Poyner, J. (2009). *J. M. Coetzee and the paradox of postcolonial authorship*. Ashgate.

Wehmeier, S., McIntosh, C., & Turnbull, J. (Eds.). (2005). Grace. In *Oxford Advanced Learner's Dictionary* (7th ed.). Oxford University Press.

SECTION TWO

Political, International, and Cultural Relations

CHAPTER SEVEN | AARON S. KING, DANIEL S. MASTERS, J. BENJAMIN TAYLOR, MANZOOR AHMAD, SADAF FAROOQ, AND AMNA MAHMOOD

Evaluating What We Know About Politics, Political Science, and International Relations

A Cross-Cultural Assessment of Political Science and International Relations Education

Scholars of political science and international relations strive to use a scientific approach to evaluate political phenomena in a variety of settings. The use of science ideally cuts across language and cultural barriers resulting in an understood baseline of evaluation of knowledge claims. Understanding the complex interactions of political institutions and human behavior is a complicated endeavor in all societies. That challenge is even greater when partisanship, ideology, and cultural difference accompany both faculty and students into the classroom (e.g., Kelly-Woessner & Woessner, 2008). Given the challenge of bias (cultural or ideological), an empirical approach to the study of politics gives us leverage to explain the world around us. More importantly, an empirical approach to the study of political science and international relations is the agreed-upon approach to the field (e.g., Johnson et al., 2015), allowing students to evaluate knowledge claims across various cultural and ideological divides. Here, we analyze the results of a survey administered to students at the University of North Carolina Wilmington (UNCW) and the International Islamic University, Islamabad (IIUI) that measures the perceptions of how we study political science and international relations. Also, we evaluate student awareness and attitudes of current events within the United States and Pakistan. Our goal is to assess cross-cultural norms in the study of political science and international relations.

Our findings suggest the perceptions of students about the fields of political science and international relations are comparable and generally aligned to the preferred values of empiricism. Additionally, knowledge of the political systems and conditions of each country is comparable when evaluating one's polity but varies when evaluating the opposite polity. More precisely, IIUI students appear to hold a greater depth of knowledge on the political system of the United States than is observed in the other direction. In an increasingly globalized world, our research offers suggestions to improve the quality of instruction, increase the substantive knowledge of our students regarding global politics, and encourage cross-cultural dialog built on the universal language of the scientific study of politics. In some sense, we are putting the discipline of political science to the test to see if the discipline itself can "travel"—or be adequately applied in more than one political context—as Kuhn (2012) so famously requires of good empirical social science theories.

In this essay, we first outline previous research on political knowledge. Next, we outline our theoretical perspective about the differences, or lack thereof, in political science knowledge and understanding in the United States and other states, particularly Pakistan. Then, we describe our research design and the basics of our survey. Finally, we report our results and conclude with some ideas for future research and ways to make political science knowledge and pedagogy more universal.

Previous Research

This project is designed to comply with several of the core objectives of the American Political Science Association (APSA), which is the preeminent professional political science organization for scholars around the world. Notably, this project promotes:

- scholarly research and communication, domestically and internationally, and
- high-quality teaching and education, *and the fostering of an environment to develop* effective citizens and political participants. (American Political Science Association, 2017; italics added)

Although our main focus is on the pedagogical side of the discipline, these teaching goals fit nicely with the main topic of the political science literature—political knowledge.

The Importance of Political Knowledge

Since at least Plato, concerns over citizens' levels of political knowledge have been at the forefront of debates about government and humans' capacity to govern themselves. Political knowledge is one of the basic building blocks for competent citizenship and is a requirement for "enlightened" citizenship as defined by most democratic theorists (e.g., see Rawls, 2009; Habermas, 2006; or Fishkin, 1991).

While the normative expectations for political knowledge as described by democratic theorists have merit, there is ample empirical evidence that political knowledge is instrumentally valuable as well. Political knowledge centers on (a) what government is and does (basic structure), (b) the basic values of government, and (c) the basic elements of government such as the party system and institutional roles (Delli Carpini & Keeter, 1993, p. 1182). Seminal works by Delli Carpini and Keeter (1996) and Page and Shapiro (1992) demonstrate that, in the American context, political knowledge generates more active and engaged citizens, and that those citizens' preferences lead public policy decisions at the national level. These works are buttressed by more evidence from Popkin and Dimock (1999) who replicate much of the previous literature with newer data. Overall, research in this area shows that those who know more about politics are more engaged and that those who are engaged are successful at getting the government to follow their stated preferences over time. The fact is, however, that some people are simply not knowledgeable about politics at all, which is different than being misinformed about politics in the first place.

While scholars agree that being knowledgeable is important, more recent work deals with the implications of being uninformed versus *mis*informed. We know that uninformed citizens can learn, and they change their behavior accordingly (see Delli Carpini & Keeter, 1996), but misinformed citizens are generally harder to correct (Kuklinski et al., 2000). This is particularly the case when information has an ideological or strongly held prior attitudinal component for the individual (Kuklinski et al., 2000; Nyhan & Reifler, 2010). Thus, understanding the extent to which students of political science are informed, uninformed, or—perhaps most importantly—misinformed is a crucial component to this research.

Knowledge of Domestic and International Affairs

Among Americans, it is knowledge of international affairs (current events, foreign policy issues/crises, and knowledge of political systems of other countries) that generally lags the most (Galston, 2001). While Americans are better informed about the rest of the world than they used to be, they still fall behind much of the world in levels of political knowledge (Dalton, 2013). This is partially due to the nature of television programming in other regions of the world, which places a premium on public affairs content rather than purely entertainment (Aalberg et al., 2010). The result is that populations outside the United States exhibit higher levels of political knowledge generally, but also higher levels of political knowledge about the rest of the world (Dalton, 2013).

Here, we investigate the extent to which each of these previous empirical findings is found in our sample, and it informs us about the pedagogical successes and areas for improvement at each institution. Furthermore, investigations of political knowledge provide an avenue for researching these important questions with a generally understudied population (i.e., the cross-national population of college students) that can provide a pathway for other studies of this kind.

Theoretical Expectations

There are important normative components to the study of politics. Political science, however, seeks to explain institutions, behaviors, and policy using the *scientific method* (Johnson et al., 2015). This perspective is central to any student's understanding of the discipline.

Regarding attitudes on the field of political science, we expected students would vary in their perspectives on the discipline. Part of student learning is a function of their instructors, each of whom has their approach based largely on their graduate training and understanding of the phenomena under investigation. Due to the cultural differences across the two countries and universities, we did not expect students at UNCW and IIUI to see the discipline in the same light. Student perspectives also vary based on their substantive area of interest. For example, some subfields within political science are more normative (e.g., political theory) in nature, while others are more empirical (e.g., political economy). Similarly, some topics lend themselves to either qualitative or quantitative analyses.

From a practical standpoint, we expected that students would know more about their own country than other nation-states around the globe. This is largely because of availability bias. Students interact with and see news about their own country more than others. However, to the extent students do know more about countries that are not the home state for a student, we expected that the Pakistani students would know more about the United States because of the primacy of international relations within the IIUI curriculum.

Research Design

Background on Grant

This project grew out of a grant from the U.S. Department of State awarded to UNCW and IIUI. The goal of the grant was to foster a collaborative model of professional development in teaching, research, and community engagement.

Description of UNCW and IIUI

This grant afforded us the opportunity to tap two convenience samples that we can compare and contrast—students in political science classes at UNCW and students in political science and international relations classes at IIUI.

UNCW is a comprehensive regional university with approximately 16,500 students (undergraduates make up about 88% of the student body). Demographically, the university is 64% female, 14.5% of students are members of a minority ethnic group, and 83% of students are from the state of North Carolina. Regarding academics, UNCW offers 55 different bachelor's degrees in addition to 30 master's degrees, and several combined/dual undergraduate/graduate degrees, and it is home to four different doctoral programs (University of North Carolina Wilmington, 2017). UNCW is located in Wilmington, North Carolina, United States, which has a population of approximately 113,910 within the city limits, and just under a half million in the southeastern region of the state (City of Wilmington, 2017).

IIUI is a national comprehensive university that offers students 120 different academic programs at the undergraduate and graduate level. With over 17,000 students, including 7,000 on a female campus, IIUI and UNCW are similar in size (International Islamic University, Islamabad, 2017). The city of Islamabad, however, is significantly larger than Wilmington with over a million residents (Staff Reports, 2011). The universities share similarities in size and composition but come from different urban environments.

Survey Design and Implementation

Our research had some goals including learning about how students perceive the academic discipline of political science and international relations as well as their perceptions on how this curriculum is delivered by the faculty at each university. Also, we sought to better understand our students' knowledge of government institutions in the United States and Pakistan. Finally, we examined the attitudes of students toward current events in both countries. To reach these goals, we designed a unique survey instrument to deliver at both universities.

The survey included four sections: (1) a standard battery of demographic questions, including information about each participant's academic standing and degree program; (2) an assessment of attitudes about political science; (3) a brief prompt about the structure of government in the United States and the current political context followed by several questions to assess attitudes toward American politics; and (4) a similar prompt focusing on Pakistani government and politics followed by questions specific to Pakistan. The location of the survey respondent determined the order of the question blocks on government and politics for each country. Students at UNCW received questions on the United States followed by questions about Pakistan and vice versa.

While the questions for each survey were mostly identical, the options to some questions varied based on the context of each country. For example, questions on partisanship reflected the partisan environment of each country, and the response alternatives for ethnicity reflected the most common ethnic groups in each country.

The surveys, approved by the Institutional Review Board at UNCW and the Quality Assurance Agency in Pakistan, were delivered electronically via Qualtrics using two different methods. In most cases, a member of our research team coordinated with faculty members from their respective department and arranged a time to come to each political science or international relations class. After an introduction to the research project, students who opted to participate accessed the survey on their electronic devices (e.g., cell phone, laptop, etc.). In some cases, we would also distribute the survey link and introduction via email to the relevant sample (i.e., an email distribution list of all political science majors). To incentivize participation in the survey, our research team offered an iPad to a randomly selected participant at UNCW and IIUI.

Analysis

Our analysis proceeds in several parts. First, we describe the samples at each university and discuss their demographic similarities and differences. Second, we examine our respondents' experience with political science classes and their views on the discipline. Third, we analyze our respondents' knowledge of political institutions within the United States and Pakistan. Finally, we compare and contrast views on the current political environment within each country.

Demographics of Samples at UNCW and IIUI

The strength of our research design lies in the two unique samples of political science and international relations students from two universities in different national and cultural settings as well as our ability to leverage these differences to better understand the knowledge of our students and their attitudes toward the different countries. There were 351 students in the UNCW sample and 512 students in the IIUI sample.

At both universities, students had the option to opt out of the survey after reading the consent form. In the end, only five students took this action. We do not know, however, the proportion of students we invited to participate in the survey who actually completed the task. By delivering the survey electronically, offering each participant the opportunity to win an iPad, and arranging with faculty to give students time to complete the survey in class, our goal was to maximize the likelihood that students would complete the task.

The two samples were quite similar in age with the average participant between 21 and 22 years old; however, the samples diverged over gender. At UNCW, about 56% of participants identified as female compared to over 87% at IIUI. Respondents from UNCW disproportionately identified as "White, non-Hispanic" (80.9%), while the students in the IIUI sample were much more ethnically diverse. About 42% of this sample identified as Punjabi, 21.6% as Urdu speaking, and 15.3% as Pakhtoon. Most students at each university studied in the country of their birth (93.3% for UNCW and 96.1% for IIUI).

Outside of their academic interests, our samples included students with a wide variety of political beliefs. First, consider partisanship. In the UNCW sample, 41.4% identified as a Democrat compared to just 27.7% Republican. Of these partisan identifiers, over half (55.1%) said they were "strong" partisans (as opposed to "weak Partisans"). While 30.9% of the UNCW sample claimed to be Independent, 75% of these individuals admitted they tended to lean toward one of the parties; these "leaners" were twice as likely to tilt toward the Democratic Party compared to the Republican Party. A quarter of all self-proclaimed Independents said they did not lean toward either party. While there are some viable political parties in Pakistan, IIUI respondents were most likely to identify with the Pakistan Tehreek-e-Insaf Party (35.8%) or the Pakistan Muslim League (20.1%). Of all partisan identifiers, over three-quarters of them identified as "strong" partisans (76.6%, compared to 55.1% of partisan identifiers at UNCW). Interestingly, 35.2% of IIUI respondents said they do not identify with any of the political parties, which was slightly higher than the percentage of Independents in the UNCW sample (30.9%).

Turning to ideology, which we measured on a seven-point scale, a plurality of UNCW respondents were liberal (49%); conservatives were about 28.6%, and 19.5% claimed to be moderate. At IIUI, a strong plurality of respondents were moderate (46.8%). Liberals were the second largest ideological group (41.8%) followed by less than 5% of the respondents who were conservative (4.85%).

Perhaps the largest disparity between the UNCW and IIUI groups was religious identification. While there was some variation in the religious affiliations at UNCW (25.7% mainline Protestant and 14.6% Roman Catholic), religious students were primarily Christian. Still, a plurality of students did not identify with any religious group. For comparison, all but one student in the IIUI sample identified as Muslim. In both samples, a majority of students said they were "somewhat religious or spiritual" (UNCW: 54.8%; IIUI: 65.0%). At UNCW, 18.8% were "very religious or spiritual," and 26.4% were "not religious or spiritual at all." By comparison, less than 2% of IIUI students surveyed said they were "not religious or spiritual at all," and just under a third were "very religious or spiritual."

Experience with Political Science

In terms of their academic standing and focus, both samples were quite diverse even though we drew both from political science and international relations classes. At UNCW, 40% of respondents were first- or second-year students compared to 60% who were upperclassmen. Similarly, about 42% of IIUI respondents were in their first or second year of study. While a majority of students in each sample had already declared their major (81.4% at UNCW and 61.3% at IIUI), not all of them were political science majors. For the UNCW sample, 48.4% were currently (or planning to be) political science majors. At IIUI, two-thirds of respondents were majoring (or planning to major) in a field related to political science. At IIUI, there were majors in both political science and international relations. Many respondents also wrote in topics like foreign policy or security studies, which we have combined together as related fields to political science. Still, many of the students declared (or intended to minor) in fields unrelated to political science.

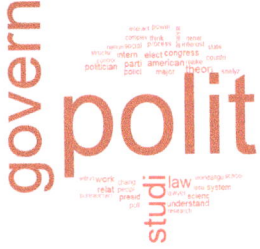 

Fig. 1. Word clouds (from left to right, UNCW and IIUI) of responses to the prompt: "What is the first word or phrase that comes to mind when you hear the term 'political science'?"

Outside of their declared or intended majors/minors, students had diverse interests within the field of political science and international relations. At UNCW, for example, 27% of respondents were interested in law, 20.1% in American politics, and 17.2% in international relations. Interestingly, 4.1% of respondents said they were not interested in political science at all. For comparison, at IIUI, only 2.5% of students were interested in law, 14.9% in Pakistani politics, and 70.3% in international relations. Less than 1% of IIUI respondents admitted having no interest in any area of political science. In short, while our samples were students in political science and international relations classes, they were not without diverse academic interests; this allowed us the opportunity to compare the different types of students in our classes.

We believe that empirically based political science should transcend political borders and cultural differences. At the same time, the knowledge of students is very much a function of the academic training of their faculty. To assess students' understanding of the discipline, we asked them several questions.

First, we asked them to give the first word or phrase that came to mind when they heard "political science." Figure 1 shows a word cloud for the responses from UNCW students (left panel) and IIUI students (right panel). The most common responses included the root words "polit" (126 mentions by UNCW sample and 204 mentions by IIUI sample) and "govern" (70 mentions by UNCW and 91 mentions by IIUI).

Next, we asked respondents to provide a short definition of political science. Figure 2 shows a comparison word cloud between the UNCW and IIUI students. This figure compares the responses between students with the size of words proportional to the maximum deviation between the rates of each word

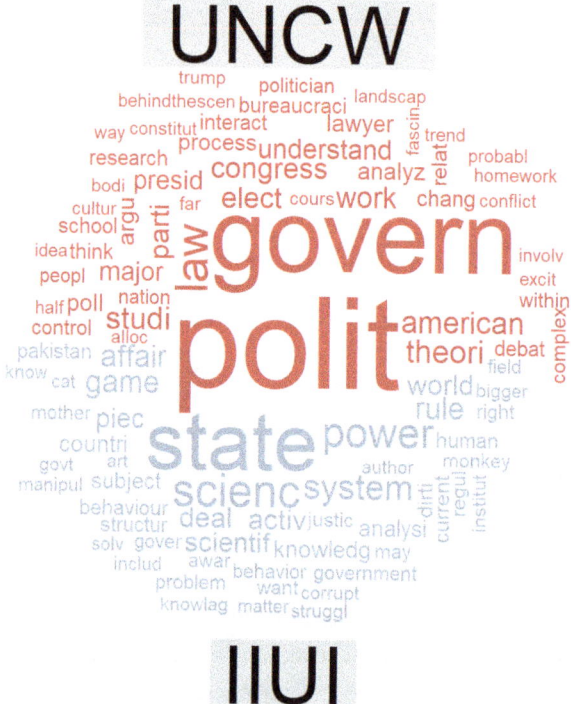

Fig. 2. Comparison cloud for the definition of political science from students at UNCW and IIUI.

appearing in one group compared to its average usage rates in both groups. Figure 2 demonstrates that the state, as a concept, loomed much larger for students in Pakistan. At UNCW, with political science students there was much wider variation among the definitions offered by students.

Figure 3 shows a commonality cloud to represent the most common words found in the definitions of political science from students in both samples. This figure demonstrates that, despite the cultural differences between IIUI and UNCW students, government and politics were still the most common words associated with the discipline.

Next, we asked students to briefly describe a question or research design they would be interested in pursuing. Figure 4 and Figure 5 show the comparison and commonality clouds for these questions. In Figure 4, the UNCW students seemed to focus more on the survey and more quantitative analysis, whereas the IIUI students had more words associated with qualitative analysis

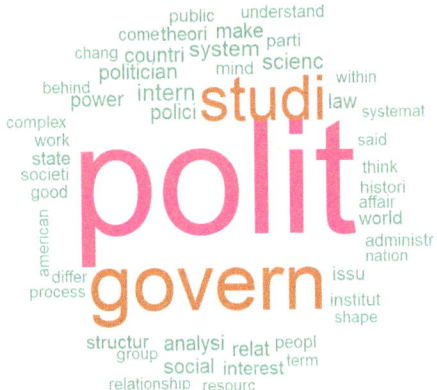

Fig. 3. Commonality cloud for the definition of political science from students at UNCW and IIUI.

and comparative politics. In Figure 5, we see that "system" and "law" are words the two student bodies used in common, but, in general, there were myriad ways students at each institution were interested in researching politics and political science. This makes sense given the variety of ways one might choose to answer a research question, but is also an instructive exercise to empirically identify this variety.

We also asked UNCW and IIUI students to give their assessment of the right balance between different approaches to the study of political phenomena using a scale between 0 and 100. First, we inquired about a normative versus empirical approach to studying political science. Here, a score of zero was given if a respondent believed political science should take a completely normative approach, while a score of 100 corresponded to a strictly empirical approach. Both samples gave nearly identical responses. At UNCW, the average score was 59.6 compared to 59.5 at IIUI; the dispersion of these distributions was also similar (UNCW standard deviation = 17.0; IIUI standard deviation = 19.0). In other words, it appears students see merit in both normative and empirical arguments, but there was a slight lean in the direction of empiricism. Once we break down students within each sample by their major, we note some differences. At IIUI, political science majors were significantly more likely to see political science as an empirical exercise compared to non-majors (62.1 versus 57.6, a difference of means p value = 0.017). Interestingly, the opposite was true comparing majors and nonmajors at UNCW. Political

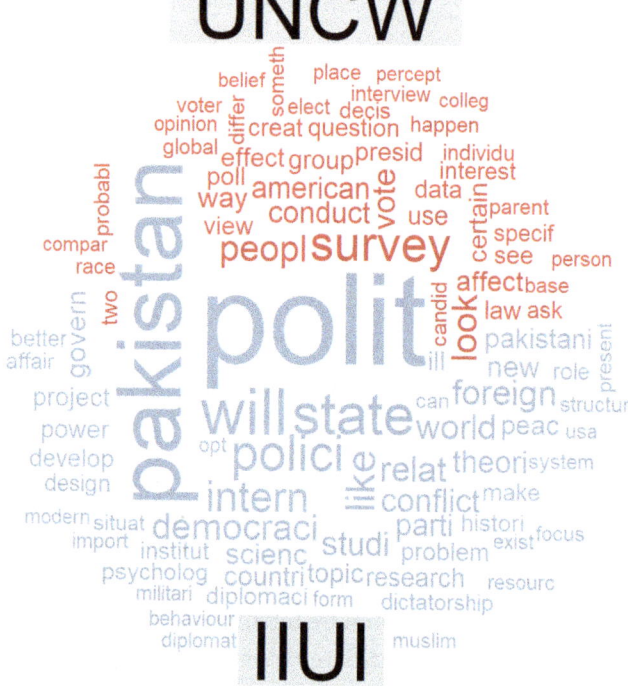

Fig. 4. Comparison cloud for research questions/designs from students at UNCW and IIUI.

science majors had a score of 58.2, while nonmajors had an average score of 62.4, which is a statistically significant difference (p value = 0.043).

Using the same scale, we asked the respondents to consider whether political scientists should take a quantitative (0) versus qualitative (100) approach to studying political phenomena. At UNCW, students were nearly in the middle with an average score of 52.9 (standard deviation = 16.2); at IIUI, students leaned toward a more qualitative assessment (average = 63.3, standard deviation = 20.5). There was no discernable difference on this question if we compared majors and nonmajors at either school.

While it is important for faculty to instruct students in the field, ultimately, most students desire an academic program to help them meet their career goals. To assess student perceptions of their preparation for the job market, we asked them to give us their level of agreement with the statement, "Political science helps prepare me for my future career." Given that many of our students may eventually enter a career outside of politics, the results were

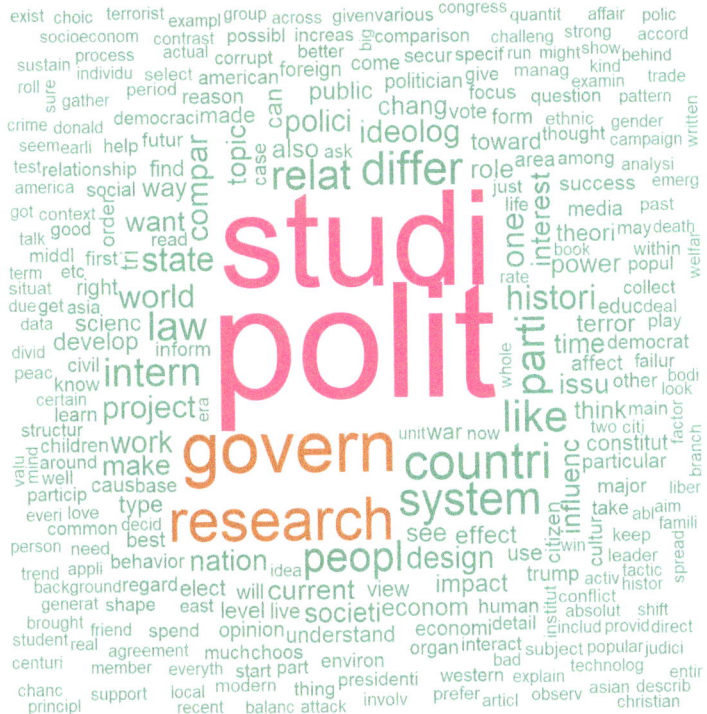

Fig. 5. Commonality cloud for research questions/designs from students at UNCW and IIUI.

encouraging. Using a seven-point scale, a majority of students in both samples reported some level of agreement with this statement. At UNCW, 27.8% "Strongly agree," 34.7% "Agree," and 24.6% "Somewhat agree." At IIUI, 29.8% "Strongly agree," 45.1% "Agree," and 19.3% "Somewhat agree." At UNCW, about 5% of respondents disagreed with the statement to some degree, while less than 2% offered any disagreement at IIUI. While students certainly self-select into academic programs and individual classes, it is encouraging to know that students feel their political science classes are valuable to their future.

Knowledge of the United States, Pakistan, and Their Political Institutions

Previous research suggests political knowledge is generally low among citizens. Contrary to this, we suspect our samples are more knowledgeable than their peers who are not enrolled in political science classes. We asked both the UNCW and IIUI samples the same sets of questions regarding their

Table 1. Self-reports of knowledge of domestic political and current events in the United States and Pakistan.

Demographic Variables	f	%
Age		
Young Adulthood (19–40 years)	95	95.0
Middle Adulthood (40–65 years)	5	5.0
Gender		
Male	50	50.0
Female	50	50.0
Family System		
Nuclear	50	50.0
Joint	50	50.0

"textbook" knowledge about the government in both the United States and Pakistan. Students at UNCW were asked first about the United States and second about Pakistan. We presented the two blocks of questions in the opposite order for students at IIUI. In sum, these questions focused on assessing each respondent's knowledge on subjects like political geography, government institutions, foreign policy, as well as their attitudes toward the current political environment in each country. In this section, we address each item in turn by comparing the survey results from students at UNCW and IIUI.

Starting with responses on U.S. politics, students at UNCW expressed a high degree of confidence with 41.6% reporting they knew "a lot" or "a great deal," and 46.4% saying they knew a "moderate amount." Only 12.1% said they only knew "a little" or "none at all." Not surprisingly, students at IIUI self-reported less knowledge about politics and current events within the United States; in fact, over 38% of respondents admitted knowing only "a little" or "none at all" (compared to 18% that indicate they knew "a lot" or "a great deal"). UNCW and IIUI students reported nearly identical results on "knowing a moderate amount" with 46.6% of UNCW students and 43.7% of IIUI students.

When we questioned each sample on their perceived knowledge about Pakistani politics and current events, the responses of IIUI students were similar to the UNCW students. Over 45% of IIUI students said they knew "a moderate amount" about Pakistani politics, and 46.2% said "a lot" or "a great deal." This shows that IIUI and UNCW students were confident about their

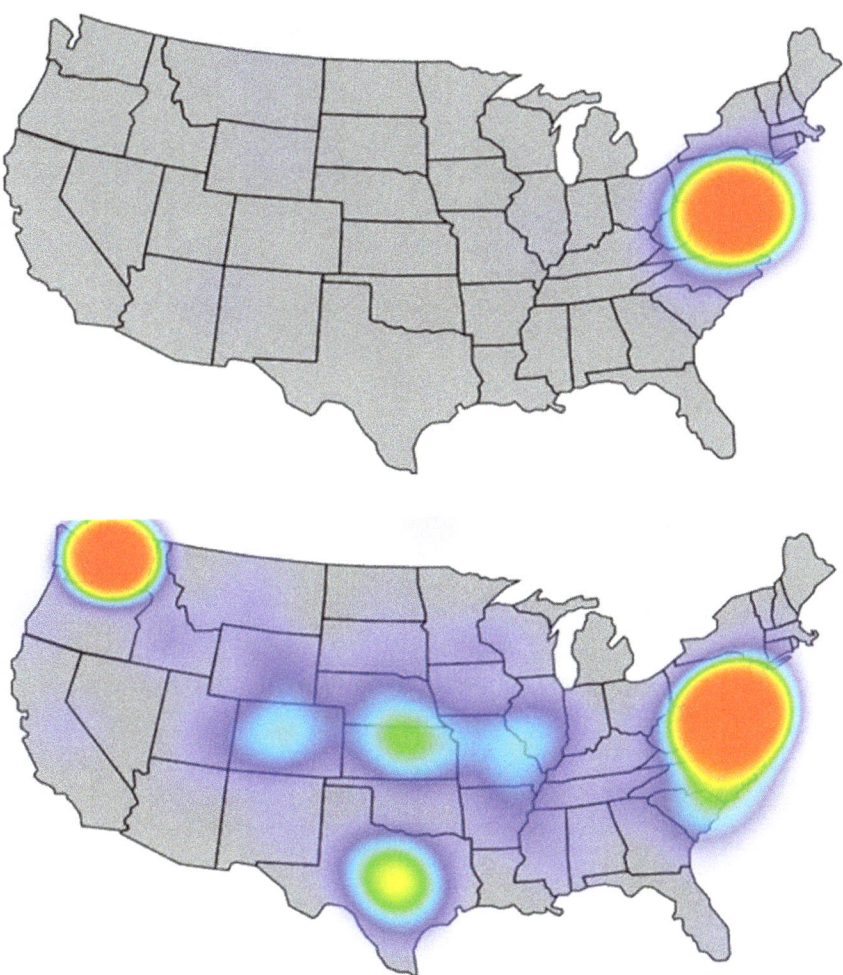

Fig. 6. Locating Washington, D.C. The top panel shows responses from UNCW students, and the bottom panel shows responses from IIUI students.

knowledge on domestic politics in their own countries. Meanwhile, IIUI students reported being more knowledgeable about politics in the United States than UNCW students reported on Pakistani politics. At UNCW, 87.1% of students said they only knew "a little" or "nothing" about Pakistani politics. Just 10.3% believed they knew "a moderate amount," and 2.6% answered "a lot" or "a great deal" about current events and politics in Pakistan, compared to 18% of IIUI students who believed they knew "a lot" or "a great deal."

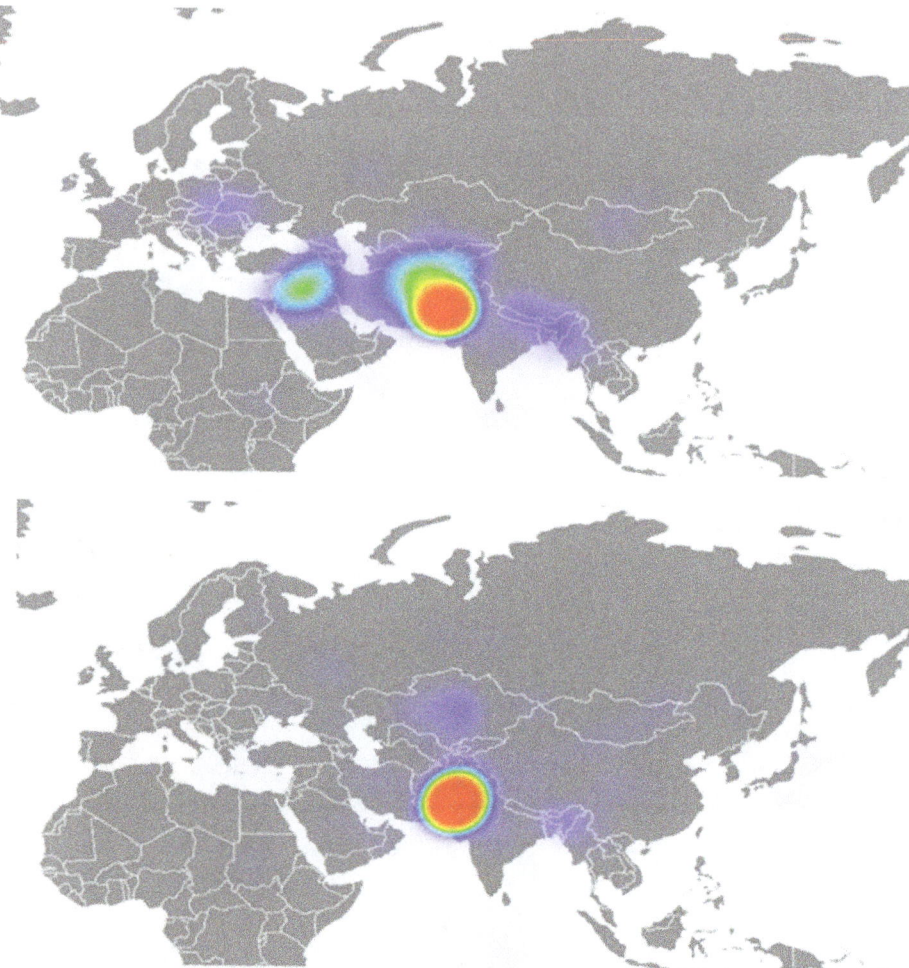

Fig. 7. Locating Pakistan. The top panel shows responses from UNCW students, and the bottom panel shows responses from IIUI students.

To assess our students' skills as political geographers, we asked all respondents to locate Washington, D.C., and Pakistan on a map. Students at UNCW had little difficulty locating Washington, D.C., just as students at IIUI had no issue locating their home country. When we asked each sample about the opposite country, the results diverged. While many students at IIUI correctly located Washington, D.C., some students misidentified the state of Washington. Some students also clicked on the state of Texas. Despite reporting they had limited knowledge about the country of Pakistan, students at UNCW did a respectable job locating Pakistan. While most students correctly identified its location, there were some students who clicked on the Middle East, specifically near the borders between Syria, Iraq, and Jordan. Figure 6 shows the heat map for locating Washington, D.C., and Figure 7 shows the results for locating Pakistan.

Next, we questioned students on the political institutions and the structure of government in each country. For the United States, a large majority of respondents at both schools answered that the United States has a presidential system (82.3% for UNCW and 90.2% for IIUI). Most UNCW respondents correctly identified the United States as a federal system (82.9%). Less than half of students at IIUI identified the United States as federal (48.9%), just over 25% indicated the United States has a unitary system, 10.4% identified the United States as a confederacy, and another 13.6% were unsure. Students at both schools struggled to correctly identify the electoral system of the United States. Only 10.9% of UNCW students and 7.7% of IIUI students answered "First past the post, single-member districts." The most common incorrect answer by UNCW was "Proportional representation, multi-member districts" (22.2%), while the most common incorrect answer from IIUI students was "Majority rule, single-member districts" (15.4%). Many students admitted they were unsure about this question (15.43% at UNCW and 30.9% at IIUI). Respondents performed better on the question about the party system of the United States. Students at UNCW were more likely to acknowledge the system as "Two-party dominant" (53.9%) compared to just 28.6% of IIUI students.

Both samples were more knowledgeable about their own country. Comparatively speaking, though, students at IIUI knew much more about the United States than UNCW students knew about Pakistan. Only 19% of UNCW students correctly identified Pakistan's parliamentary system of government compared to 87.9% of IIUI students. Even when guessing, first reporting they were unsure, less than a third of UNCW students gave the correct answer. Even though the federal structure of Pakistan is similar to that of the United States, only 10.4% of UNCW students recognized this (compared to nearly 90% of IIUI students). Just as before, the most difficult question about Pakistan related to its electoral system. Just under 70% of UNCW students said they were "unsure" about this question; the second most common answer was "Majority rule, single-member districts" (9.84%). Even students at IIUI seemed quite unsure about this answer; the most common answer was "Majority rule, multi-member districts" (30.2%). Turning to the party system, only 19.6% of the UNCW sample correctly identified the multiparty system in Pakistan (compared to 81.8% of students in the IIUI sample).

Attitudes on Current Events Within the United States and Pakistan

With foreign affairs playing a significant role in the politics of each country, we first asked students how they perceived the role each country plays on the world stage. A significant plurality of both samples saw Pakistan as a "regional power" (44.9% at UNCW and 54.4% at IIUI), and nearly all respondents saw the United States as a "global power" (96.5% at UNCW and 95.9% at IIUI). There was less agreement, however, when it came to identifying each country's allies around the world.

We presented respondents with a list of 11 different countries, including the United Stated (for the IIUI survey) or Pakistan (for the UNCW survey), Iran, Germany, Saudi Arabia, China, India, Russia, Israel, France, Japan, and the United Kingdom. Focusing first on the United States, students at UNCW were most likely to select the United Kingdom (16.4%) or France (16.1%), while students at IIUI were most likely to select Israel (16.3%) or India (15.4%). For the perceived allies of Pakistan, nearly a fifth of UNCW students were unsure (18.4%), and 16.4% identified Saudi Arabia. IIUI students were most likely to select China (34.8%) or Saudi Arabia (20.5%).

Turning to domestic politics within each nation, we asked all respondents their level of agreement with five different statements, including topics like government responsiveness, representation, equality of citizens, the ability of political parties to work together, and the role of the media. In each case, the agreement was associated with traditional democratic ideals. Focusing first on attitudes on the United States, generally speaking, IIUI students were more likely to agree or strongly agree with these statements than students at UNCW. For example, only 7.7% of UNCW students strongly agreed or agreed with the statement that "The government responds to the wishes of its citizens" compared to over 60% of students at IIUI.

In another example, two-thirds of UNCW students had at least some level of disagreement with the statement "The government treats all citizens equally" compared to just 14.5% of IIUI students. When we asked our samples about the level of agreement to the same statement regarding Pakistan, the most common answer from UNCW students was "Neither agree nor disagree" (about half of all respondents for each question). Similar to their peers in America, Pakistani students had mixed attitudes on these questions. The IIUI students were most likely to agree regarding the ability of the media to monitor and report on the actions of government (85.8%). The most significant disagreement occurred when they were asked about equality for all citizens (68% offered some level of disagreement).

Finally, we measured the approval ratings for (then-current) President Donald Trump and Prime Minister Nawaz Sharif. Among students at UNCW, Donald Trump was struggling, with the average feeling thermometer score of 31.8 (standard deviation = 31.3). Students at IIUI were also hesitant to approve of Donald Trump; the average score was 38.3 (standard deviation = 28.3). The average thermometer score for Prime Minister Nawaz by UNCW students was 44.8 (standard deviation of 13.6) and 44.6 for IIUI students (standard deviation of 29.3).

Conclusion

The results of this study demonstrate that the understanding of political science does travel across cultural and international boundaries. Students at both IIUI and UNCW understood political science as an empirical field with normative components. Regarding research choices, students at IIUI had a clear preference for studies related to Pakistani politics, which is reflective of the general focus of the IIUI curriculum preparing students to enter government service or otherwise deal with practical political issues. At UNCW, research questions generally focused on the type of study students might want to pursue, which likely subsumed the preferences for most students to study American politics though they did not specifically state this.

When it comes to political knowledge, our basic expectations were borne out here as well. IIUI students were much more knowledgeable about the United States than UNCW students were knowledgeable about Pakistan. Both sets of students had some difficulty with the map question, but IIUI students performed much better than UNCW students on the non–home country- and government-specific questions. Overall, these findings replicate previous research on American and non-American political knowledge overall.

Finally, on attitudes toward current events, there were some interesting findings worth exploring more in the future. Understandings about the relationships between nation states and the levels of efficacy, trust in government, and the role of government all varied quite widely between the UNCW and IIUI samples. To be sure, some of this was expected, but a more important question to answer is whether these differences can be replicated in the wider population of either country. This is to say: How representative are these responses of the wider population in the United States or Pakistan? At this time, we cannot answer this question, but it does provide an interesting avenue for future research.

Limitations

There are some significant limitations to consider. First, these samples were convenience samples of college students at single institutions in both the United States and Pakistan. Therefore, we are cautious when generalizing from such samples in a nonexperimental setting. Our conclusions need to be replicated before we put too much stock into these findings.

A second limitation was that, invariably, when doing cross-national, cross-cultural research, some nuances of political circumstances are unintentionally obscured. Continued refinement of the survey instrument and replication can ease some of these issues and make sure that inadvertent misunderstanding of the survey does not hinder the results. Furthermore, exogenous events—such as the resignation of the Pakistani prime minister while the survey was in the field—are always a complication in political science. Replication is crucial to ensure that the effects of these events are effectively controlled in our understanding of the attitudes we report here.

Suggestions to Improve Teaching Instruction

While our results are rather preliminary given the limitations outlined above, our research does suggest several avenues to improve our teaching of political science. While each nation's political context and the interests of students and faculty can hamper their willingness to expand their knowledge to other regions around the world, our skills as political scientists do not stop at the boundaries of our substantive area of inquiry.

Whether we study American politics, international relations, or another subfield, our shared training in the science of politics serves as a bridge to connect our interests and leads to a broader understanding of political phenomena. For example, in the Introductory Research Methods class at UNCW, students have the flexibility to choose individual research topics from across the field of political science. However, we work collectively to apply the course material to these diverse research questions. Even if instructors are not experts in each subfield of the discipline, a strong foundation in research methods (e.g., developing empirical research questions, incorporating the extant literature, crafting a theoretical argument, and designing a method for systematic data collection and analysis) is a language that is universal, regardless of the subfield.

It is not surprising that students are more knowledgeable about their home country in comparison to others around the globe. However, this project shows that students in the United States are not as knowledgeable about Pakistan. We suspect this result would be similar if we looked at other nations around the world as well. While we do not expect students to be experts in every country, increased emphasis on the themes of comparative politics could help students, regardless of the class topic. Consider an introductory class on American government. An explanation of the "first past the post" electoral system and "single-member districts" is enhanced once students can compare it to countries that rely on proportional representation and multi-member districts. As instructors, we must not see ourselves as scholars and teachers of specific regions or subfields; rather, we should define ourselves by our methods.

While empiricism has a strong foothold in political science curricula, these concepts are likely taught explicitly in one or two classes focused on research methods. Faculty in substantive classes should be more intentional about highlighting the concepts first taught in methods courses within their other classes. For example, when reading a scholarly article for a class on international relations, we should reinforce our students' understanding of the central question or relationship of the research (i.e., key independent and dependent variables), its contribution to the literature, and the specific hypotheses under investigation.

Our participation in activities surrounding this grant offers one additional suggestion to improve our teaching in political science. As educators, we should continuously engage in dialogue with our colleagues—both within our institution and outside of it—to better understand our unique perspectives and best practices on the delivery of our curricula. Through activities like research colloquia and workshops as well as observing the classrooms of our colleagues, participants in this grant gained valuable perspective on teaching political science in different settings. We have benefited greatly from these activities, and we encourage all educators to seek out similar opportunities to continue to improve the quality of their instruction and the delivery of their curricula.

Future Research

Our reading of the literature demonstrates that there is much to be gained from research of this kind, particularly through avenues like *The Journal of Political Science Education*, which is a pedagogy journal sponsored by the American Political Science Association. We think this essay is an important extension of traditional pedagogy research because it combines both questions important to the field—political knowledge, efficacy, and political trust—and a consideration of the pedagogical causes and implications of these questions. We suggest that future research in these areas follow our lead. In an era of budget constraints, questions about the value of social science, and concerns about the stability of modern post-Cold War government norms, research similar to this can serve as the "canary in the coal mine" for understanding the evolution in training and attitudes students have about political science and government.

Our major limitations stem from the representativeness of our data, and our use of only two institutions in two different countries. Future research should leverage additional data from diverse contexts to systematically study our delivery of a consistent political science curriculum despite cultural differences and international borders, and how it affects the knowledge and attitudes of our students.

REFERENCES

Aalberg, T., van Aelst, P., & Curran, J. (2010). Media systems and the political information environment: A cross-national comparison. *The International Journal of Press/Politics, 15*(3), 255–271.

American Political Science Association. (2017). About APSA. https://apsanet.org/ABOUT/About-APSA.

City of Wilmington. (2017). City of Wilmington, NC | Home. https://www.wilmingtonnc.gov/home/

Dalton, R. J. (2013). *Citizen politics: Public opinion and political parties in advanced industrial democracies* (6th ed.). CQ Press.

Delli Carpini, M. X., & Keeter, S. (1993). Measuring political knowledge: Putting first things first. *American Journal of Political Science, 37*(4), 1179–1206.

Delli Carpini, M. X., & Keeter, S. (1996). *What Americans know about politics and why it matters*. Yale University Press.

Fishkin, J. S. (1991). *Democracy and deliberation: New directions for democratic reform*. Yale University Press.

Galston, W. A. (2001). Political knowledge, political engagement, and civic education. *Annual Review of Political Science, 4*(1), 217–234.

Habermas, J. (2006). Political communication in media society: Does democracy still enjoy an epistemic dimension? The impact of normative theory on empirical research. *Communication Theory, 16*, 411–426.

International Islamic University, Islamabad. (2017). History. http://www.iiu.edu.pk/?page_id=30

International Political Science Association. (2017). Constitution & mission statements. https://www.ipsa.org/organization/mission-statement

Johnson, J. B., Reynolds, H. T., & Mycoff, J. D. (2015). *Political science research methods* (8th ed.). CQ Press.

Kelly-Woessner, A., & Woessner, M. (2008). Conflict in the classroom: Considering the effects of partisan difference on political education. *Journal of Political Science Education, 4*(3), 265–285.

Kuhn, T. S. (2012). *The structure of scientific revolutions: 50th anniversary edition*. University of Chicago Press.

Kuklinski, J. H., Quirk, P. J., Jerit, J., Schwieder, D., & Rich, R. F. (2000). Misinformation and the currency of democratic citizenship. *Journal of Politics, 62*, 790–816.

Luskin, R. C. (1990). Explaining political sophistication. *Political Behavior, 12*, 331–361.

Nyhan, B., & Reifler, J. (2010). When corrections fail: The persistence of political misperceptions. *Political Behavior, 32*, 303–330.

Page, B. I., & Shapiro, R. Y. (1992). *The rational public: Fifty years of trends in Americans' policy preferences*. University of Chicago Press.

Popkin, S. L., & Dimock, M. A. (1999). Political knowledge and citizen competence. In S. L. Elkin & K. E. Soltan (Eds.), *Citizen competence and democratic institutions* (pp. 117-145). Penn State University Press.

Rawls, J. (2009). *A theory of justice* (rev. ed.). Harvard University Press.
Staff Reports. (2011). *Islamabad's population surges*. Dawn. http://www.dawn.com/news/623105
University of North Carolina Wilmington. (2017). Just the facts: UNCW. https://www.uncw.edu/aboutuncw/aboutJustthefacts.html

CHAPTER EIGHT | MUHAMMAD SULEMAN

The Post-9/11 Politicization of Sufi Islam and the Rise of Barelvi Extremism in Pakistan

Since the 1980s, Pakistan's society has been marred by religious extremism and terrorism, especially after initiation of the Afghan Jihad. The underlying cause of religious extremism in Pakistan is mainly due to the practice of employing religion for strategic, political, and vested interests by institutions, different political groups, as well as religious organizations. The worrisome point is that when one client faction of a religious extremist group becomes a threat, the patrons craft a new group to counter the dissident group rather than rectifying its policies. When the state counters or tries to counter the first faction with the assistance of a second group, then that second group occupies the space vacated by the first, and later it also, perhaps, creates challenges to centrist and normative values of state and society. In this way, the cycle of religious extremism and counter-extremism has continued in one form or another since the 1980s. Generally, after achieving the required results, the patrons become disinterested in guarding their client groups or those who have organically developed roots among the people, and the patrons abandon them.

Sufi Islam as a Counterweight to Extremism

After the 9/11 incident, General Musharraf decided to support the United States-led war as a key non-NATO ally in combating terrorists while taking different measures domestically to tackle the threat of extremism and terrorism. Employing soft measures, President Musharraf started institutionalizing Sufi Islam, mainly followed by a Barelvi school of thought, perceived to be more flexible, tolerant, and peaceful. This was intended to suppress the Wahabi and Deobandi school of thought, perceived to be sowing the seeds of extremism through the promotion of armed Jihad. It is noteworthy that the followers of Sufi and orthodox schools of thought have long historical differences with each other over their respective religious beliefs. The long history of segregation between the Barelvis and Deobandis has left divisive impacts on the society.

In the history of Pakistan, President Ayub Khan and Zulfiqar Ali Bhutto had a major role in politicizing Sufi Islam and employed this ideology for their political ends (Ewing, 1983). Decades later, the Musharraf government perceived the ideology of Sufism as one presenting a gentler face of Islam and hence decided to promote it as more accommodative toward the culture and as more natural to Pakistan (Shaikh, 2012), which is based on pluralism. It was also viewed as more tolerant and patient in the context of interfaith and intrafaith harmony, and as more resilient and progressive for the state of Pakistan. In addition to the Musharraf government, the United States was also interested in promoting Sufi Islam to tackle the threat of religious extremism in Muslim countries, especially in Pakistan. The prominent U.S. think tanks also conducted studies on Sufi Islam and termed it as fit to counter the growing orthodoxy and militancy in the country. In 2003, the Rand Corporation concluded in a study that Sufi Islam was helpful for American interests in building modern democratic Islam in the Muslim states, aimed at countering religious fanatics. In 2007, the Rand Corporation reexamined its report and termed Sufi Islam as a "natural ally" (Rabasa et al., 2007) to the West in countering the threat of radical Islamists. However, this time the report also warned that due to the emergence of radical mindsets, there was room for radical and extremist tendencies in popular Islam, too.

The Heritage Foundation, a conservative U.S. think tank, published a report in 2009 on Sufi Islam and recommended that it was the best option for Pakistan's internal stability, as it not only restores local traditions and culture but also counters the threat of extremism (Curtis & Mullick, 2009). Another think tank, World Organization for Resources Development and Education, a Washington-based institute, published a report in 2010 (Mirahmadi et al.) that emphasized that to defeat the radical tendencies in Muslims and project the U.S. foreign policy in the region, the mainstream Barelvi politicoreligious parties promoting the Sufis and *pirs* should be encouraged in Pakistan. However, these studies neither covered all the aspects nor indicated the fault lines in ideologies of clerics and followers of popular Islam, which can birth intolerance and extremism in the society.

Assimilation of Sufism Into National Ideology

In Pakistan, history reveals that during politically turbulent times, governments resort to the doors of the Sufis and Shrines. In response, the Shrine custodians fully extend their support to the rulers due to their vested interests (Sherani, 1991). To tackle the menace of extremism, like his predecessors, the Musharraf regime also sought help from pirs and Barelvi clerics of the country. This time, the state employed Sufism as a symbol against extremism and terrorism. State officials and political leaders issued statements to propagate the idea that Sufi Islam was the actual version of Islam while Deobandi and Wahabi Islam was an imported version that spoiled society. It was rationalized that Sufi Islam had great relevance with the local culture, based on its teachings of coexistence, and the promotion of tolerance and peace in society.

Musharraf's purpose was not only to bring stability to an extremism-affected country, but also the consolidation of his regime. During that time mostly Deobandis were against Musharraf's decision to participate in the War on Terror against the Taliban and Al-Qaeda because the Taliban belongs to the Deobandi school of thought, so Deobandis had their support with their sect fellows, the Taliban. In that scenario, Deobandis had become a liability for the government, and the elimination of their influence became necessary. Barelvi who are in the majority and were living peacefully had been supported by the Musharraf regime to counter extremism, decrease Deobandis' influence, and consolidate the Musharraf regime as well. To achieve the anticipated goals, Musharraf was largely dependent on Barelvi clerics, pirs (holy saints), and leaders of different Barelvi politicoreligious parties.

In 2004, Musharraf promoted his doctrine of "enlightened moderation" (Musharraf, 2004). To make it successful, he implored his fellow countrymen to "shun militancy and extremism" and "promote Islam, as the flag-bearer of just, lawful, tolerant and value-oriented society." The initiative of promoting Sufism against extremism started in 2006 when extremism and terrorism were at their culminating point in Pakistan. Yousaf Salahudin, the grandson of Pakistani national poet Allama Iqbal, suggested to General Pervez Musharraf that Sufism was the best weapon to counter the threat of extremism in the country owing to its liberal, secular, and tolerating nature, which suited Pakistan's pluralist society. He also opined that Western countries were mystic hungry, and Pakistan had the potential to export its Sufi music to the West

(Philippon, 2015). As a result, General Musharraf established the National Council for Promotion of Sufism in 2006 to implement the idea. The main motive of the council was to promote Sufi philosophy and culture, which had common values of society, especially tolerance and pluralism, to project a soft image of the country. General Musharraf was appointed patron-in-chief of the council, while Chaudhary Shujat Hussain (president of the then-ruling party PMLQ, or Pakistan Muslim League/Quaid e Azam Group) became chairman, Mushahid Hussain Syed (secretary general of PMLQ) represented Islamabad, Yousaf Salahudin the Punjab, Jam Muhammad Yousaf (chief minister of Baluchistan) the Baluchistan, Hameed Haroon (chief executive of Dawn Media Group) the Sindh, and Abbas Sarfraz (ex-senator and ex-federal minister) the Khyber Pakhtunkhwa (KP) region. Shrine custodian of the famous Indian Shrine of Khwaja Moeen-ud-Din Chishti of Ajmair Sharif, PirSarwar Chishti tied the turban on Chaudhri Shujat Hussain. He also blessed him with the authority of being a Sufi along with authorizing him to promote the values of Sufism in the country (Philippon, 2015). All the major positions of the council were occupied by state elites and non-Sufis. However, the shrine custodians and Barelvi clerics also got involved in serving their own purpose. In the first meeting of the council, Chaudhary Shujat said that the message of Sufism was "peace, love and brotherhood" and steps must be taken to this end ("Sufism to Be Promoted," 2006). In the same year, Musharraf inaugurated the ceremony of the National Council for Promoting Sufism on the birthday of national poet Allama Muhammad Iqbal at Lahore. The chief minister of Punjab, Chaudhri Pervez Elahi, also arranged an International Sufi Conference in Lahore. During the conference, Punjab's home secretary said that it was necessary to promote the Sufi philosophy of peace, love, and tolerance to counter the "Mullah Islam" (Philippon, 2015). One way or the other, the Musharraf government started the politicization of Sufism and instrumentalized pirs and Barelvi clerics to ensure internal stability.

In this regard, a two-facet strategy was adopted by the government to disseminate Sufi ideology. One was on a social level to penetrate Sufi ideology into the social structure of the state. The second was on the political front to incorporate Sufis, pirs, and Barelvi clerics into the national politics. On the social front, the Sufi ideology was promoted through celebrations of *urs*. It encouraged spiritual poetry and Sufi music shows at different shrines and arts councils to mold people toward moderation and a soft version of Islam so that they could not fall into the hands of extremist forces. Government officials started paying homage to Sufi shrines. On the political front, pro-Sufi religious parties were promoted and strengthened to defy religious extremism and ideology of terrorists through demonstrations. These pro-Sufi politicoreligious parties arranged processions throughout the country and openly condemned Talibanization. Even these groups also termed the Taliban as *Khawarji* (outside of Islam) and terrorists. Among them, the politicoreligious party of Dr. Tahir-ul-Qadri, Pakistan Awami Tehreek, and his religious organization Minhaj-ul-Quran, also played an important role.

To promote Sufi ideology and shrine culture in the country, Musharraf himself visited shrines located in Punjab and Sindh. During his visits, he advised the public that Sufism was the real face, not only compatible with Islam but also the country's traditions and culture. He also termed Punjab and Sindh as the lands of Sufis, which emphasized peace, tolerance, and liberal and moderate values. He also prayed at different shrines for the protection of the country from religious fanatics that challenged its existence. Government officials, leaders, and politicians started active participation in the urs of different shrines, where they used to lay shrouds on the grave of enshrined pirs, offered prayers, and addressed the people over the importance of shrines and Sufism in the country and religion (Philippon, 2015). The former governor of Punjab, Khalid Maqbool, also supported the idea to counter extremism through the soft approach of Sufi Islam. He met with different shrine custodians and gave them instructions to promote unity among Muslims. Sheikh Rasheed Ahmad, then the railway minister of Musharraf's cabinet, praised the importance of Sufism in the country and emphasized getting rid of the evil powers who wanted to disrupt the social machinery. Musharraf also, for the first time, appointed a shrine custodian, Sahibzada Saeedul Hassan Shah, as minister of the *Awqaf* department. Before him, the slots were occupied by all nonpirs, who used to criticize the role of pirs in the country's social landscape (Philippon, 2015).

To achieve anticipated goals, some government institutes have also assisted in disseminating Sufi ideology. These include the Pakistan Academy of Letters, Ministry of Culture, Ministry of Education, and Pakistan National Council of the Arts. These institutes emphasized promoting cultural values through different initiatives such as seminars, conferences, workshops, literature festivals, and music and art exhibitions. Different Sufi music nights were also arranged in which prominent singers from across the country participated. Among such singers, Sain Zahoor, Abida Perveen, and Rahat Fateh Ali Khan are notable.

To promote Sufi culture and music, Musharraf also approached the Rafi Peer Theatre Workshop to bring out the soft image of Pakistan at the domestic level and in front of an international audience. The U.S. government also took great interest in Pakistan's new policy of incorporating Sufi ideology into nationalism. In this context, calendars were distributed among the officials that contained fascinating pictures of different Sufi shrines, and interestingly, these pictures were captured by an American photographer (Philippon, 2015). In 2008, with the ending of Musharraf's tenure, the National Council for Promotion of Sufism also lost its functioning.

Role of Pakistan People's Party Government

The left-wing Pakistan's People's Party (PPP) has several shrine custodians as its active members, occupying a central position in the party, which emphasizes pluralistic values and religious harmony. In this context, it is also said that shrine custodians are natural allies to the PPP. Before the 2008 general election, the PPP had pledged in its manifesto (Ispahani, 2010) to promote Islam as a peaceful religion. Its manifesto stated:

> The message of Islam is the message of Peace. It is a message of brotherhood and tolerance. These are symbolized in the words and verses of Data Sahib, Shah Abdul Latif of Bhittai, Baba Farid Ganj Shakar and Lal Shahbaz Qalander. The sufi saints adopted a life of simple living and high thinking. It's time that we do the same. By no means did they use or preach the use of force. The PPP commits itself to religious tolerance.

After coming into power, the PPP government took several initiatives to promote Sufism in the country. In this regard, they also followed the footprints of the Musharraf government by establishing the Sufi council with a new name, Sufi Advisory Council, on June 8, 2009. The council (Hassan, 2009) consisted of seven members, dominated by clerics of the Barelvi political party Jamiat-e-Ulemai-e-Pakistan (JUP). Head of the JUP, Haji Muhammad Hanif Tayab, was appointed as chairman of the council. The PPP government also nominated a descendant of the Moosa Pak Shaheed shrine, Syed Yousaf Raza Gilani, as the prime minister of Pakistan. In addition to this, Shah Mehmud Qureshi, shrine custodian of Shah Rukn-e-Aalim, was appointed as foreign minister, and Hamid Saeed Kazmi, shrine custodian of the Ahmad Saeed Kazmi shrine of Multan, was appointed as the federal minister for religious affairs to handle the religious issues, Awqaf, and interfaith harmony. This indicated the PPP's policy to promote harmony through believers of Sufi Islam. Kazmi was very vocal against the Taliban and survived a murder attempt. Meanwhile, on the political front, the Sunni Tehreek and Sunni Ittehad Council (alliance of different Barelvi religious parties) had also strengthened and activated against extremism and terrorism in the country. In May 2009, the then-foreign minister and shrine custodian of one of the influential shrines of the country, Shah Mehmud Qureshi ("Anti-Terror Consensus Shaping Up," 2009), while addressing the ceremony of urs of the Shah Rukn-e-Alim, said,

> Sunni Tehreek has decided to play an active role in the fight against Talibanisation…. We will not surrender to forces harming the interests of the country and distorting the image of Islam… people of the country loved Islam, but their Islam was different from the brand which troublemakers were trying to impose at gunpoint.

Prime Minister Yousuf Raza Gilani and his cabinet members also used to visit many shrines across the country and stressed promoting the values of Sufism. In March 2010, he officially participated in Okara's famous shrine Karmanwali Sarkar's urs ceremony. While addressing ("Saints, Not Army Generals Spread Islam," 2010) the ceremony, Gilani said, "*Khankahi* [monastery] system was vital to eliminate terrorism from the country." Nonetheless, experts believe that the Sufi ideology has the potential to curtail the menace of extremism and terrorism from across the country due to its pluralistic nature, but they also raise questions on rewarding greater authority to pro-Sufis, which may put negative impact on the social sector by exploiting the people of their pirs. Ayesha Siddiqa, a well-known Pakistani writer, warned (2009) about this issue as she wrote, "Greater power not only enhanced the greed for more power but also resulted in the corruption of the Sufi order." Some termed it as "not good news" and considered it as a sort of politicization of religion that has already created many issues for the country. It was also perceived that state-sponsored Sufism (Eteraz, 2009) gets everything back especially in the environment where religion is used for political purposes. On August 29, 2011, the PPP government ceased the function of the council due, apparently, to nonavailability of the funds (Senate Secretariat of Pakistan, 2017). It is also worth mentioning that at that time, the radical and extremist sentiments were penetrated into the Barelvi followers, especially on the issue of blasphemy.

Symptoms of Extremism

Arguably, Barelvis are more flexible and peaceful than the Deobandis and Salafi schools of thought. However, they also encompass fundamental views regarding their religious beliefs and practices. Whenever they feel their belief system is being threatened, they try to defend it from other beliefs, especially secular views. The theorists claim that when fundamentalists perceive a threat to their beliefs, they react to perceived threats in three ways (Gregg, 2016): isolating themselves from the threat, attempting to change government policies, and using violence to counter the perceived threat and protect their fundamental beliefs. As the Barelvi school of thought started gaining more prominence on the national landscape, they felt a threat being imposed to their fundamental beliefs. In this context, they used violence as a means to counter the influence of other systems and tried to challenge governmental policies.

The faction that had been perceived as most tolerant, peaceful, and natural to the pluralistic values of Pakistan during the Musharraf era abruptly turned to violent activities over the issue of a suggested amendment in the blasphemy law. In 2010, the former governor of Punjab Salman Taseer expressed his support for Asia Bibi, a Christian woman sentenced to death for alleged blasphemy of Prophet (PBUH). During a TV interview, Taseer called Article 295-C of the Pakistan Penal Code (PPC), the blasphemy law, "*kala qanoon*" (black code) and said that many people use this law just for the sake of their enmities against other people. The PPC Article 295-C says that anyone who utters derogatory remarks about the Prophet Muhammad (PBUH) "shall be punished with death, or imprisonment for life, and shall also be liable to fine." Taseer suggested amendments to the blasphemy law. After this, many clerics, including Barelvi clerics, issued fatwas (religious decrees) against Taseer (Siddiqui, 2011), claiming that he had committed blasphemy by using inappropriate words where the blasphemy law was concerned. Moreover, they perceived this measure as a threat to their belief system from the seculars. Some clerics even set a bounty on Taseer's head. The fallout of these fatwas was detrimental. In 2011, Taseer was shot down by his bodyguard Mumtaz Qadri, who was a Punjab police personnel. Mumtaz Qadri was a follower of the Karachi-based nonpolitical Barelvi religious organization, Dawat-e-Islami, which is mostly considered a peaceful organization. Later in the court, Mumtaz Qadri said that he had no links with any extremist organization. However, he admitted that he was "impressed" (Associated Press, 2011) by the speeches of two Barelvi clerics, Mufti Qari Haneef Qureshi and Imtiaz Shah. However, as soon as Mumtaz Qadri was arrested, the Sunni Ittehad Council (SIC), which primarily was established to counter extremism and terrorism in the country, started a proper movement for his acquittal, but it bore no results. The court declared Mumtaz Qadri a terrorist for the killing of the sitting governor of Punjab and sentenced him to the death penalty. On February 29, 2016, Mumtaz Qadri was executed in a Rawalpindi jail, and thousands of people across the country participated in his funeral prayers. Sunni Tehreek organized Qadri's funeral prayer in which many influential clerics, from different sects, participated.

The funeral prayer was led by Pir Haseenud Deen Shah, a powerful Barelvi saint in Rawalpindi who administers a seminary in Rawalpindi and is the chief caretaker of Tanzeemul Mudaris Ahl-e-Sunnat Pakistan. The most prominent among the attendees were Jamat-e-Islami Chief Siraj-ul Haq, Mufti Muneebur Rehman, the head of the country's Ruet-e-Hilal Committee, and former Federal Minister for Religious Affairs Hamid Saeed Kazmi. Many other prominent leaders of various Sunni organizations, pirs, and custodians of different famous Sufi shrines also participated. Among these, Pir Muhamamd Afzal Qadri, Dr. Ashraf Asif Jilali, Allama Khadim Hussain Rizvi, Sahibzada Abu Al-Khair Muhammad Zubair, Pir Muhammad Naqib, Allama Kokab Noorani, Syed Riaz Hussain Shah, Engineer Sarwat Ijaz Qadri, Shah Muhammad Awais Noorani, Hafiz Ahmed Raza Qadri, Sahibzada Hamid Raza Hashmi, Qari Hanif Qurehsi, and Sahibzada Usman Qadri were prominent in religious circle of society. Ironically, many of these clerics had already been engaged in counter extremist activities by the state.

After Qadri's execution, many religious parties emerged on the political landscape, especially on social media, in support of Mumtaz Qadri's cause. Today, Mumtaz Qadri has attained the status of a saint in society, dozens of people pay homage at his shrine daily (Pasha, 2016), and his first urs ceremony was celebrated by a large number of people in February 2017. In this context, a coalition party under the name of Tehreek Labaik Ya Rasool Allah (TLYRA) (Movement of "We Are Present, Messenger of God") was formed by Barelvi Ulema in which Sarwat Ijaz Qadri, chief of Sunni Tehreek; Mualna Khadim Rizvi, chief of Fidayeen-i-Khatam-i-Nabuwat (willing to martyr on the issue of prophet finality); Pir Afzal Qadri, chief of Aalmi Tanzeem-e-Ahl-e-Suna; and

Mualna Ashraf Asif Jalali, chief of Sirat-e-Mustaqeem, were the main founders. Since then, the party has arranged processions and rallies in different cities of the country in which they provoked people not to compromise on Article 295-C of the PPC, and proclaimed that if anyone committed blasphemy, the government should execute them, or the people will do it otherwise. They always raised slogans in their processions, including their main narrative, objective, and motto, "*Gustakh-e-Rasool ki aik saza, sar tan say juda*" (There is only one punishment for the blasphemer, they should be beheaded). Their narratives and actions left a deep impact on society by radicalizing people on the issue. As a result of these activities, the years 2016 and 2017 saw a dramatic rise in human rights abuse under the garb of blasphemy issues in the country. One of the pupils of Khadim Rizvi, leader of TLYRA, Tanveer Qadri, who resides in the United Kingdom, killed an Ahmadi person on the issue of blasphemy in Glasgow, Scotland. Later, Tanveer released audio messages in which he admitted Khadim Rizvi was his mentor. His audio messages (Iqbal & McKay, 2017) have been played at the processions of TLYRA to incite the audience. Khadim Hussian Rizvi also calls himself Ameer-ul-Mujahidin (commander of holy warriors).

The extremist ideas of Barelvi clerics over the issue of blasphemy have gradually penetrated societal structure and further divided society on a sectarian basis as well. In March 2016, the pop singer turned Deobandi cleric, Junaid Jamshed, was also victimized by a Barelvi mob at Islamabad Airport on the issue of alleged blasphemy. Before that, Junaid sought forgiveness for any misunderstanding, but he was beaten and abused. When he died in a plane crash in December 2016, the TLYRA clerics and followers abused him and called the accident a punishment of God to the blasphemer. The members of TLYRA also warned and threatened Pakistan Tehreek-e-Insaf Chairman Imran Khan over saying inappropriate words about the Prophet due to a slip of the tongue. After this, Imran immediately sought forgiveness from the Barelvi clerics and visited the Dawat-e-Islami headquarters in Karachi. A fatwa of *wajib-ulqatil* (deserving death) was also issued against Shaan Taseer, son of Salman Taseer, over his support of Asia Bibi.

The Labaik Party has also continuously arranged religious gatherings across the country, the most famous of which was held in the capital in March 2016 and then in November 2017, which compelled the state to capitulate in the face of the furious Barelvis protestors' demands. Subsequently, the federal law minister resigned from his post. The Labaik organization commits hate speeches and provokes people, directly violating the much-publicized Nation Action Plan (NAP)—established after the 2014 Army Public School incident to counter the threat of extremism and terrorism in the country.

The emerging trends of Barelvi extremism specifically on the blasphemy issue have shaken the entire Pakistani society. The instigative speeches by members of the Labaik Party have resulted in some horrendous incidents where violent mobs have killed people under the pretext of blasphemy charges. The "mob justice" witnessed during the Masahil Khan murder, a Chitral incident, resulted in two sisters killing a man booked for blasphemy in Sialkot. At the same time, the murderers are always glorified and treated like "holy warriors" and heroes.

What is alarming is that the Labaik Party registered itself as a political party with the Election Commission of Pakistan in 2017 with the name of Tehreek Labaik Pakistan. A Labaik Party member secured the third position and left the traditional political party, the PPP, far behind. During their election campaign, they openly used Mumtaz Qadri posters to attract voters. The salient features of their main political manifesto are to impose the Nizam-e-Mustafa (government system of the Prophet) in the country, secure the sanctity of the Prophet (PBUH), and if anyone commits blasphemy, punish them with death. The *ameer* (chief) of Tehreek Labaik Pakistan, Moulvi Khadim Hussian Rizvi—who also called himself *Ameer-ul-Mujahdin* (commander of holy warriors)—openly stages processions and provokes police officers and other followers to kill the blasphemers.

Conclusion

The politicization of religion, especially in the context where one faction is strengthened at the cost of the other, has proved to be a fatal gamble. This trend implies that the state has indulged in pitting one sect against the other on an ideological basis rather countering the threat of terrorism. Barelvis, no doubt, are in the majority but have been marginalized since independence; however, after 2001, they got the opportunity to reinforce themselves over other sects, especially Deobandi, on ideological grounds when they had been promoted. The politicization of religion, especially in the context of marginalizing other sects, results in the destabilization of society. Diverse societies like

Pakistan house people belonging to different religions, sects, ethnicities, and cultural backgrounds, so they need a holistic approach and more pluralistic norms based on democratic and liberal values in order to peacefully progress.

The party, like Labaik, with its ideological narrative built and based on the pillars of extremism, is being allowed to operate by the state despite committing violations against the rule of law (NAP specifically) in the form of hate speeches, processions, and sit-ins in different cities across the country. It is becoming mainstream in the country's politics, by default or design. It is ironic that even after losing scores of innocent people and after billions of dollars in damages to the economic infrastructure in this war against extremism and terrorism, it seems the state of Pakistan is still not serious about countering the plague of extremism being disseminated by organizations like Labaik. The country, which already faced multiple dimensions of religious extremism and terrorism, is now indulged in another dimension of violent extremism on the issue of blasphemy.

REFERENCES

Anti-terror consensus shaping up: Qureshi. (2009, May 4). In *Dawn*. https://www.dawn.com/news/856494

Associated Press. (2011, January 10). *Sermons motivated killer of Governor Taseer*. Dawn. https://www.dawn.com/news/597628/sermons-motivated-killer-of-governor-taseer

Curtis, L., & Mullick, A. H. (2009). *Reviving Pakistan's pluralist traditions to fight extremism*. Heritage Foundation. http://www.heritage.org/asia/report/reviving-pakistans-pluralist-traditions-fight-extremism

Eteraz, A. (2009, June 10). *State-sponsored Sufism: Why are U.S. think tanks pushing for state-sponsored Islam in Pakistan?* Foreign Policy. http://foreignpolicy.com/2009/06/10/state-sponsored-sufism/

Ewing, K. (1983). The politics of Sufism: Redefining the saints of Pakistan. *The Journal of Asian Studies*, 42(2), 251–268.

Gregg, H. S. (2016). Three theories of religious activism and violence: Social movements, fundamentalists, and apocalyptic warriors. *Terrorism and Political Violence*, 28(2), 338–360.

Hassan, A. (2009, June 8). *Sufi Advisory Council set up to fight extremism*. Dawn. https://www.dawn.com/news/469894/sufi-advisory-council-set-up-to-fight-extremsim

Iqbal, S., & McKay, C. (2017, January 31). *Asad Shah murder: Killer Tanveer Ahmed releases prison message*. BBC. http://www.bbc.com/news/uk-scotland-38815366

Ispahani, F. (2010, November 30). *The PPP—hope for a new Pakistan.* Express Tribune. https://tribune.com.pk/story/84092/the-ppp--hope-for-a-new-pakistan/

Mirahmadi, H., Farooq, M., & Ziad W. (2010). *Traditional Muslim networks: Pakistan's untapped resource in the fight against terrorism.* World Organization for Resources Development and Education. http://www.worde.org/publications/worde_reports/traditional-muslim-networks-pakistans-untapped-resource-in-the-fight-against-terrorism/

Musharraf, P. (2004, June 1). *A plea for enlightened moderation.* Washington Post. http://www.washingtonpost.com/wp-dyn/articles/A5081-2004May31.html

Pasha, A. (2016, December 19). *Mumtaz Qadri's shrine: In memory of Salmaan Taseer's assassin.* Dawn. https://www.dawn.com/news/1302289

Philippon, A. (2015). A sublime, yet disputed, object of political ideology? Sufism in Pakistan at the crossroads. In R. D. Long, G. Singh, Y. Samad, & I. Talbot (Eds.), *State and nation-building in Pakistan: Beyond Islam and security* (pp. 146–165). Routledge.

Rabasa, A., Benard, C., Schwartz, L. H, & Sickle, P. (2007). *Building moderate Muslim networks.* Rand Corporation for Middle East Public Policy. https://www.rand.org/pubs/monographs/MG574.readonline.html

Saints, not Army generals spread Islam: Gilani. (1 March 2010). In *The News.* https://www.thenews.com.pk/archive/print/669853-saints,-not-army-generals-spread-islam-gilani

Senate Secretariat of Pakistan. (2017). Questions for oral answers and their replies: 259th Session, 15. http://www.senate.gov.pk/uploads/documents/questions/1487233258_245.pdf

Shaikh, F. (2012). Will Sufi Islam save Pakistan? In S. Bashir & R. D. Crews (Eds.), *Under the drones: Modern lives in the Afghanistan–Pakistan borderlands* (pp. 174-191). Harvard University Press.

Sherani, S. R. (1991). Ulema and *pir* in the politics of Pakistan. In H. Donnan & P. Werbner (Eds.), *Economy and culture in Pakistan: Migrants and cities in a Muslim society* (pp. 216-218). Palgrave Macmillan.

Siddiqa, A. (2009, February 14). *Faith wars.* Dawn. https://www.dawn.com/news/833136

Siddiqui, S. (2011, January 5). *Hardline stance: Religious bloc condones murder.* Express Tribune. https://tribune.com.pk/story/99313/hardline-stance-religious-bloc-condones-murder/

Sufism to be promoted, says Shujaat. (2006, October 13). In *Dawn.* https://www.dawn.com/news/214641

CHAPTER NINE | MUHAMMAD KHALID MASUD

Globalization of Islamic Law

A Muslim Perspective on International Law

Globalism has been posing questions about a host of hitherto long-held legal doctrines like the sovereignty of nation-states and the exception of national law in the domain of international law. Debates on new concepts like legal pluralism have led to calls for revisiting the ideas of the universality of law and the rule of law and state exception. The international law of human rights has set global standards against religious, cultural, and gender discrimination. Muslims are singularized for calling for an exception on behalf of Sharia in international law. Consequently, the globalization of universal human rights, international conventions and treaties relating to the judicialization and legality of women's rights, protection, and custody of children, and marriage, divorce, and inheritance are considered clashes between global and local law.

Globalism: Multiple Definitions

The term globalism is still in the process of legal definition. In current discussions, the following five ideas are described as characteristics of globalism (Steger, 2004, pp. 1–2):

1. Complexity,
2. Multidimensionality,
3. Magnitude: a process in which masses are involved,
4. Restructuring: the weakening of state actors and the rise of nonstate actors, and
5. Relativity: rule of law and sovereignty are no longer relevant.

Recent mass migrations, global terrorism, ethnic genocide, climate change, destruction of the ozone layer, and immense poverty are examples of the complex phenomena of globalism. Ideas of governance, states, and the rule of law do not go along with these disasters. Most of us think in ethical and moral paradigms about these disasters. Consequently, movements like global ethics are emerging to deal with issues arising from the abovementioned characteristics of globalism.

Globalism is extremely relative, and in that sense, it is no longer ethically oriented. Naturally, we then turn to the ideas of powerful states and hegemons to prevent disorder. If we look at the genealogy of these terms and the history of this process, we find that globalism is an idea that envisages the future to which human societies are moving, and globalization as a process is continuously translating this idea into practice.

In this essay, I prefer the following as a working definition: A growing perception that a formerly state-centered political process is evolving toward a mere multilayered one where other actors interplay in the pursuit of public goals and the fulfillment of public tasks.

History

The term "globalism" came to be used in the 1940s in war-stricken Europe that looked for a peaceful new world order without war and conflict. The United States emerged as a hope, imagined as a global power. It was a mighty power as Europe was before the 1940s. Europe's imagination reflected not only the despair but also its position of disparity. The United States, with 6.3% of the world population, held 50% of the world's wealth (U.S. Department of State, 1948). It was in this process of thought and action that by 1948 globalism also came to mean "globalization," a process of discovering legal instruments to put globalism into practice and to build institutions to institutionalize global sovereignty and rule of law.

Studies during the next 50 years that examined ideas and theories of the global world found that they were not global in reality; they were still utopias of a global world that reflected the local dreams and anxieties. Critical analyses of these theories mention six perspectives. I need not go into details because they are Euro-centered and restricted to the Kantian philosophy of universality. This globalism was lopsided because the ideas of universal citizenship, civil society, and multiculturality were conceived along with the necessity of global hegemony.

Six Perspectives of the Theory (MacLean, 2013):

1. Global conditions of sociocultural interpretations
2. Kantian philosophy of the Universal Citizen
3. Political project founded as transnational institutions like civil society
4. The notion of Citizen with multiple identities
5. International orientation toward global engagement
6. Multicultural competence and practice

Genealogically speaking, globalism was related to the ideas like cosmopolitanism and citizens of the world, but ironically the globalized world is still conceived in the image of a village. Wide differences exist between globalism as ideal and policy and globalization as practice and politics.

Major Studies of Globalism

It is almost impossible today to explain that the phenomena of globalism and the "clash of civilizations" are not synonymous, as often claimed. Let me introduce some of the major studies on the subject to show how the current perceptions of globalism and globalization have changed from internationalism to transnationalism to globalism as globalization and ideology in the 1960s.

Joseph Nye, an American political scientist, in his co-edited book with Robert Keohane, *Transnational Relations and World Politics* (1972) observed an increasing decline in the degree of globalization as one world. It was developing through various economic, social, and cultural networks. He defined globalism in 1972 as a network of transnational interactive connections. He continues to believe in the United States as global power (Nye, 2005). His *Governance in a Globalizing World* in 2000 marked a huge shift from his earlier idealist approach to a more realistic and pragmatic understanding of the phenomenon.

In 2005, Manfred B. Steger's *Globalism: Market Ideology Meets Terrorism* observed that the globalization process was not monolithic; different types of globalization were happening, and dominant among them was the global economy or globalization of the market. Liberalism in trade gave rise to the power of nonstate actors. In "Ideologies of Globalization" (2005), he considered terrorism as a form of globalism because terrorists as nonstate actors were largely facilitated by the global economy market.

Paul James argued that globalism is an ideology that is a product of various ideas contesting for dominance. He considered Western modernity and capitalism were the driving force of colonization like the ancient Greek and

Roman empires. His book, *Globalism, Nationalism, Tribalism: Bringing Theory Back In* (2006), traces these links to the ideologies of empires in the past.

These diverse analyses of globalism call for avoiding the tendency to essentialize the concepts. Not only the phenomena but also the perspectives of analyses are diverse.

History: Waves of Globalization

Studies on globalization divide its history into three waves. The first wave came in the 18th century in the shape of colonialism. In this period, the national laws of the colonizing nations were considered normative for law reforms in the colonies and interstate relations.

The second wave came in the 19th century when national laws were upgraded to serve as international law in the conduct of war and peace treaties. The second wave transformed the world war into a cold war, polarizing the world order.

The third wave came at the end of the Cold War in the 1980s. Fortunately, globalism has been comparatively more real in international law. Globalization of international law succeeded in establishing international law institutions. Political theorists believe that this process of globalization is specific to the third wave. Historians use different epithets to describe them: "end of the division of the world," "New World Order," "denationalization," "pluralism," "liberalism triumphant," and "emancipation of nonstate actors."

The following are some of the benchmark institutionalizations in this period:

- Multilateral international relations and laws
- Transfer of government functions to other levels of governance
- Trade liberalization
- Development of information technology
- Open market economy
- Transnational business
- Strengthening democratic values
- The interaction between global and local
- The emergence of new norm-generating actors
- Blurring state and civil society, public and private
- The rise of the standard of living; an increase in levels of poverty

Now, then the question is: What is wrong with globalization?

International Law

The paradigm of globalization simplifies the status of state, comparing it to the status of a citizen in a nation-state. In old international law, sovereignty was considered the central legal principle in relations between states. The current international law describes the sovereignty of nation-states as normative but horizontally. Its purpose is the state's liberty. In real politics, however, sovereignty is claimed by powerful states.

International law was minimal and contingent in its early phase; it was based on the variable will of the states. Its only concern was ensuring coexistence between states. It lacked institutions to adjudicate and to enforce compliance on rogue states. Hence, there was a dependence on powerful states. International law was accidental and structurally weak. It depended on states. Power continued to be a fact of life. The principle of the rule of law is still based not on domestic but on a transnational society level. States, especially powerful states, are in a state of exception, an exception to the rule of law.

Rule of Law

Paulo Canelas de Castro's (2007) detailed analysis of the principle of the rule of law uncovers its two paradigms in national and international law. To him, this principle relates to the modern state and its legal order. Connected with the principle of sovereignty, it became the central principle of international law. The rule of law, as a superior, hierarchical principle, justifies the coercive power of the state and its representatives over the national civil society. It helps enforce legislative commands of the state. Sovereignty is the normative principle that protects the liberty of the state, justifying its horizontal supremacy. The principle of sovereignty has been so compelling that it made international society appear in a state of anarchy, powerful states struggling for hegemony. The state used sovereignty in national law to support its armed authority. International law, then, properly called "law of nations," remained minimal to ensure only the coexistence of states and was contingent, based on the variable will of the states. It was "toothless," lacking institutions to solve conflicts.

de Castro finds diversity in practice and approaches as an essential trait of the rule of law. He discusses in detail the formal and substantive approaches, also respectively called thick and thin. Formal refers to concepts of legality, clarity, and quality, and substantive to quality, positive values, and substantive fairness. Legality is discussed next.

The substantive aspect of the rule of law has developed significantly in the last 50 years. The substantive international law is no longer only ethically normative; it has developed institutions, like courts that are independent and ensure compliance of the law, according to law. International law has also developed substantive methods of analysis. Transformation in this area has taken place, for example, in trade and environmental laws. There have been dramatic legal and institutional developments in trade and laws on the environment and climate change. Regarding method, development in the areas of legality, legislation, and judicialization are substantive. Judicialization means institutionalization and procedure.

Legality

Legality means that the rule of law is viable, robust, and comprehensive. The term refers to formal and substantive aspects of law, not merely theoretical but also material. As Ronald Dworkin (1998) would say, the rule of law cannot truly exist without law's empire. It means specified areas of life and issues must be properly regulated. Only then can one claim that human conduct is governed by right, and not by might. That is what Dworkin calls law's empire: rule-oriented, not diplomatic-oriented.

Formal aspects refer to requirements such as authority and clarity, but no rule of law exists without positive values and demands of substantive fairness (Raz, 1977, p. 195; Summers, 1988, pp. 154–161), enforceable by courts or other institutions charged with the control of legality (Dworkin, 1985, pp. 11–12). The rule of law necessarily means that politics yields to law, and diplomacy in international law yields to jurisprudence. Oscar Schachter warns that it is not possible to reduce law to politics "without eliminating it as law" (1991, p. 4).

In formal practice, however, international law tends to yield to diplomacy as jurisprudence yields to politics. Politics is arbitrary, variable, but law is not arbitrary. It is written and known in advance. The rule of law means that law applies to all equally and that all are equal before the law. Others argue that contrast between law and politics.

Islamic Law

Concerning the globalization of international law, critical studies focus on Europe and North Africa. Muslim liberals are contrasted with fundamentalists, liberals as Westernized, and the fundamentalists as representatives of orthodox and authentic Islam.

Ann Elizabeth Mayer's *Islam and Human Rights, Traditions and Politics*, went into its fifth edition in 2012 since its first printing in 1991. She critically appraises various Islamic human rights schemes that dilute the human rights afforded by international law. She compares Muslim human rights schemes with the complex Islamic legal heritage and international human rights law and challenges them as stereotypes about a supposedly monolithic Islam and finds them inherently incompatible with human rights. Mayer dissects the political motives behind the selective deployment of elements of the Islamic tradition by conservative forces seeking to delegitimize demands for democracy and human rights (2012, p. 211).

Sharia Exception

Let us look at the following table to see how Mayer's analysis is generally exaggerated and is only partly true. She is right in her observation that the political and conservative elements in Muslim societies exploit this kind of argument to resist reforms (Mayer, 1998, pp. 25–45).

There are three myths about Islam and human rights:

First myth: Muslim countries have rejected human rights. In fact, as Table 1 shows, out of 57 countries, 33 have no reservations.

Second myth: All Muslim countries have reservations about human rights. Only 24 entered reservations (see Table 1).

Third myth: These reservations are based on Sharia. Table 1 shows that only 11 countries refer to Sharia in their reservations. These Sharia reservations are also limited to two or three clauses. As family laws are continuously revised in Muslim countries to bring them in accordance with the Quran and Sunna, providing justice to the vulnerable, there will be fewer conflicts with universal laws.

During this period, some Muslim countries have already withdrawn reservations. Meanwhile, the legality of reservations has also been challenged, and reservation as an exception has become debatable.

The government institutions in Muslim countries and scholars in research institutions are also keenly interacting with the questions of globalism and

Table 1. Reservations and Sharia (Freeman, 2009).

Reservations and Sharia	Number	Proportion
Total number of Muslim countries	57	
Muslim countries that have no reservations	33	58%
Muslim countries that have reservations	24	42%
Muslim countries that referred to Sharia as reason for reservation	11	19%
Muslim countries that mentioned other reasons	13	23%
Non-Muslim countries that referred to religion as reason for reservation	2	India, Israel

globalization. I will only refer to two such efforts by the Organization of Islamic Cooperation's (OIC's) resolution in 2005, and the Salzburg Global Seminar in 2010 and its publication in 2012.

In an extraordinary session held at Makkah on September 9–11, 2005, an OIC committee of Muslim scholars and intellectuals observed that international order is in a transitional period and the Islamic world must effectively participate in the shaping of the evolving international system. Islamic legal education in Madrasas and universities requires training in research methodologies and critical studies of Islamic legal tradition and joining international conventions to enable Muslim lawyers and jurists to fully participate in this process of globalization of international law.

The committee recommended that:

> Since globalization is a fact of life today, it should be appropriately made use of against its adverse effects which dominate international and commercial relations. Following the example of developing countries, particularly the European Union, the formation of regional economic groupings among the OIC member states are strongly recommended. (Masud, 2006, p. 106)

The Salzburg Global Seminar on "Islamic Law and International Law: Searching for Common Ground," held in Salzburg, Austria, in 2010 noted that contemporary scholarship on Islamic law and human rights had evolved four different approaches and methods in the search for common ground.

1. To identify those instances where Islamic legal doctrines coincide with the content of human rights law while proclaiming as outdated those which conflict with international human rights.
2. To argue, in an apologetic fashion, that Islamic legal tradition espoused human rights protections centuries before Western international law.

3. To suggest that no common ground exists and accept the reality that they are two distinct systems of meaning and value and must be evaluated on their terms.
4. The final approach, "Clearing Ground" (Masud, 2012, pp. 104–114), situates the dialogue about the common ground at a more abstract level, positing parallel lists of core values in both Islamic law and international human rights law.

Accordingly, contributions to this seminar, published by Oxford University Press in 2012 with the title *Islamic Law and International Human Rights Law, Searching for Common Ground?*, on freedom of speech, freedom of religion, women's equality, and minority rights help deepen the understanding of the relationship between Islam and human rights and provide a challenging, original starting point for studying the subject.

Conclusions: Global and Local

Globalism in the Muslim world, and concerning Muslims, is often perceived as "Western globalism." This perception has localized globalism in the West politically, culturally, and economically. Consequently, globalism is often perceived regarding colonialism, empire, clash, conflict, dominance, and Westernization. The idea that other nations must only follow denies the sense of belonging to this idea. Due to this perception, globalism has not been successfully localized in Muslim societies.

Globalism has not been able to meet its ideal of peace, progress, and world order. Nations are still resorting to war to solve political differences, even maneuvering regime changes in the hope of democratization. Clashes are still militant and are dependent on the use of lethal weapons. Tremendous prosperity and abject poverty appear to be features of globalization of economy.

It is wrong to conclude that resistance to globalism in Muslim societies is rooted in their religious and cultural values. Islamic civilization in history has been a global movement. It was global with a difference. I will mention three features in which it differed with this third wave of globalization.

1. Islam's capacity to localize itself was immense; it recognized the diversity of languages, culture, custom, and even local perceptions of religion.
2. Islam empowered the local. It rehabilitated and restored the local political, physical, cultural systems and adopted them to its global needs.

3. Islamic thinking continuously defined and redefined the global as and when it encountered the local (Masud, 2006, p. v).

To conclude, I must invite your attention to the OIC recommendation I mentioned earlier about enhancing Islamic legal education in Madrasas and universities, including training in research methodologies and critical studies of Islamic legal tradition. I congratulate the organizers of this conference, International Islamic University, for hosting it. I would like to propose that universities in Muslim countries should likewise host, participate, and collaborate with other institutions of learning in the world to organize conventions on the Islamic and international law to enable Muslim lawyers and jurists, muftis and educators to fully participate in this process of globalization. These conventions may help activate dynamic regional economic, legal, and juridical groupings to benefit the globalizing world.

REFERENCES

Cavanaugh, K. (2012). Narrating law. In A. M. Emon, M. S. Ellis, & B. Glahn (Eds.), *Islamic law and international human rights law: Searching for common ground?* (pp. 17–51). Oxford University Press.

de Castro, P. C. (2007). Globalization and its impact on international law: Consolidating an international rule of law, constitutionally reconfiguring international law? *Boletim da Faculdade de Direito do Universidad de Macau, 20*, 223–282. http://studylib.net/doc/7247498/globalization-and-its-impact-on-international-law

Dworkin, R. (1985). *A matter of principle.* Harvard University Press.

Dworkin, R. (1998) *Law's empire.* Belknap Press.

Emon, A. M., Ellis, M. S., and Glahn, B. (2012a). Editors' introduction—From "common ground" to "clearing ground": A model for engagement in the 21st century. In A. M. Emon, M. S. Ellis, and B. Glahn (Eds.), *Islamic law and international human rights law: Searching for common ground?* (pp. 1–4). Oxford University Press.

Emon, A. M., Ellis, M. S., and Glahn, B. (2012b). *Islamic law and international human rights law: Searching for common ground?* Oxford University Press.

Freeman, M. (2009). *Reservations to CEDAW: An analysis for UNICEF.* UNICEF. https://www.unicef.org/gender/files/Reservations_to_CEDAW-an_Analysis_for_UNICEF.pdf

James, P. (2006). *Globalism, nationalism, tribalism: Bringing theory back in.* Sage.

Keohane, R. O., & Nye, J. S. (1972). *Transnational relations and world politics.* Harvard University Press.

MacLean, D. N. (2013). *Cosmopolitanisms in Muslim contexts*. Edinburgh University Press.

Masud, M. K. (2006). Concluding address at the International Conference, Karachi, December 2005. In N. A. Tahir (Ed.), *Different facets of the Islamic Ummah in a globalized world*. Goethe-Institut.

Masud, M. K. (2012). Clearing ground: Commentary to "Shari'a and the modern state." In A. M. Emon, M. S. Ellis, & B. Glahn (Eds.), *Islamic law and international human rights law: Searching for common ground?* (pp. 104–114). Oxford University Press.

Mayer, A. E. (1998). Islamic reservations to human rights conventions, a critical assessment. *Recht van de Islam, 15*, 25–45.

Mayer, A. E. (2012). *Islam and human rights: Traditions and politics*. Avalon Publishing.

Nye, J. (2000). *Governance in a globalizing world*. Brookings Institution.

Nye, J. (2002, April 15). *Globalism versus globalization*. The Globalist. https://www.theglobalist.com/globalism-versus-globalization/

Nye, J. (2005) On the rise and fall of American soft power. *New Perspectives Quarterly, 22*(3), 75–77.

Raz, J. (1977). The rule of law and its virtue. *Law Quarterly Review, 93*, 195, ff.

Saul, J. R. (2009). *The collapse of globalism*. Penguin UK.

Schachter, O. (1991). *International law in theory and practice*. Martinus Nijhoff.

Steger, M. (2002). *Globalism: The new market ideology*. Rowman and Littlefield.

Steger, M. (2005). *Globalism: Market ideology meets terrorism* (2nd ed.). Rowman and Littlefield.

Steger, M. (2010). *Globalization: A brief insight*. Sterling Publishing Company, Inc.

Steger, M. (2005). Ideologies of globalization. Journal of Political Ideologies 10(1):11-30.

Steger, M. (Ed.). (2004). *Rethinking globalism*. Rowman and Littlefield.

Summers, R. (1988). The ideal socio-legal order. Its "rule of law" dimension. *Ratio Juris, 1*(2), 154–161.

U.S. Department of State. (1948). *Foreign relations of the United States, 1948, General: The United Nations, Vol. 1, Part 2* (p. 524). United States Government Printing Office.

CHAPTER TEN | DAVID GRABER

World Cultural Heritage

Does the World Embrace "World Cultural Heritage"? Evidence From the Online Presence of UNESCO National Commissions

Theoretically, all humankind should be allowed to experience and appreciate the array of extraordinary cultural accomplishments of civilization. Similarly, it seems a given that the international community should do the best it can to ensure that those manifestations of culture that are in danger of being lost are preserved for future generations to enjoy, as a sort of global "public good." This is the sentiment behind the *World Cultural Heritage List*,[1] which is managed by the United Nations Educational, Scientific, and Cultural Organization (UNESCO). The concept is an extrapolation of the view that is behind most archives and many museums; as sociologist Thomas Schwinn notes, the list of sites that UNESCO has established is an attempt to represent and preserve "the diversity and variation of cultures" by establishing "a reservoir of those cultural forms of expression." Schwinn calls this "the pool model" (2006, p. 205).

The extent to which the countries of the world embrace "world cultural heritage" is an important question and one worth trying to answer, not least as part of an attempt to understand the global spread and reach of cultural values. It would be an enormous undertaking to try and conduct opinion polls of entire countries and governments across the globe. However, we do have what has been called "the global standard" for "world cultural heritage" (Keough, 2011, p. 599; Manuel, 2004, p. 6): The *World Cultural Heritage List* is the world's premiere effort to institutionalize the notion of "world cultural heritage" on a transnational level. There are many criticisms of the *List*, including some which question its worth (Steiner & Frey, 2012, pp. 6–11); however, there is nothing similar in existence that could compete with it regarding global prestige, recognition, and country participation. A facile answer to the major question of the study is that because 194 countries have signed the treaty establishing the program, the 1972 *Convention Concerning the Protection of the World Cultural and Natural Heritage* (UNESCO World Heritage Center, n.d.), the overwhelming majority of countries of the world must by definition support "world cultural heritage." It is one thing to sign a treaty and yet another to subscribe to the spirit of the document and to demonstrate fealty to the principles enshrined within it.

For a comparison to be valid, there must be a basis with some sort of level playing field, and this study argues that to answer the question for all 194 of the participating countries in the World Cultural Heritage Program, the best approximation for such a basis can be found in the part of the program that links the countries to the program: the National Commissions. Each state party to the convention is expected to have a National Commission to the UNESCO World Cultural Heritage Center, and it is this commission that serves as a liaison in charge of identifying potential sites for the nation and shepherding them through the nomination process, among other tasks. The National Commission directory reserves a spot for each National Commission to link to a website that highlights the work and achievements of the commission on behalf of the country (http://pax.unesco.org/countries/NationalCommissions.html). This study examines the online presence (or absence) of those liaisons as a set of texts.

The texts for this study should be understood in connection with the larger and broadly acknowledged story of the current troubled state of the World Heritage Program (although broad critique of the World Heritage Program itself is beyond the scope of this study). At the time of the founding of the program, the international community was assured that it would incorporate basic principles of international cooperation, democratic process, and equal representation to ensure that candidate sites of exceptional worth were selected in an unbiased manner. To implement those principles into the selection process, the convention defines "cultural heritage" as "monuments ... groups of buildings ... or sites" with the distinctive qualifying term "of outstanding universal value" (UNESCO World Heritage Center, n.d.) and calls for "an equitable representation of the different regions and cultures of the world" (http://whc.unesco.org/en/conventiontext/). Criticisms of the World Heritage Program and the *List* have come primarily over accusations that participants are subordinating the program principles to economic interests and that this is occurring to the detriment of some of the sites themselves and also of the integrity of the *List*.

It is not unsurprising that the material realization of an idealistic vision may be disappointing to some. Similarly, it is to be expected that in a world of diverse cultures there will be differing opinions on what is worthy of being chosen as an outstanding cultural manifestation. The *World Cultural Heritage List* seems to have inspired particular vehemence. Attacks have come over the principles mentioned above, with allegations that impartiality has been sacrificed, that there is an unequal representation of countries and regions in the *List*, and that national interests have hijacked the system for selecting candidate sites of exceptional value. Anthropologist Lynn Meskell describes the committee that rules on World Heritage site nominations as suffering from "overt politicization" in the form of disregard for expert opinions and advisory bodies in decision making. In her account, many states are simply interested in getting as many sites as possible inscribed to attract more tourists or for other economic reasons, or states are blocking inscription onto the endangered site list out of fear that protection might limit the economic activity that is allegedly causing damage to a particular site (Meskell, 2013).

Most criticisms are mostly focused on the *practice* of how the sites are selected for the *World Cultural Heritage List* and the representation and the consequences, and they offer some interesting commentary on what has happened to the *spirit* of the program. While the scholarship on "world cultural heritage" has focused heavily on the practice behind the *List* and the effects on designated heritage sites, there has been less attention paid to what has happened to the spirit that inspired the creation of the *List*. To approach that question, it is worth taking a brief look at where the concept of a "world culture" comes from and the spirit behind it.

One of the first thinkers to popularize "world culture" as a set of outstanding cultural works taken from multiple national traditions is German writer Johann Wolfgang Goethe (1749–1832). In the 1820s, Goethe began referring to "world literature," which he described as "universally human," a tradition that includes works not just from Europe but also from Persian and other cultures (Pizer, 2000). Additionally, the idea of "world culture" bears connotations from a concept often linked to the late 19th-century British cultural critic Matthew Arnold (1822–1888): the idea that every national tradition has a set of texts that are superior and yet exemplary for that culture. Arnold's name is often used concerning his idea of preserving and promoting culture as "the best that has been thought and said" (Arnold, 2006, p. 5). However, Goethe's collection was his selections of works, and the heirs to Arnold are generally to be found in sets of classics of a national or world regional tradition of "great books." Goethe's and Arnold's vision remained largely an ideal that is far more modest than the extraordinary undertaking of the UNESCO *World Cultural Heritage List*.[2]

That spirit as it was formulated by Goethe and Arnold was invoked by various agents within the international community as they sought to found the UNESCO *World Cultural Heritage List*. The origins of the *List* are well documented, and it is not necessary to go over them in depth (see, for example, Betts, 2015). Before the establishment of the convention in 1972, there were several campaigns to preserve monuments in danger of destruction, of which the most important for this study was the effort to save Nubian statues in Egypt, finally achieved by 1980 and involving more than 50 nations. The inspirational rhetoric about the importance of cultural heritage reflects the ideas that Goethe and Arnold helped popularize. This rhetoric played an important role in the effort to win over the public, with its message that there is a precious set of unique and extraordinary, yet vulnerable, cultural accomplishments that belongs to all people. U.S. President John Kennedy echoed the words of Arnold when speaking to Congress in 1961 in support of funding the campaign to save the Nubian statues: "The United States, one of the newest civilizations, has long had … a concern for the preservation of man's great achievements in art and thoughts" (qtd. in Betts, 2015, p. 111). In a speech from 1960, UNESCO General Director Vittorio Veronese called the campaign to save the Nubian statues part of the organization's mission "to safeguard world civilization." These monuments, he emphasized, "do not belong solely to the countries that hold them in trust. The whole world has the right to see them endure. They are part of a common heritage…. Treasures of universal value are entitled to universal protection" (qtd. in Betts, 2015, p. 109).

It is beyond the scope of this study to present a detailed analysis of how the World Heritage Program and the *List* developed and where and why changes occurred. Instead, it is enough to look to current scholarly assessments of the program to give us an overview of where the program is today vis-à-vis the principles on which it was founded. Over the past decade, numerous experts within and outside the program have sounded the alarm over its perceived failure to honor those original principles and guarantee the integrity of the *List*. Anthropologists, economists, legal scholars, and others have produced a litany of problems with bias in the selection process, political interference, adverse consequences for sites, and financial difficulties (see, for example, Keough, 2011; Meskell, 2013; Manuel, 2004; Steiner & Frey, 2012). Additionally, the program, like most UNESCO projects, appears to be in "dire" financial straits, particularly following the U.S. withdrawal from the organization over UNESCO's recognition of Palestine (Meskell, 2013, pp. 490–492). After weighing the advantages and the disadvantages of inscribing a site on the *List*, Swiss economists Bruno Steiner and Lasse Frey recommend various alternatives to the inscription (2012).

The actual language used by observers of the program is striking. In her 2013 overview of the program, anthropologist Lynn Meskell calls the selection process "deeply imperfect" and warns of "an emergent crisis" and "an impossible situation" (2013, pp. 492, 484, 490). She cites the assessment (unattributed) at the World Heritage Committee in 2011 that due to the dysfunctional nature of the program, the convention may have reached its "death" (2013, p. 493). In an article entitled "Heritage in Peril," lawyer Elisabeth Keough states that the program is "in desperate need of an overhaul" (2011, p. 8) and has fallen victim to "the proliferation of greed and power-hungry politics" (2011, p. 9). Frey and Steiner (2010) call into question the rationale for the entire endeavor by titling their article, "The World Heritage List: Does It Make Sense?" A loss of idealism can be detected in the word choice and tone of the articles. For scholarly prose, much of this language might seem unnecessarily hyperbolic, which in turn suggests that there is a strong sentiment among observers that the spirit of the program has in some way been violated.

Much criticism of the *List*'s content focuses on the "lack of balance" in the representation of countries and regions, and some scholarly observers view the *List* and its very understanding of heritage as fundamentally Eurocentric (Meskell, 2002, p. 28; Manuel, 2004, p. 3). Although the caretakers have sought to make the *List* more representative of the various world regions, critics such as Frey and Steiner claim that it heavily favors European-nominated sites, due to a "biased" nominating process (2010, p. 36). Meskell notes that "the properties being proposed still inhabit the familiar taxonomies of chateaux, churches, mosques, historic cities, forts, and, to a lesser extent, archaeological excavations" (2013, p. 489). Manuel (2004) goes even further, claiming that the notion of global cultural heritage is itself "Westernized" and "[t]he imbalance of [*World Heritage List*] sites can be explained as a result of heritage being defined through an established Eurocentric museological lens." He contends that "museology, as an international standard, is a Western social construction" (2004, p. 3).

To address the question of "does the world embrace its world cultural heritage?" this study seeks to relate evidence from the National Commission websites to some of these criticisms that others have already identified, moving through a short series of subquestions. However, a word of caution is in order here. Although the number of member states the study investigates is comprehensive in regard to the signatories to the convention establishing the *List*, this study makes an assumption that some might find questionable: that the member state's National Commission website and its content are somehow representative of the country in question and the attitude of the government and elite groups within that state. It is true that there are various possibilities for why this might not be the case, such as conflicting interests or the degree of engagement of certain individuals or collective entities involved. However, this study claims that it is not unreasonable to assume that in most cases the National Commission website is in fact to some degree indicative of a set of national priorities, even when there is no site or if the government seems to have invested little effort in creating the site. However, more research would be needed to reach more certainty in these matters.[3] these reasons, the analysis here is meant merely to suggest preliminary and not definitive answers.

Do we see countries using their UNESCO National Commission website to celebrate their contribution to world cultural heritage?

It is difficult to establish rigid, mutually exclusive categories for the types of online presence we can observe for the various National Commissions. Under the method used for this study, it is posited that a site can be said to "fully embrace" "world cultural heritage" if it presents the nation's contribution to the *List* in the form of pictures or descriptions and explanations, and/or with direct statements on the importance of preserving these and other sites for the world. There is one more criterion: to qualify for "fully embraces" under this study, the site must include this information in more than the native language of the country (or in more than one language). For the sake of consistency, the language rule is applied to all websites, even those in one of the most commonly used and spoken world languages, such as English or Spanish, as well as to a website solely in a language less studied globally, such as Polish. In addition to the category "fully embraces," the study identifies the following categories of criteria: some National Commission sites are only in the country's native language, or have very little information on "world cultural heritage," or make little or no reference to the *List*, or merely link to a ministry in the country's government—or have some combination of those possibilities. Finally, the study establishes one remaining category, "no functioning site." This was the case for many states: either there is no National Commission website listed in the National Commission database (or none can be located using a search engine), or the web address is provided but does not work, or ownership of the site has lapsed and is now held by a third party.

Of the 194 states parties that have signed the World Heritage Convention, approximately a quarter of them qualify as "fully embracing" the world cultural heritage concept. If we break the global figures down into the five "regions" that UNESCO assigns the countries to, we see that there is one "region" that has a significantly higher rate of an online presence, Europe and North America (which includes Israel, the Russian Federation, and the states of the Caucasus). If that "region" is excluded, the portion of signatories with a National Commission website that promotes "world cultural heritage" in more than the native language goes down to less than one in five. (The other four "regions" are Africa, the Arab States, Asia and the Pacific, and Latin America and the Caribbean.) The "region" of Europe and North America has a "fully embraces" rate (36%) that is roughly twice or more than that of any of the other regions: the next highest rate is the Arab states (19%). At the other end of the spectrum, all the states from Latin America and the Caribbean were solely in native Spanish (Portuguese in Brazil), or had little to no information on "world cultural heritage," or had no functioning website. For this reason, none of those qualified under the study criteria as having a National Commission website "fully embracing" "world cultural heritage."

Is existence of an online presence embracing "world cultural heritage" something that can be linked to how wealthy a country is or what region it is in?

At first consideration, one might assume that wealthier, more developed countries would have National Commission websites, and the poorer, less developed countries would be most likely not to have a website. Are the high number of absent websites, in fact, a matter of not having or not wanting to devote the resources to create such an online presence, and a reflection of the standard of living in the country? This is not necessarily the case. Limiting the analysis to the National Commission websites of members of the Organization for Economic Cooperation and Development (OECD), the so-called "rich countries club," reveals that the percentage rate does not go up substantially (from 36% to 40%), and if we focus solely on the countries that were OECD members before the collapse of the Communist bloc, the rate does not go up but instead goes down slightly (38%). This suggests that it is not merely a country's lack of financial resources or level of development that keeps it from establishing an online presence celebrating its contribution to "world cultural heritage." There are some possible reasons why a state might not have a functioning National Commission website, and for this brief study, it would be prohibitively time consuming to track down those reasons for the more than 150 governments that fall into that category. One example from close to home will serve to illustrate how complex the issue may be. In the United States, matters of culture, and particularly government funding of culture, often fall victim to broad ideological disagreements in domestic politics. There was no National Commission to UNESCO sites for the United States under the Trump Administration, and under the Obama Administration, the U.S. website ignored the country's cultural contributions to the *List* and focused instead solely on the *nature* sites (before 2017: https://www.state.gov/p/io/unesco/). The relationship of the U.S. government to UNESCO has long been complicated (Meskell, 2013, pp. 490–491), and treatment of the reasons for that relationship would require more space than is available. In addition to the possibility that there is some sort of antagonism on the part of the member state toward the organization or a lack of consensus within the country, there is also theoretically the possibility of administrative or other oversight. Although countries from the "region" of Europe and North America are more likely to embrace "world cultural heritage" than countries from other regions, there are other factors that determine whether the National Commission website is created and maintained.

The fact that so many National Commissions have no functioning website or only a link to a related ministry could be indicative of perceived lack of financial resources due to insularity, indifference toward the international community, or lack of awareness of the purpose and importance of the website. Also, even though it is not always necessarily the case, having the website only in one language might correspond to an attitude that there is no need to reach out to those who do not know that language—a sort of language chauvinism that suggests that much of the country may operate under a similar national mindset.

If the World Cultural Heritage Program and the concept informing its practices are in fact Eurocentric, and if the program practices have been misappropriated as some observers claim, is it the case that at least a "core of countries" with the closest ties to the European cultural tradition, that is to say, from the "region" of Europe and North America as defined by UNESCO, are embracing "world cultural heritage" in the original spirit, based on what we can observe from their National Commission website content?

There are National Commission sites that "fully embrace" the concept of "world cultural heritage" and demonstrate allegiance to the principles of the program and the original spirit. Germany's website, for example, foregrounds broad representation of international heritage sites with examples such as the Great Wall of China, the Pyramids of Giza, and the Taj Mahal—sites that are not German or even European. Elsewhere at that website, it is possible to see a list of the German sites on the *List*, and the website emphasizes that the sites on the *List* are for "humanity as a whole." The website highlights international cooperation, exchange, transparency, and conservation, and it offers the information in several languages—German, English, and French (http://www.unesco.de/home.html).

However, websites that "fully embrace" the concept in this way form a minority among those within the Europe and North America "region," and instead we encounter a range of ways in which that spirit appears to have been subordinated to other purposes. On several websites, instead of celebrating the cosmopolitan ethos of the *List*, it is apparent that the exceptionality of the country's heritage sites is being used to assert some sort of national uniqueness or superiority for the country itself. For example, the U.S. National Commission website (prior to 2017, when it was removed under the Trump Administration) had almost nothing to say about culture, but noted that the United States proposed the convention and was the first state to ratify it, and stated that the convention "is the most widely accepted international conservation treaty in the world, which has resulted in the American concept of national parks being implemented worldwide" (before 2017: https://www.state.gov/p/io/unesco/). With this wording, the sentence is written in such a way as to highlight the expansion of American influence over the world, as opposed to any of the principles or the purpose of the heritage program. It suggests that the U.S. National Commission website in its pre-2017 incarnation was more about promoting the United States and its image than contributing to and sharing "world cultural heritage." Similarly, until 2017, the Italian National Commission website stated (correctly, at that time and following the results of the most recent selection committee session in Paris) that Italy is the country with the greatest number of sites on the *World Cultural Heritage List*. (The language on the Italian website has since been revised.) The Russian National Commission website is full of information on UNESCO and "world cultural heritage," yet it also contains "Stories of Famous Russian Teachers, Scientists, and Cultural Workers" and "Weighty Opinions of Russian Politicians and Public Figures" under a picture of Russian President Vladimir Putin. The Russian site also features an article by the minister of foreign affairs, Sergei Lavrov, with the description "Russia finds itself again at the crossroads of key trends that determine the vector of future global development" (http://www.unesco.ru/en/). In all three of these cases, the Russian Federation, Italy, and the United States, a sense of national importance seems to have taken precedence over appreciation of global cultural achievement, even in these "core countries" with ties to European cultural heritage.

The UNESCO World Heritage Program was intended to incorporate principles of fairness and equal representation, impartiality, and expert evaluation and advice. It was called forth by a spirit of cosmopolitanism. The National Commission websites, as a set of texts, while broadly comparable by their context, form only one measure for approaching an answer to the question of the extent to which countries embrace this concept, and thus the study does not make any claims to being comprehensive. As we have seen above, despite the near-universal adoption of the convention establishing the program, three-quarters to four-fifths of the world's countries do not "fully embrace" the concept of "world cultural heritage" under the study criteria. Similarly, among all the National Commission websites, the relatively high numbers that are not functioning, or offer no information on the *List* and the program, or are only in the country's native language, suggests that in most countries of the world, the cosmopolitan spirit of sharing in the cultural achievements of all countries is not highly valued. Further, the study finds that the majority of the countries in the "region" of Europe and North America cannot be said to "fully embrace" "world cultural heritage," even though the program and its practices are considered Eurocentric and despite the fact that these countries have the greatest affinity for European cultural ideals and possess the greatest financial resources to draw on. Instead, some websites from the region of Europe and North America reveal not a cosmopolitan spirit, but a national agenda.

NOTES

1. Although the full title is the *World Cultural and Natural Heritage List*, this study is concerned exclusively with the *List's* preservation of culture and not sites of natural significance.

2. Of course, Goethe and Arnold are talking about "culture" in general, whereas "world cultural heritage" is concerned with what Lynn Meskell calls, more precisely, "the preservation of cultural properties" (2013, p. 483). As Frey and Steiner point out, for the preservation of documents in written, audio, or video format, UNESCO has created the *List of the World's Documentary Heritage* (2010, p. 7).

3. In a personal email communication, a representative from the Danish National Commission wrote the following: "In the Danish National Commission for UNESCO we do not have the resources to maintain a website, so we try to communicate to a wider audience through mail networks and a dedicated Facebook page: UNESCO Danmark" (J. Dalsgaard, personal communication, 29 January 2018).

REFERENCES

Arnold, M. (2006). *Culture and anarchy*. Oxford University Press.
Betts, P. (2015). The warden of world heritage: UNESCO and the rescue of the Nubian monuments. *Past & Present, 226,* 100–125.
Frey, B. S., & Steiner, L. (2010). The *World Heritage List*: Does it make sense? *University of Zurich Working Paper Series*. Institute for Empirical Research in Economics.
Keough, E. B. (2011). Heritage in peril: A critique of UNESCO's World Heritage Program. *Washington University Global Studies Law Review, 10,* 593–615.
Manuel, K. (2004). *Governing cultural heritage: UNESCO's World Heritage Convention* (Publication No. 2241) [Master's thesis, University of Windsor]. Electronic Theses and Dissertations.
Meskell, L. (2002). Negative heritage and past mastering in archeology. *Anthropological Quarterly, 75,* 557–574.
Meskell, L. (2013). UNESCO's World Heritage Convention at 40: Challenging the economic and political order of international heritage conservation. *Current Anthropology, 54,* 483–494.
Pizer, J. (2000). Goethe's "world literature" paradigm and contemporary cultural globalization. *Comparative Literature, 52,* 213–227.

Schwinn, T. (2006). Konvergenz, Divergenz oder Hybridisierung? Voraussetzungen und Erscheinungsformen von Weltkultur [Convergence, divergence, or hybridization? Preconditions and manifestations of world culture]. *Kölner Zeitschrift für Soziologie und Sozialpsychologie, 58,* 201–232.

Steiner, L., & Frey, B. (2012). Correcting the imbalances of the *World Heritage List*: Did the UNESCO strategy work? *EBLA Working Papers.* University of Turin.

UNESCO World Heritage Center. (n.d.). http://whc.unesco.org/en/about

CHAPTER ELEVEN | NAEEM QURBAN

Terrorism and Politics
The Strategic Dimension of the Saudi-Led Islamic Military Alliance

The Strategic Dimension of the Saudi-Led Military Alliance

The announcement of the Islamic Military Counter-Terrorism Coalition (IMCTC), which is also known as the Islamic Military Alliance (IMA), was announced on December 15, 2015, by the young Defense Minister Prince Muhammad bin Salman, now the Crown Prince of the Kingdom of Saudi Arabia. Initially, only 34 Muslim states were part of this coalition, while more than 10 Muslims states were vigilant to join in the initial phase. So far 41 countries are aligned under IMCTC. This coalition was formed in the post-Arab Spring scenario when the Middle East was apprehended in the quagmire of radicalization and extremism by Da'esh (ISIS). Libya, Syria, and Iraq were blazing due to civil wars and the terrorist activities by ISIS.

In March 2016, in Riyadh, the first meeting of the chiefs of staff of the armed forces of IMCTC affirmed their intention to intensify their efforts in the fight against terrorism through joint action in accordance with their capabilities and at the request of each member state to participate in initiatives, programs within the framework of the IMA to combat terrorism in accordance with the policies and procedures of each state, without prejudice to the sovereignty of the member states of the coalition. They also stressed the importance of activating the launch of the coalition through a meeting of defense ministers of the member states.

During the U.S.-Arab-Islamic summit on May 20–21, 2017, in the Riyadh Declaration, it was revealed that the coalition would be based on the reserve force of 34,000 troops to support operations against terrorism. The leaders welcomed the readiness of some Islamic countries to participate and the progress achieved so far. The coalition forces will be led under the command of General (r) Raheel Sharif, who earlier served as the chief of the Pakistan Army.

The first meeting of the defense ministers and representatives of IMCTC member states was held in Riyadh under the theme "Allied Against Terrorism" on November 26, 2017. It was formally announced that the coalition of 41 Islamic countries is together against terrorism, with the aim to focus on four dimensions: ideology, media, counter-terrorism financing, and military fields.

Background

In December 2010, the Arab Spring sparked in the Middle East and shook the governments of the longtime rulers in the region, such as Bin Ali in Tunisia, Hosni Mubarak in Egypt, and Muammar Gaddafi in Libya. Soon after Libyan civil war in 2011, Syrian President Bashar al Assad's government also came under severe pressure to step down. But due to the use of force, the Syrian revolution turned into massive civil war in 2012–2013. Meanwhile, Iraq was already battling with the terrorism and insurgency by Al-Qaeda.

Viewing this gap in the transitional phase in the Middle East, Al-Qaeda and its other outfits seized the opportunity to escalate their presence in the other parts of the Middle East. With the rise of Al-Qaeda in Iraq (AQI) and later Al-Qaeda in Iraq and Syria (ISIS), also known as Islamic State (IS), the dynamics of Syrian civil war and Iraq changed dramatically. It gained more prominence than the Syrian opposition and its Free Syrian Army when they captured the Syrian city of Raqqa in January 2014, and in June 2014, Da'esh (IS) captured Mosul in Iraq with a few thousand members and heavy equipment of ammunition.

Da'esh (IS) started recruiting new members to increase its force and to hold their so-called caliphate. They started using the latest means of communication to spread their ideology around the world. They knew their targets and how to radicalize the minds of people. Interestingly, people started joining Da'esh (IS) from around the world. In September 2015, the *New York Times* reported that around 30,000 fighters had most probably joined Da'esh (IS) from around 100 countries (Schmitt & Sengupta, 2015). It was only because of the unprecedented ability of Da'esh (IS) to recruit the radicalized followers through social media.

Meanwhile, when Iran saw the falling Syrian regime of Bashar al Assad, they came forward to rescue his legitimacy. It was an ideological support that was viewed in the Middle East after the Arab Spring by Saudi Arabia and Iran, taking sides to their respective ideological regimes to hold their influence in the region. Saudi Arabia supported the Bahraini minority Sunni regime against the Shi'ite revolution, while Iran supported Alawite's minority regime of Bashar al Assad in Syria. Iran, along with Quds Force and Hezbollah, gave all means of technical, financial, and military support to Syria during its worst time of civil war when Damascus was about to fall in the hands of rebel Sunni majority opposition groups. Tehran's clandestine support to Damascus was already there in 2012–2013, which eventually increased after Iran's nuclear deal with P5+1+EU (China, France, Russia, the United Kingdom, the United States, and Germany, plus the European Union) in July 2015. With this agreement on a nuclear deal, the United States seemed to shift its direction to include Iran in the efforts to end the conflict in Syria. "I view this week as a major opportunity for any number of countries to play an important role," U.S. Secretary of State John Kerry (2015) said at the start of a meeting at the United Nations headquarters with Mohammad Javad Zarif, Iran's foreign minister. "We need to achieve peace and a way forward in Syria, in Yemen, in the region itself" (qtd. in Gordon, 2015, p. 12).

Viewing the above scenario and changing dynamics in the region, on December 15, 2015, just five months after Iran's nuclear deal, suddenly an announcement was made by the young Saudi defense minister about the IMA of 34 Sunni states and excluding the destabilized states like Syria, Iraq, and Yemen, while Iran was also excluded. Many critics viewed this alliance as anti-Iran or anti-Shia, while many called it Islamic-NATO or Muslim-NATO.

The perception of IMCTC is still prevailing as an anti-Iran coalition. This is because of the current happenings in the region, specifically between Saudi Arabia and Iran, since the start of Arab Spring to the Syrian and Yemeni civil wars and from the execution of Shia Shiekh Nimr Baqir al Nimr by Saudi Arabia to the blazing of the Saudi embassy in Tehran, which ultimately led them to sever ties with each other.

Key Components of the Islamic Military Alliance

The Saudi-led counter-terrorism coalition has had its clear objective since it was announced in December 2015. Its target is not just specific to Da'esh (IS), but any terrorist organization that appears in front of the coalition. There will be a joint operations center based in Riyadh for the coordination and support of efforts to fight terrorism in many parts of the Islamic world. The coalition will pursue terrorist organizations, regardless of their classification.

On the occasion of the first meeting of defense ministers and their representatives of the 41 states of IMCTC at Riyadh on November 26, 2017, commander-in-chief of IMCTC General (r) Raheel Sharif categorically said that "IMCTC's sole objective is to fight against terrorism, and it is not against any country, sect or religion" (Saudi Press Agency, 2017c).

The joint statement of the alliance affirms,

> The principles and objectives of the Charter of the Organization of the Islamic Cooperation, which calls on Member States to cooperate in combating terrorism in all its forms and manifestations, and rejects any justification or excuse for terrorism, and to achieve integration and alignment of efforts to combat terrorism, which undermines the inviolability of the self and threatens regional security and peace. And is a threat to the vital interests of the nation, and violates the system of coexistence. (Embassy of the Kingdom of Saudi Arabia, 2015)

The strategic determinants of the alliance are:

1. Legitimacy: The coalition draws its legitimacy through the accession of the majority of Muslim countries and enjoys the support and respect of the international community.
2. Localization: The use of local culture to combat terrorism in the Member States through the formulation of regional and local solutions.
3. Partnership: Building partnerships with international organizations and supporting countries with advanced capabilities in the fight against terrorism.
4. Securing Resources: Participation of coalition members in financing anti-terrorism initiatives according to their potential and willingness to participate.
5. Effectiveness: The speed in making the required decisions and the flexibility of moving to meet the developments in a timely manner.
6. Cooperation: Emphasis on the principle of coordination and cooperation among the Member States, supporting States and international organizations.
7. Participation: Alliance Member States participate in the planning process.
8. Common Goal: Member States agree on the importance of alliance and alignment between Alliance vision and strategic objectives.

9. Sovereignty: Emphasis on respect for the sovereignty of the Member States and the independence of their laws and regulations. (Islamic Military Counter-Terrorism Coalition, 2017)

The above-mentioned nine core principles of IMCTC show its aim and goals that it does not just contain itself on the battlefield but its sphere will spread to every aspect of life to counter terrorism and extremism from within society. With the extermination of ambiguity, it is clear that the coalition will work under the four counter-terrorism domains that were adopted as IMCTC's declaration as follow:

1. The ideology aspect will work on the glorification of the true ideology of Islam and in preserving the universal message of Islam, which will also encourage the true essence of moderate, tolerant, and to counter radical ideology.
   The Crown Prince of Saudi Arabia Muhammad bin Salman has also orchestrated a "Vision 2030" for the Kingdom of Saudi Arabia, which is not just an economic package and reforming the economy, but it will also restructure the society particularly in Saudi Arabia with the true ideology of Islam to transform the hardline society into a moderate and open society.

2. The media and communication aspect will develop cyber and media space on the disseminate facts from Quran and Hadith and scholarly, knowledge-based factual content to refute the rhetoric and claims of extremists and terrorist organizations that have been misleading and propagating on cyber and media space.
   The media and cyber warfare is the essential component in the contemporary scenario of the globalized world. The terrorists and extremists such as ISIS have been reaching the people through the cyber space and media. Therefore, there must be a phenomenon to curtail the propagated material and let positive and factual communication be given wider space to reach to the people.

3. The third aspect is financial cooperation in terrorism. It has become now the most threatening stage for most of the states in Europe who are already working on the counter-terror financing. IMCTC will develop legal, regulatory, and operational frameworks and facilitate the exchange of information to support the fight against the financing of

terrorism. Monetary policies, legislation, and financial controls must be developed and enforced along with the improvement in compliance to align with international standards. Increase in the technical and security cooperation in the exchange of data and information, the transfer of knowledge and expertise, in areas focused on combating the financing of terrorism is needed. The importance of ensuring the adequacy and effectiveness of systems and procedures to block terrorist financing is essential. Increased levels of awareness of the various ways terrorists finance their operations must be enhanced, to find the best and most successful solution to eliminate terrorist financing. (Saudi Press Agency, 2017b)

In the military sphere, most of the Islamic states do not possess trained and equipped military to fight against terrorism. The coalition will help coordinate efforts, resources, and planning, facilitate military exchanges, and contribute to facilitating the building of military capabilities of member states to fight terrorism. It will promote and accelerate the strength of the allied state to fill the gap to the counter-terrorism fight. The fight against terrorism cannot be won in the battlefield unless you are equipped with intelligence information and proper training, which will be integrated into the military effort through the Counter-Terrorism Center.

Formation and Mechanism of the Military Alliance

Pakistan's former Army Chief General (r) Raheel Sharif formally joined the IMA as the commander-in-chief in April 2017, after the nonobjection certificate by the government of Pakistan. It was revealed by Pakistan's then-Defense Minister Khawaja Asif in January 2017 that General Sharif was appointed as a commander-in-chief of IMCTC and was formally announced in the first meeting of defense ministers and the inaugural session of IMCTC on November 26, 2017.

I had an opportunity to interview Lt. General (r) Amjad Shoaib of the Pakistan Army, who has been in touch with former Chief of Army Staff (COAS) of the Pakistan Army and first commander-in-chief of IMCTC General (r) Raheel Sharif and was also present at the inaugural session of IMCTC in Riyadh. "It is not a one-day job to structure the framework of any professional institute," he said. There are certain rules and regulations to be adopted, upon which the whole alliance should be in agreement. There will be the body of defense ministers of IMCTC who will examine the progress of the framework and its rules and regulations. There are various components that are to be addressed such as who will decide to dispatch the force on the request of any allied nation. There must be a board or a body that will monitor the situation and the sensitivity in a particular country. Do they just need advisors or commanders to maneuver? Or are their capabilities not up to the mark and require the help from an allied force?

Similarly, the body will also decide, what will be the mission of task forces. Should it act like a peace keeping force, or should it act as a response force along with the local forces against their enemies, particularly terrorist groups?

- How will the appointment of the next commander-in-chief be made?
- How long will the term of the chief be?
- Will the regular army of any allied nation be sent for a mission, or will a new force from reserves participate in the missions?
- Where are these forces to be used?
- What will be the conditions to request assistance?
- How will the funding be generated?

Most of the above concerns and questions regarding the mechanisms of IMCTC were addressed during the inaugural session of the defense ministers, who agreed on the following.

The center headquarters for IMCTC will be in Riyadh, while Saudi Arabia will meet the coalition's needs and will ensure the fulfillment of all necessary legal, procedural, and regulatory obligations. After getting the approval of the respective governments, the coalition members will also nominate their representatives and delegates to the center.

The chairman (the Crown Prince and Defense Minister of Saudi Arabia Muhammad bin Salman) of the IMCTC Ministers of Defense Council will appoint the secretary-general (president of the center) and the military commander of the coalition. The first (acting) secretary-general appointed by the chairman of IMCTC is Saudi Lt. Gen. Abdullah Al Saleh, and the military commander is Pakistan's ex-Army Chief General (r) Raheel Sahrif.

There is no regular army of IMCTC so far, and its framework is still under consideration, which was revealed in November 2017 at the defense ministers meeting in Riyadh. However, it was hinted in the U.S.-Arab-Islamic summit's declaration in May 2017 that IMCTC will provide a reserve force of 34,000 troops to support operations against terrorist organizations (Saudi Press Agency, 2017a).

The aim was particularly against the ISIS activities in Iraq and Syria, who are now almost on the run but are reported to spread in the region, which could cause more damage in the society if not curtailed. Concerns have been raised by Pakistan, China, and Russia over ISIS's presence in Afghanistan. Many European countries have also expressed their concerns that it might have dispersed into Turkey and will enter into Europe, which is an alarming situation for them (O'Connor, 2017).

At the defense ministers meeting in November 2017, the ministers emphasized the strategic importance of the trained, organized, and well-equipped military's role in contributing and combating the threat of terrorism and enhancing regional and international security and peace.

> Within the framework of the Islamic Military Counter-Terrorism Coalition, the participation of the coalition states will be defined in accordance by each country's capabilities and resources, in accordance by each country's desire to participate in a given military operation. (Saudi Press Agency, 2017b)

As far as the annual budget, regulations, and procedural rules are concerned, they will be under the discretion of the chairman of IMCTC. So far, Saudi Arabia itself is bearing the expenses of IMCTC Headquarters and the Center of Counter-Terrorism in Riyadh.

The meeting of the IMCTC Ministers of Defense Council will be held annually and whenever necessary, under the chairmanship of Muhammad bin Salman. It will follow up on the strategies, policies, plans, and programs to achieve IMCTC's objectives and to review the reports submitted by the IMCTC's Counter-Terrorism Center, to pursue concerted efforts in various areas to combat terrorism.

The ministers intend to redouble their efforts to promote joint action in operations, programs, and initiatives within the framework of IMCTC and in line with IMCTC's organizational structure and mechanisms (Saudi Press Agency, 2017b).

Many have called this alliance the NATO of Muslim States. The motives of NATO were well-known. It was formed during the Cold War era to counter communism and the threats from the Soviet Union. NATO stayed in existence even after the fall of the Union of Soviet Socialist Republics. Such concerns regarding the creation of a Muslim force are understandable. But in a current scenario of the fight against terrorism and ideological warfare, especially in a

Muslim world, there was a dire need of such a forum to deal with this disease of terrorism and radicalization in a Muslim country led by Muslim countries.

Saudi Arabia's ambassador to Islamabad, Nawaf Ahmad Al-Maliki, said in an interview that we would continue efforts for the eradication of terrorism from the platform of IMCTC, adding that in this regard General (r) Raheel Sharif has rendered great services in Pakistan during his tenure. Al-Maliki said we would take benefit from the experiences of General (r) Raheel Sharif. He further said that the IMA is not against any country, but this alliance has been formed for the eradication of terrorism ("Exclusive Interview of Saudi Arabia's Ambassador to Islamabad," 2017).

Along with the sharing of information, IMCTC will also train, equip, and provide forces if necessary for the fight against militants. It is an opportunity for many countries who do not have access to advanced equipment and technologies that Saudi Arabia is acquiring. Pakistan has an opportunity to excel its expertise and lead IMCTC in the fight against terrorism.

The joining of General (r) Raheel Sharif was on the assurance by Saudi Arabia that this alliance will not be used against any Islamic state, including Iran. The purpose of this force was told to General (r) Raheel Sharif in clear words that it will only deal with the terrorist activities on the request of a particular country, and the mission of the force will be well defined.

Deradicalization

IMCTC does not just aim to combat terrorists on the battlefield but has also formulated a framework to combat terrorism on the ideological front. The terrorist organizations are radicalizing people and have recruited a large number of people through social media and the internet. Various organizations are working on this ideological front to radicalize people for their interests. It includes Sunnis as well as Shi'ites.

To confront the radicalization through social media and the internet, the Kingdom of Saudi Arabia has developed the Ideological Warfare Center (IWC), which provides intellectual initiatives to IMCTC to combat terrorism. Its main tasks are:

1. To detect the errors, allegations, suspicions, and deception techniques promoted by extremism and terrorism.
2. To clarify the Islamic approach to cases relating to extremism and terrorism.

3. To provide the intellectual initiative to the IMA to fight terrorism.
4. To offer similar intellectual initiative to multiple authorities within Saudi Arabia and abroad.
5. To raise the level of public awareness regarding the true nature of Islam within the Muslim world and outside of it.
6. To provide further support toward the positive mental image about the truth of Islam worldwide.
7. To inoculate youth against extremist ideologies through a variety of programs.
8. To dismantle the means by which terrorists recruit their targeted demography.
9. To showcase the correct understanding about the attempt of extremism toward distorting religion, including its false interpretation and its corrupt and heinous crimes.
10. Finally, to showcase the values of moderation and tolerance in Islam.

The IWC embarked on posting its electronic messages focusing on the extremist ideologies, fighting from all over the world. The IWC managed to attract people who have been persuaded by extremism from more than 100 countries, including individuals who were born, lived, and grew up in non-Muslim countries. They have been affected by the messages and literature of extremism exchanged electronically among them due to a lack of knowledge and basic understanding. Some of these messages and literature focused on stirring religious fervor or taking advantage of financial difficulties ("Saudi Ideological War Center Launches Initiatives," 2017).

> "Al Qaeda did not collapse after the fall of the Taliban because its ideology still existed," said Mohammad al Issa, who also directs the defense ministry's new Ideological Warfare Center and has a seat on the kingdom's Council of Senior Scholars, said Saudi Arabia had already took initiatives to discredit and dismantle extremist websites. ("Saudi to Open Militant-Monitoring Center," 2017)

Similarly, Da'esh (IS) will also be dispersed within our society after being defeated in Iraq and Syria. This will lead to continuous destabilization in the region because the ideology of Da'esh still exists. We have seen in the past when Mujahedeen were left on their own after the Soviet–Afghan War. As a result of such negligence, Afghanistan and Pakistan remained unstable for so long. In 2002 after the United States started the Afghan war, General

Musharraf, former president of Pakistan, prescribed various militant organizations that were sympathizing with or facilitating Mujahedeen. They were neither accommodated in the social activities nor were they monitored or briefed about their approach toward militancy and extremism. Consequently, many tribal militant groups joined the Afghan war. The Haqqani network, which has become the most threatening and violent force against the United States and allied forces in Afghanistan, was previously trained and equipped by the United States and the Pakistani government itself, but was left on its own without mainstreaming its members into society or handing over to Mujahedeen a stable and peaceful Afghanistan, which former U.S. Secretary of State Hillary Clinton also admitted. Pakistan's involvement and allegiance with the United States in the Afghan War resulted in the formation of Tehreek e Taliban Pakistan in 2007, comprised of various militant groups such as Punjabi Taliban, Lashkar-e-Jhangvi, and other tribal militant organizations. Therefore, it is necessary for the governments and authorities to monitor those radicalized entities in the society and to establish centers of rehabilitation for the continuous counseling of jihadists.

Iranian Thwart to Counter-Terrorism and Radicalization

The notion that has triumphed since the announcement of Saudi-led IMCTC is that it is an anti-Shi'ite alliance. It prevailed because Saudi Arabia did not include Iran, Iraq, Syria, and Yemen. First, Iraq and Syria were not included in this alliance because they were troubled and destabilized regions, and it could not be done without the collaboration of local authorities and the international community. Second, knowing the fact that Iran has been covertly supporting Bashar al Assad's regime in Syria, even before the Iran nuclear deal in mid-2015, it is quite easy to understand that Riyadh would not collaborate in such a way with Tehran to include them in IMCTC. Third, there are numerous Shi'ite organizations from around the Muslim states that are paid and facilitated by Iran to participate in Iraq and Syrian wars.

Syrian President Bashar al Assad wrote a letter to the supreme leader of Iran, Ayatollah Khamenei, in September 2017, to thank and acknowledge the support of Iran in partnering with Syria in the fight against terrorism on its request. President al Assad also expressed his deep gratitude for the continuous military assistance of Iran since 2011, which helped turn the tables (al Assad, 2017).

According to various sources, Iran has been sponsoring foreign fighters in Syria and Iraq. Many senior commanders and retired military specialists of Iran's Islamic Revolutionary Guards Corps (IRGC) and Quds Force have been deployed in Syria. The primary role of the Iranian forces is to gather intelligence, plan the strategies for the two-front war, and manage the logistics of the battle for the Syrian regime to fight against the rebel insurgency and the Islamic State terrorists (Saul & Hafezi, 2014).

Iranian forces and officials of IRGC assisting the al Assad regime in Syria could be in the few thousands, but the matter of concern is that Iran is also sponsoring and recruiting militant Shia organizations and foreign fighters from around the Muslim states. This is a similar pattern to what Da'esh has adopted to recruit its combats by radicalization. It is already an open secret that Quds Force and Hezbollah are always strengthened and backed by Iran. It was reported that in March 2011, "Turkish officials seized light weapons—including assault rifles and grenade launchers—on an Iranian cargo plane bound for Syria. ... Syria received other Iranian shipments that included riot control gear and computer equipment for internet surveillance, the U.S. and allied sources claimed (Warrick, 2011).

Dr. Matthew Levitt discussed the implications of the nuclear agreement in the Council on Foreign Relations. He is of the view that even before the nuclear agreement, Iran not just pledged but also provided billions of dollars to assist the Syrian regime by funding, training, and equipping foreign fighters and proregime Shia militias while it was under financial and economic sanctions. As sanctions are lifted and Iran has more money, it is likely to spend more to keep the regime afloat (Laub, 2015). This can be seen from the surprising increase in the military budget of Iran in the middle of the fiscal year 2017–2018, allocating US$5 billion with half of it being utilized in the fight against terrorism to IRGC Quds Force (Warrick, 2011).

The increase in Iranian expenditures over Quds Force and Hezbollah, and the promotion of other Shia militant organizations will not just benefit Hezbollah's regional and international operations but will also provide the opportunity to expand Iran's network around the region. The radicalization and convincing of Shi'ite communities through its ideology is a matter of concern. With more money, Iran has raised its aid to Shia militias from around the Muslim world who are gathering in Iraq and Syria, while Quds Force and Hezbollah are training the foreign fighters of Shia militias. Though they are fighting on behalf of the regimes, their tactics could exacerbate sectarian tensions.

Similar to Da'esh, Iran is also working on its ideology and radicalizing people to join the Syrian war to safeguard Shi'ites' interests in the region. The number of foreign fighters in Syria is not confirmed, but it is estimated that it could be from 50,000 to 88,000 who are being recruited, financed, and trained by Iran. It was revealed by the pro-opposition Syrian news website Zaman Al Wasel in May 2015 that they have accessed Syrian defense ministry documents in which the Syrian government requested Iran to handle the matters related to supervision and payroll of thousands of Shia militias and foreign fighters (Jedinia & Al Hendi, 2017). The number might have doubled as Iran is now spending more and more under its defense budget after the financial and economic sanctions have been lifted since the implementation of the Iran nuclear deal. According to an estimate, around 65 Shia militia organizations from Iran, Iraq, Syria, Lebanon, Palestine, Bahrain, Yemen, Afghanistan, and Pakistan are recruiting radicalized people under the banner of their Shi'ite ideology and are sponsored by Iran ("How Much Is Iran Paying," 2017).

Iran has not just recruited the volunteer fighters to fight against Da'esh and the Syrian rebel forces; Iran is paying them with heavy salaries, and the families of the martyred are being awarded the nationality of Iran with a handsome stipend. The martyred are buried with honor in dedicated graveyards in Iran.

Once the Syrian war is over, these militant organizations will be dispersed in society. Their radicalized minds could affect the states like Pakistan, Afghanistan, Central Asian nations, and particularly Saudi Arabia. It is the same pattern that is being followed by Da'esh and has been destabilizing society through its ideology. Many terrorist activities against Shia communities reported in Pakistan were conducted by Da'esh through their highly qualified but radicalized young generation fighters.

Saudi Arabia is currently facing many problems in its Shia majority Eastern Province where radicalized people have raised arms against the monarchs. The fight in Saudi Arabia is not just for democratic rights or minorities' privileges, but this struggle has been transformed into ideological dominance in the region. Similarly, the Zeinabiyoun brigade and Fatemiyoun brigade recruit Shi'ites from Pakistan and Afghanistan, respectively. It could be a disaster for Pakistan if not dealt with in time. It is estimated that Iran spends US$6 billion to US$20 billion to support foreign fighters and IRGC forces fighting to secure the Syrian regime (Lake, 2015). Alternatively, the official figure approved by Iran's parliament in August 2017 is US$2.5 billion, as quoted earlier. Such intensified and deep interests of Iran to dominate Shia ideology and influence in the region must be the scope of IMCTC along with the fight against Da'esh.

Pakistan's Concern

Being members of IMCTC, Pakistan and Afghanistan are not just facing the threats from the Taliban and Da'esh; the inciting sectarian clashes among the Sunni and Shia jihadists could become a quandary for IMCTC. Reportedly, the Zeinabiyoun brigade is being recruited from the Hazara community and Turi tribe of Kurram agency in Pakistan (Dehghanpisheh, 2015).

Da'esh has found that by playing the anti-Shia card, it can win sympathy and support from among anti-Shia groups in Pakistan such as Lashkar-e-Jhangvi and Jammat-ul-Ahrar. The presence of Da'esh in Afghanistan and Pakistan and its continuous sectarian violence will prompt to grow the membership of the Fatemiyoun and Zainabiyoun brigades. Iran will get the opportunity to stretch its influence and network from the Levant to South Asia, while IMCTC in that scenario will find it difficult to tackle the sectarian conflict with the resistance from Pakistan not to act against any sect. Pakistan's Interior Ministry has banned the outfits, which were reportedly operating in the Shia majority area of tribal agencies, recruiting Shi'ites for the Syrian war from Pakistan. As per National Counter-Terrorism Authority's (NACTA) notification, Ansar-ul-Hussain was outlawed on December 30, 2016, while Jamat ul Ahrar (JuA) and Lashkar-e-Jhangvi Al-Almi (LeJA), which are associated with Da'esh, were proscribed in November 2016 (National Counter-Terrorism Authority, n.d.).

For Pakistan, it is perplexing to counter terrorism as well as sectarianism being part of IMCTC. Since the joining of Pakistan as a member of IMCTC, Iran has been raising its concerns with the government regarding the purpose and intentions of the coalition. Earlier in April 2015, Pakistan's parliament decided not to be a part of any coalition against Yemen. The decision was appreciated by Iran as well as many other stakeholders in Pakistan. On the issue of joining IMCTC, Pakistan's Defense Minister Khawaja Asif has briefed the Senate and National Assembly of Pakistan regarding Terms of Reference (ToRs) and the appointment of General Raheel Sharif as commander-in-chief of IMCTC. The major concern of Pakistan remained the anti-Iran impression of the coalition, although it has been clarified many times by the government and authorities. According to Khawaja Asif (Ghumman, 2016), Pakistan will never be part of an anti-Iran coalition nor will it send its troops to take part in any anti-Iran or anti-Shia campaign.

Pakistan is the second largest Shia population after Iran. Pakistan also acknowledges the fault line between Sunni and Shia sects. Therefore, it is very much necessary to be aware of ToRs of IMCTC and how much involvement of Pakistan and its forces it requires to fight terrorism. Keeping in view that Pakistan had rejected Saudi Arabia's request to participate in the Yemen war and later joined the Saudi-led IMA, Pakistan must keep its relationship balanced with Iran and Saudi Arabia.

The Iranian concern at the time of General Raheel's appointment as commander-in-chief of IMCTC was also addressed by Pakistan's civil and military leadership. The successor of General Sharif, Chief of Army Staff General Qamar Javed Bajwa's extensive visit to Iran in early November 2017 also worked to make Iran understand that Pakistan will never indulge in any drive against Iran. During his three-day historic visit, General Bajwa met Iranian Chief of General Staff Major General Muhammad Bagheri at General Staff HQ and Iranian Defense Minister Brigadier General Amir Hatami, and he visited the IRGC HQ, where he met the commander-in-chief of IRGC, Major General Mohammad Ali Jafari, which was the first time for any Pakistani general. Pakistan and Iran expressed their commitment to fight against Da'esh and any threat of terrorism against each other, and at the same time, it expressed its concerns regarding recruitment from Pakistan. According to the Inter-Services Public Relations (ISPR), "Both sides agreed to ensure that their soil is not used by any third party against any of the two countries" (ISPR, 2017).

The very next day, General Bajwa, along with Prime Minister of Pakistan Shahid Khaqan Abbasi, visited Saudi Arabia for the formal inauguration of IMCTC. Director General of Inter-Services Intelligence (ISI) Lt. Gen. Naveed Mukhtar was also with the delegation. Pakistan pledged its commitment to cooperate and strengthen the security and defense sector and discussed the entire spectrum of regional and international issues with Saudi King Salman bin Abdulaziz and Crown Prince Muhammad bin Salman. Pakistan's efforts in routing the menace of terrorism and extremism from its soil were also appreciated.

Conclusion

IMCTC is the need of the hour. Most of the terror-affected countries around the world are Muslim states, and its enemies were also portraying themselves as Muslims but have extremist and radicalized ideology. They have also become proxies in the hands of the enemies of Islam and the actors who want to destabilize the regions.

The OIC could not deliver anything effective since the war against terrorism and unrest in the Middle East erupted. Nor did any Muslim state take the lead to organize any joint force or mechanism to fight the radicalization. IMCTC is the platform where it will be possible for all regional countries to cooperate, coordinate, and build their trust among each other to counter terrorism and radicalized ideology.

Afghanistan and Pakistan have been fighting a war against terrorism since 2001. And it faced the most casualties and losses in the world. But neither country has jointly operated at their respective border region. Despite the intelligence-sharing mechanism among both neighbors, there is still a lack of coordination and trust between the two member countries of IMCTC.

With the fall of Da'esh, the strategy of terrorists will be changed from conventional to guerilla tactics and urban warfare. The war against terrorism will not be just a single-front war against Da'esh, but it will be fought on all the four fronts discussed under the domain of IMCTC: ideology, media, financing, and military. The sectarian conflicts will be the most sensitive areas to be dealt with. Members of IMCTC have a clear stance that none of the states will provide its assistance and troops against any particular state. Therefore, there is no chance that IMCTC will act against Iran or any other Shia state. The only dilemma it will face is the radicalization of Sunni as well as Shia, which could lead toward sectarian conflict. So it must be made clear whether terrorism and sectarianism will fall under the same category or not and how IMCTC will deal with it.

General (r) Raheel Sharif, one of the most popular military chiefs Pakistan has seen, is now commanding IMCTC. In his tenure as army chief, Gen. Sharif effectively devised new war strategies against Tehrik-i-Taliban (TTP) strongholds in terror-infested areas. Statistics show that under his regime, Pakistan saw a major improvement in the peace process and the armed forces cleared out previously controlled and infested areas and are now working toward rehabilitation and normalcy. The most prominent example is the state of affairs in North Waziristan. The final draw-out was in the Shakai valley, north of the city of Wana, where the final reinforcements of TTP were eliminated. Gen. Sharif devised a policy of treating abettors and facilitators as terrorists, who were spared in exchange for information on the previous doctrines. His appointment as the chief of IMCTC has been internationally recognized as an element of Pakistan's contribution to the global peace process. Furthermore, Gen. Sharif can also be utilized in the future to negotiate terms between Saudi Arabia and Iran for a probable peace process between the two countries.

The appointment of Gen. Sharif can also be viewed as Pakistan's assurance that Pakistan will not take part in an extension of the Kingdom of Saudi Arabia (KSA)–Iran conflict. As the Pakistani premier and current army chief's visit highlighted, Pakistan is clear on its nonpartisan stance in any due conflict. Defense Minister Khawaja Asif's clarification in the parliament further emboldens the writ of the state on the matter.

The dynamics of Pakistan are sensitive concerning its relationship with its neighbor Iran and Saudi Arabia. It is of deep concern for the state of Pakistan that Iran has been recruiting Shia militia from Pakistan and Afghanistan. This could prove to be a strategic setback to Pakistan as the war in Iraq and Syria draws to a conclusion, as the Shia militias might become a threat for their respective states just like ISIS is. Trained and battle-hardened recruits might be utilized to fill a vacuum that ISIS might create, just as Mujahedeen, initially recruited from Pakistan and trained to fight against the Soviet Union, turned into what the Taliban are today and waged war against Pakistan. In conclusion, the radicalization of Shias is not too different from the methodology of ISIS itself. Ideological conflict resolution is the most important battlefront for IMCTC. IMCTC will not be a conventional warfare military; rather it will be committed to the deradicalization of aforementioned groups, ensuring the closure of loopholes for terror financing, rooting out support from minority groups in attempts to resurrect diminished radicals, and strategically using media for eliminating cyber warfare and malignancy.

REFERENCES

al Assad, B. (2017). *Iran a partner in Syrian victory: Assad's letter to Ayatollah Khamenei*. Press TV. http://www.presstv.com/Detail/2017/09/14/535154/Iran-Syria-Bashar-Assad

Dehghanpisheh, B. (2015, December 10). *Iran recruits Pakistani Shi'ites for combat in Syria*. Reuters. https://www.reuters.com/article/us-mideast-crisis-syria-pakistan-iran/iran-recruits-pakistani-shiites-for-combat-in-syria-idUSKBN0TT22S20151210

Embassy of the Kingdom of Saudi Arabia. (2015, December 15). *Joint statement on the formation of the Islamic Military Alliance*. Embassy of the Kingdom of Saudi Arabia. https://www.saudiembassy.net/statements/joint-statement-formation-islamic-military-alliance

Exclusive interview of Saudi Arabia's ambassador to Islamabad, Nawaf Ahmad Al-Maliki. (2017, September 11). In *Sabah News*.

Ghumman, K. (2016, January 20). *Pakistan not joining any anti-Iran coalition, Asif tells NA*. Dawn. https://www.dawn.com/news/1234169

Gordon, M. (2015, September 26). *Shifting direction, Kerry aims to include Iran in efforts to end the conflict in Syria*. New York Times.

How much is Iran paying for Assad's foreign fighters? (2017, May 29). In *TRT World*. http://www.trtworld.com/mea/how-much-is-iran-paying-for-assads-foreign-fighters-368090

IRNA. (2017, August 13). *Iran Parliament firmly approves anti-US bill*. IRNA. http://www.irna.ir/en/News/82629764

Islamic Military Counter-Terrorism Coalition. (2017). About IMCTC. https://imctc.org/English/About

ISPR. (2017, November 17). *No. PR-546/2017-ISPR* [Press release]. https://ispr.gov.pk/press-release-detail.php?id=4363

Jedinia, M., & Al Hendi, A. (2017, May 28). *Iran to bankroll pro-government militia fighters in Syria*. Voice of America. https://www.voanews.com/a/sources-iran-to-bankroll-pro-government-militia-fighters-in-syria/3874390.html

Lake, E. (2015, June 9). *Iran spends billions to prop up Assad*. Bloomberg. https://www.bloomberg.com/view/articles/2015-06-09/iran-spends-billions-to-prop-up-assad

Laub, Z. (2015, September 3). *The Middle East after the Iran Nuclear Deal*. Council on Foreign Relations. https://www.cfr.org/expert-roundup/middle-east-after-iran-nuclear-deal

National Counter-Terrorism Authority (NACTA). (n.d.). *Proscribed organizations*. NACTA. https://nacta.gov.pk/proscribed-organizations/

O'Connor, T. (2017, August 18). *End of ISIS means more attacks like Barcelona in U.S. and Europe*. Newsweek. http://www.newsweek.com/end-isis-middle-east-more-attacks-barcelona-us-europe-652247

Saudi Ideological War Center launches initiatives to fight terrorism. (2017, May 2). In *Arab News*. http://www.arabnews.com/node/1093386/saudi-arabia

Saudi Press Agency. (2017a, May 21). *Riyadh declaration: Arab-Islamic-American Summit succeeds in building close partnership to confront extremism, terrorism, fostering regionally, int'l peace, stability, development* [Press release]. http://www.spa.gov.sa/viewfullstory.php?lang=en&newsid=1632551

Saudi Press Agency. (2017b, November 26). *IMCTC issues final declaration Riyadh* [Press release]. http://www.spa.gov.sa/viewstory.php?lang=en&newsid=1691870

Saudi Press Agency. (2017c, November 27). *Crown Prince opens inaugural meeting of IMCTC Ministers of Defense Council in Riyadh* [Press release]. http://www.spa.gov.sa/viewstory.php?lang=en&newsid=1691846

Saudi to open militant-monitoring center during Trump visit. (2017, May 20). In *Reuters*. https://www.reuters.com/article/us-usa-trump-gulf-centre/saudi-to-open-militant-monitoring-center-during-trump-visit-idUSKCN18G09P

Saul, J., & Hafezi, P. (2014, February 21). *Iran boosts support to Syria to bolster Assad*. Reuters. https://www.reuters.com/article/us-syria-crisis-iran/iran-boosts-military-support-in-syria-to-bolster-assad-idUSBREA1K09U20140221

Schmitt, E., & Sengupta, S. (2015, September 26). *Thousands enter Syria to join ISIS despite global efforts*. New York Times.

Warrick, Joby. (2011, May 27). *Iran reportedly aiding Syrian crackdown*. Washington Post. https://www.washingtonpost.com/world/national-security/iran-reportedly-aiding-syrian-crackdown/2011/05/27/AGUJe0CH_story.html?utm_term=.9e0b8984c12e

CHAPTER TWELVE | MANZOOR KHAN AFRIDI

Pakistan's Role in Interregional Connectivity Between South Asia and Central Asia

Opportunities and Challenges
in the Age of Globalization

Regional Connectivity in a Globalized World

Globalization can be considered as the process of integration and interaction among people and different nations. Globalization is a process that is driven by investment and international trade, supported by technology. The process of globalization is holistic and has impacted almost every section of human society. Globalization is not entirely new as people and companies have been investing in other countries for thousands of years. However, it is the technological advancement that is primarily responsible for increased global economic and cultural connection during the last few decades. Many observers note that the world has qualitatively entered a new phase. The new wave of globalization has opened economies in countries as well as at the global level. Now, many governments prefer the free-market economy, developing their own production systems and encouraging investment and trade (Council on Foreign Relations Education, 2016).

Regional integration is the main driver of globalization. The nature of integration may be economic or political, but economic integration is usually the main engine of regionalism. Through regional integration, states overcome the hurdles of geography through shared norms, resources, and common accords (Fujimura, 2004). Regionalism can be considered as an approach through which states liberalize trade and create market for capital, people, and services. For example, the European Union is a regional approach that has greatly helped the countries of Western Europe in achieving peace, prosperity, and security (European Commission, 2022). The English School of International Relations suggests that countries have been successful in devising an international "anarchical society" in which they do not have to surrender their will before some powerful entity. Furthermore, the English School suggests that there is a low level of conflict and high level of order in "international society" (Bull, 2012). However, the primary concern of the classical English School theorists was international society, not regional societies, because they took "international society" as universally homogenous. However, contemporary English School theorists, like Barry Buzan, are highlighting the importance of regions in global politics (Buzan, 2014).

In the discourse of globalization and regional integration, lack of infrastructure links is a primary problem. Recent research in the field of development has emphasized the significance of improving infrastructure linkages between countries (Roland-Holst, 2009). The governments of developing countries should focus on improving links of infrastructure because their economies are becoming highly integrated. In this process, cross-border goods will play a crucial role as goals of development cannot be realized through weak infrastructural linkages with neighbor states. In addition to goods, the prevention of diseases, environmental protection, and developmental research can also cross borders through improving links of infrastructure. A regional integration approach requires many other policies like reduced tariffs, nontariff barriers, and improved custom procedures. Emerging regional institutions are playing central roles in regional approaches. There is widespread agreement that regional integration is very difficult to realize without improving regional and transport infrastructure (Fujimura, 2004).

Central Asia is a region that has a population of 70 million and is comprised of six states: Kazakhstan, Kyrgyzstan, Turkmenistan, Tajikistan, Uzbekistan, and sometimes Afghanistan. Nomadic people have historically ruled over the region. Central Asia has served as the crossroads for movement of ideas, people, and goods among Western Asia, Europe, East Asia, and South Asia. Most of Central Asia was part of the Russian Empire and then the Soviet Union (Roland-Holst, 2009). Central Asia is known for its importance of geostrategic location. It is located at the intersection of some of the great civilizations like Chinese, Persian, Arabian, and European civilizations, and links various parts of Eurasia. The states of Central Asia were part of the Soviet Union and got independence after the disintegration of the Soviet Union. Central Asia has become a hot spot for major power rivalry in the post-Cold War era due to its rich natural and hydrocarbon resources.

The countries of Bangladesh, Afghanistan, Pakistan, India, Bhutan, Maldives, Nepal, and Sri Lanka are included in South Asia. The countries of South

Asia became members of the South Asian Association for Regional Cooperation (SAARC) in 1985. However, due to the rivalry between India and Pakistan, the states of South Asia could not form an integrated regional economic block. The region has great potential for economic development, but security concerns do not allow a genuinely integrated region of South Asia. The China Pakistan Economic Corridor (CPEC) can provide a platform that can integrate the economies of South Asia as well as economies of Central Asia. Thus, CPEC can function as an engine for regional integration in Central and South Asia.

Central Asia and South Asia have a long history of cultural and economic relations that goes back countless millennia to at least 1500 BC. Religious–cultural exchanges, invasions, and trade were important factors that strengthened relations between the two regions (Dixit, 2015). Mahmud Ghaznavi of Afghanistan made the first major assault, against India, between Central and South Asia. After the first wave of attacks from Central Asia against South Asia (India), they continued unabated until the 12th century. These incursions from Central Asian states in South Asia galvanized Central Asia–South Asia cultural and economic relations. The disintegration of the USSR in 1991 ended in the independence of five states from Central Asia, which can provide rich energy resources and raw material like industrial goods and communication. Turkmenistan owns the world's fifth largest reserves of natural gas. The output of oil in Turkmenistan can reach to 48 million tons a year. Pakistan wants to improve its relations with Central Asian states through two strategies: using Muslim culture to build deep connections with Central Asian states and improving its economic links. Pakistan is the country that has a great importance for Eurasia. Pakistan has the potential to integrate a pan-Eurasian economic zone by connecting the economies of the Eurasian Union, Iran, SAARC, and China.

CPEC is a part of the massive and ambitious Chinese One Belt One Road (OBOR) program. Through six corridors, OBOR aims to connect South Asia, China, West Asia, Central Asia, the Middle East, Russia, Africa, and Europe to improve the timely flow of trade. CPEC is comprised of networks of railways, roads, airports, economic zones, energy projects, industrial parks, and fire optics. Special economic zones have been designed along the route of CPEC. CPEC is a framework that promotes regional connectivity (Hanif, n.d.). The vision of CPEC is to expand the Karakoram Highway between Pakistan and China and construct rail, pipeline, and industrial networks from Gwadar to the Chinese border. The energy requirements of this ambitious project will be filled by the Iran–Pakistan–China pipeline. In addition to Iran–Pakistan–China pipeline project, the world's largest solar farm will also be built to provide energy to CPEC. CPEC will provide China access to the Arabian Sea by avoiding trips to the Strait of Malacca. CPEC will also provide China easy access to energy resources of the Middle East, which will be badly needed by the export-oriented economy of China. Furthermore, CPEC will provide Central Asia a link to Southeast Asia that will prove highly beneficial for exports for lesser-developed and far-flung areas inside China. The important intersections in China like Xinjiang will become a vital Eurasian hub of trade that will connect China, the Eurasian Union, SAARC, and Iran.

Only China and Pakistan will not only reap the benefit of CPEC as the project will prove beneficial for the whole region. The improvement in geographic connections will occur through the new projects of railways, roads, and air transportation. Such improved communications will promote economic, academic, and cultural links. This will cause a positive influence on the volume of business and trade and regional resources and will move toward optimal utilization and will culminate in a shared harmony, development, and destiny (China Pakistan Economic Corridor, n.d.). Central Asian states have always looked toward finding new markets in Pakistan, India, China, and other countries of West Asia. However, their landlocked geography makes the task very difficult. CPEC can offer a valuable chance to Uzbekistan, Turkmenistan, Kyrgyzstan, and Tajikistan to find access to regional and global markets. At the same time, Pakistan is also keen to gain access to the energy-rich resources of Central Asia through Afghanistan to transport its goods to Central Asia. China has been a main investor in infrastructure in Central Asia since the mid-1990s. Chinese companies have built bridges, highways, and telecommunication systems in Uzbekistan, Kyrgyzstan, and Tajikistan. China hopes to expel Islamic insurgency in the region through economic integration. CPEC can prove a natural extension to that program.

Several leaders of Central Asian states have welcomed CPEC. The president of Turkmenistan has promised to work along with Pakistan and emphasized the role of CPEC. Turkmenistan is allowed to use CPEC to access the Indian Ocean. With access to CPEC, Tajikistan also desires to gain access to the Indian Ocean; this will allow Tajikistan to connect with the rest of world, thus surmounting the geographic barriers of its landlocked geography. However, currently road and railway links between Dushanbe and Islamabad are not satisfactory. At the same time, Tajikistan can also provide Pakistan a road link to other Central Asian states through its Murghab Province. Tajikistan President Emomali Rahmanov and Pakistan Prime Minister Nawaz Sharif agreed on creating three highway projects that would prove extensions to CPEC. Uzbekistan Prime Minister Ulugbek Rozukulov expressed positive views about CPEC in his December visit to Islamabad. Uzbekistan's participation in CPEC can double the energy outputs of Pakistan and can ensure permanent access to electricity for Pakistan. Similarly, Kazakhstan Prime Minister Karim Massimov highlighted the importance of CPEC for his country (Ali, 2016).

The Eurasian Union can be considered as a Russia-led trade block that is comprised of Armenia, Belarus, Kazakhstan, and Kyrgyzstan. Kazakhstan and Kyrgyzstan are geographically close to South Asia. But, due to the unwillingness of Uzbekistan and war-torn Afghanistan, trade links of these Central Asian states and South Asia are not fully developed. Alternatives to deal with this problem of linking Central Asian economies with regional markets of South Asia are the North–South corridor between Russia, Iran, and India through the Caspian and Arabian Seas, and CPEC. Iran's energy importance cannot be ignored, and energy resources of Iran will attract Asia's two powerful economies—China and India. Both China and India prefer to invest in real sectors, therefore, physical connective infrastructure will play a key role in fully utilizing the natural resources of Iran. India is also trying to develop physical linkages with Iran like the Chabahar Port investment and the undersea Iran–India gas pipeline. However, for economic efficacy, overland routes will be best for energy trade options between Iran and India.

Though Bangladesh–China–India–Myanmar and SAARC can increase their trade volume with China, the scope of the project is limited to the northern areas of India and the Yunnan Province in China. Therefore, another corridor is pertinent that can link more areas, for which CPEC is the most appropriate choice. The logistical project of the North–South Corridor is envisioned to connect India and Russia, but bimodal form of transportation makes this project less efficient. Thus, a land link between India and Russia seems a viable option, which will require passage through Pakistan, as railroad may traverse from India to Russia through Iran and Central Asia. This link of India to Russia via Pakistan will save the circuitous route of sea–land (Korybko, 2015).

India has desired to reach the economies of Central Asia through Pakistan. However, because of Indo–Pak rivalry, this desire could not be materialized.

Therefore, India has focused on the Iranian port of Chabahar to find access to Central Asia and Afghanistan. The ports of CPEC and Chabahar can accomplish the goal. Iran has already made the offer to Pakistan to become a part of Chabahar and Tehran; at the same time, Iran has been offered to be a part of CPEC. The TAPI (Turkmenistan, Afghanistan, Pakistan, and India) gas pipeline was signed in 2015. Such a project can reduce trust deficit among the states. However, due to political rivalry, TAPI did not materialize. Similarly, the genuine regional integration in South Asia cannot be materialized despite SAARC. SAARC was envisioned to be a regional integration platform that would improve economic relations of the member countries. Nonetheless, due to the rivalry between India and Pakistan, the dream could not be fulfilled. However, if differences between India and Pakistan are resolved, then economic capability of the region will be improved and SAARC can be fully integrated with the rest of Eurasia (Korybko, 2015).

Pakistan, despite its important strategic location, was unable to form well-established trade links with the countries to the east and its northwestern neighbors. Pakistan's access to Central Asia is in jeopardy unless Pakistan allows an Afghanistan exit to India. North–South trade among India, Afghanistan, Central Asian states, and Pakistan can be served through CPEC. The connectivity among Gwadar Port, Chabahar Port in Iran, CPEC, and Bangladesh–China–India–Myanmar can form a new era of trade and economic integration in South, Central, West, and East Asia. The connectivity between Chabahar and CPEC will change the bitter feeling between Pakistan, India, and Iran. India's inclusion in CPEC will change India's perception about claims that CPEC passes through the disputed territory of Gilgit–Baltistan. South Asia has been one of the least integrated regions in the world, though the region has huge potential for economic growth. The regional cooperation in CPEC would improve the overall status of cross-border electricity and trade volumes between the countries of the region, thus removing the trade barriers.

Pakistan is geopolitically the most suitable corridor for transit and trade activities, and it provides a gateway to South Asia, Central Asia, West Asia, and East Asia. Pakistan's role in the Cold War and post-Cold War was important due to its geostrategic position near the two powerful countries of China and India. But it was not successful in utilizing its strategic position in the region in such a way that can prove beneficial for itself as well for the whole region. The states of Central Asia have always looked for regional markets like India, Pakistan, China, and West Asia. Tajikistan and Afghanistan both have transient agreements signed with Pakistan and China as a part of the CPEC program, which will allow their goods to reach regional as well as global markets. Pakistan also desires to reach resource-rich countries of Central Asia for trade and energy. Pakistan should move toward an export-oriented economy and must search for new markets in India and its neighboring countries. CPEC seems to be the best asset that Pakistan has to expand its trade with China, Central Asia, and South Asia.

The economic and infrastructure connection of CPEC can resolve the political and security problems in Southeast Asia. CPEC can ease tensions between China and the countries of East Asia who have conflicting claims of the Spratly Islands in the South China Sea. The presence of the global hegemon—the United States—may deteriorate the security tensions between China and its neighbors that are at odds with China. Gwadar Port is only 400 kilometers away from the Strait of Hormuz, thus reducing China's maritime transportation costs and distance from 12,000 kilometers to 3,000 kilometers. Currently China imports 80% of its oil and energy through Malacca Strait. But, after President Obama's rebalance policy, the Asia Pacific has achieved a higher strategic importance. The trans-Pacific treaty between the United States and some countries in East Asia bears witness to this (Ali, 2016).

Russia, which has been a historic friend of India and an adversary to Pakistan, has realized the strategic importance of Pakistan in an emerging multipolar world. The relations between Russia and Pakistan are improving. After the end of the ideological rivalries of the Cold War, the strategic alignment in South Asia has changed. Pakistan has turned eastward toward China while India has moved toward the Western world. In contemporary global politics, Pakistan is understood as the staunch ally of China, and India is being considered as a balancer between Russia and the United States. India is keen in supporting the U.S. policy of containing China. In addition to this, India considers Pakistan as a Chinese proxy and, therefore, a threat for its western borders. Though rivalry between India and Pakistan has not been reduced, they are ready to give Eurasian multilateral institutions a chance to improve the overall status of regionalism in South Asia; that is witnessed from India and Pakistan's entry into the Shanghai Cooperation Organization.

It is easy for India to develop friendly relations with the states of Central Asia, as India was close to the Soviets during the Cold War, of which India was a part of the Central Asian states. India has no direct access to Central Asia; but it needs new markets for its industrial products and energy to fuel its own industries. Pakistan is located at such a geographic position that it can function as a transit corridor between Central Asia and South Asia. Although a security tension in Afghanistan is the main problem, almost every Central Asian and South Asian link will have to traverse through Afghanistan. With the completion of the Gwadar Port in 2005, China was given permission to station its navy at Gwadar to project its power in the Arabian Sea and the Persian Gulf. The states of Central Asia have deep religious, cultural, and economic bonds with South Asian states, mainly with Pakistan and India. If Central Asia and South Asia improve their geoeconomic ties, they can assist each other in overcoming economic crisis (Naseem & Younas, 2016).

Problems of Regional Connectivity

Pakistan, with its geographic position, has the potential to transform the landlocked countries of Central Asia as progressive centers for trade and energy, thus giving them a regional connection with South Asia. The energy reserves of Central Asia are pertinent for industrial demands of "Shining India" (Naseem & Younas, 2016). However, India has no physical connection to Central Asia. Therefore, the land link of India to Central Asia is only possible through Pakistan and China. However, India and Pakistan are still thinking through the lens of neorealism that relative gains can be turned into aggressive military behavior. Therefore, India is trying to create hurdles in CPEC by supporting the separatists in Baluchistan Province in Pakistan and is claiming that CPEC passes through disputed territories of Gilgit and Baltistan. Pakistan should make a genuine attempt to include India in CPEC as currently Pakistan can connect CPEC with the Central Asian states. However, to connect CPEC with the South Asian states, India must be taken on board. Therefore, to utilize CPEC and the geographic location of Pakistan, the countries of Central and South Asia should try to come up with cooperative strategies with the desire to economically integrate the regions of Central and South Asia, and then the region can witness genuine peace and prosperity.

Conclusion

Central Asia and South Asia will have to form regional connections if they want to improve their economies in a globalized world. Pakistan offers a best option for regional connectivity between Central Asia and South Asia through the Chinese-funded CPEC program. The major hurdle in any such Central Asia–South Asia regional integration may stem from Indo–Pak rivalry. However, it is expected that economic benefits may quell the security concerns in the region and lead to regional integration; Central Asia and South Asia will witness stability, peace, and prosperity.

REFERENCES

Ali, A. (2016). China Pakistan Economic Corridor: Prospects and challenges for regional integration. *Arts and Social Sciences Journal, 7*(4). https://www.omicsonline.org/open-access/china-pakistan-economic-corridor-prospects-and-challenges-for-regionalintegration-2151-6200-1000204.php?aid=77852&view=mobile

Bull, H. (2012). *The anarchical society: A study of order in world politics.* Palgrave Macmillan.

Buzan, B. (2014). *An introduction to the English School of International Relations: The societal approach.* John Wiley & Sons.

China Pakistan Economic Corridor. (n.d.). *Introduction.* CPEC. http://cpec.gov.pk/introduction/1

Dixit, S. (2015). *Central Asia South Asia interface: Issues and challenges* [LinkedIn post]. Linked In. https://www.linkedin.com/pulse/central-asia-south-interface-issues-challenges-dr-sonam-dixit

European Commission. (2022). *The European Union: What it is and what it does.* https://op.europa.eu/webpub/com/eu-what-it-is/en/

Fujimura, M. (2004, November). *Cross-border transport infrastructure, regional integration, and development.* Think Asia. https://think-asia.org/handle/11540/3604

Council on Foreign Relations Education. (2016). *What is globalization?* Globalization 101. http://www.globalization101.org/what-is-globalization/

Hanif, M. (n.d.). *CPEC: Its impact on peace making in South Asia.* Pakistan Observer. https://pakobserver.net/cpec-impact-peace-making-south-asia/

Korybko, A. (2015). *Pakistan is the "zipper" of pan-Eurasian integration.* Russia Institute of Regional Studies.

Naseem, N., & Younas, I. (2016) Regional bonds between Central Asia and South Asia. *Journal of Political Studies, 29*(2), 168–180.

Roland-Holst, D. (2009). Infrastructure as a catalyst for regional integration, growth, and economic convergence: Scenario analysis for Asia. In F. Zhai (Ed.), *From Growth to Convergence* (pp. 108–149). Palgrave Macmillan.

CHAPTER THIRTEEN | ASMA SHAHEEN AND
NAZIA IQBAL

The Role of Family Systems on Couples' Life Satisfaction and Anxiety Levels

Marriage is a social contract that bonds together the single unit often known as a family. It is important to note that it is not only a legal contract, but also a social contract, as a mere legal contract could not provide such a strong sense of emotional bonding and feelings of possession for their relation. Although marriage is considered one of the strongest relationships, more recently marriage has become increasingly difficult for such reasons as more awareness and information available to spouses regarding their rights, increased lack of tolerance, industrial and corporate growth making people more materialistic, and stress, which is increasing day by day.

There is no systematic definition of the term "family"; the term has different meanings for everyone. One may define family as consisting of only a husband, wife, and their dependent children; others may define family as consisting of all close relatives, including sisters, brothers, nephews, parents, grandparents, in-laws, and more. It depends on the circumstances of each individual's environment and perceptions (Pimentel, 2000).

Family systems theory posited by Ludwig von Bertalanffy (1975) widened the span of family research to include all members of the family, instead of only the mother. Family is primarily classified into the following two categories:

- Nuclear
- Joint family

A nuclear family system is defined as a husband, wife, and their dependent children. There are many advantages of living in a nuclear family system, including the freedom to make decisions and engaging in personal growth for the well-being of oneself and one's family. However, in a nuclear family system, neither the husband nor wife have additional supports to fulfill their duties and must manage the tasks and challenges of their lives without any external support (Caruso & Timmermann, 2013).

Joint family systems do not have a clear-cut scientific definition. Generally, those living together have significant influence on each other, have direct or indirect blood relation, and offer unconditional support. One of the many advantages of joint family systems is that in difficult times, one has the support of multiple family members. All members of the family do not have similar skills and potential to grow themselves due to individual differences; that is why with the support of joint family systems, opportunities can be expanded to become a successful person. There are noticeable disadvantages of joint family systems as well. Sometimes one member of the family may have to work harder and sacrifice comfort for the betterment of other family members, but other family members do not agree to work hard and sacrifice the same, beyond a certain level, which leads to injustice (Caruso & Timmermann, 2013).

Some other factors related to joint family systems can lead to dissatisfaction as well as lack of freedom, more formal behaviors, interference, conflict of interests, generation gaps, and more. A commonly observed problem is that each member of the family feels that they sacrifice more than the other family members and deserve more praise, care, and recognition. There are no standardized parameters to determine which family system is superior to the other, but rather it depends on the nature of the familial relationships, circumstances, and behaviors of all members of the family (Caruso & Timmermann, 2013).

In the 1960s, the term "life satisfaction" gained attention in the field of research. Life satisfaction is a term used to describe the way an individual evaluates their existence as well as life and the way an individual perceives themself in the future. Well-being can be described as the measure of life satisfaction and can be evaluated in terms of self-concepts, self-perceived ability to cope with daily life, mood, and satisfaction with relations as well as with their achieved goals. It measures the overall behaviors and attitudes of one's life rather than just focusing on current feelings (Bailey et al., 2007).

Anxiety can be stated as the feelings of dread in anticipation of events, some somatic symptoms, inner conflicts, and some nervous behaviors such as confusion. There is a difference in the meanings of fear and anxiety. Anxiety is the anticipation of future threat, while fear is a response to a real, immediate threat. It is the overreactions to the situations that usually become generalized as a whole and subjectively anticipated threatening situation (Davison et al., 2008).

According to the American Psychological Association, dissatisfaction leads to anxiety in the family system in which one is living. Anxiety has both psychological and physical impacts on one's life. Psychological symptoms can include feeling worried; remaining uneasy most of the time; having difficulties in sleep and concentration, which make one tired; remaining overalert and irritable; and feelings of dependency on others and needing frequent reassurance from them. Physical symptoms are also obviously noticed in an anxious person because in a stressful situation, the body releases stress hormones such as adrenaline and cortisol. These hormonal releases turn into some physical symptoms like increased heart rate and sweating, fast breathing, palpitations, feeling sick, chest pains, headaches, loss of appetite, and feeling faint (American Psychological Association, 2013).

Premilla D'Cruz and Shalini Bharat (2001) investigated joint and nuclear family systems in Indian family setups. Pakistan and India were divided into two parts after the division of the subcontinent. Their traditions, living styles, and a few customs are similar. D'Cruz and Bharat found that while many believe that the joint family system was joint, overtaken more recently by the nuclear family system due to the flourishing of industrialization and urbanization, the truth is more complex. The main idea behind that study was to examine and explore the diversity in Indian family types, which tells us that "a multiplicity of family patterns including joint families, nuclear families, single parent families, dual earner families and adoptive families have always coexisted, illustrating the presence of family plurality in the Indian context" (2001, p. 185).

Because in the 20th century people had limited access to information, the joint family system was believed to be the best living system, but later on that perspective was complicated by having more understanding, information, and perceptions. This additional information also drew attention to some of the negative aspects of the joint family system (i.e., it can restrict the capabilities that make a person unique). The joint family system makes everyone dependent on each other, but today's world is a world of ambitions for everyone. Individuality is not possible in joint families. Now persons are familiar with their needs, rights, and desires due to education, which makes them ready to live on their own rather than just depending on families.

A study of the influence of marital quality of life and family patterns of nuclear and joint family systems on adolescents' mental health was conducted by Sumaira Rashid (2014). Adolescents' age ranged from 17 to 19 years, and they belonged to different socioeconomic statuses. The conclusion of the study revealed the phenomenon that parental marital satisfaction is greater in a joint family system than nuclear family system. Moreover, parental marital satisfaction was found to have a great influence on the mental health of adolescents, whether they grew up in a joint or nuclear family system.

A study of life satisfaction and family strengths of couples was carried out by Gregory F. Sanders and James Walters (1985). The quality of family interaction was investigated among married elderly adults and their offspring. Three factors were mainly analyzed: health status, family strengths, and job prestige. The phenomenon of life satisfaction was found to be different among men and women. Women rated high on perceptions about health, family strengths, and job strength. Men scored high in family strengths, job prestige, and financial aid.

Emilia Oprisan and Daniel Cristea (2012) proposed a study to find influential factors in successful marital relationships. Although much research has been done on finding life satisfaction among couples, there still is not any way of keeping marital relationships secure. The researchers found some factors for unsuccessful marriages like low self-esteem, difficulty in communication between couples, and unhappy thought patterns, regardless of their relationship duration. The crux of the study was that duration of relationships does not matter for having life satisfaction; rather, there are other factors involved in dissatisfaction, for example, healthy communication between couples, strong self-esteem, and thought patterns.

Another study was conducted by Nadia Arif (2011 to find out the relation of life satisfaction with different types of marriages. The researcher distributed her research in three studies. In the first study, she explored three marriage types: marriage without parental approval, arranged marriage, and marriage by choice with parental approval. In the second study, views of single and married men and women were investigated to determine what views they have about how life satisfaction correlates to different marriage types. The views of single and married persons were quite opposite. Married persons significantly scored higher marital satisfaction in marriage by their own choice, while bachelors scored high on marital satisfaction in marriage by choice with parental permission. A third study explored the marital satisfaction in existing marriage types, whatever it was. Study results showed that marriage by choice with parental approval scored higher than the other two types of marriages (arranged or marriage by choice without parental approval).

Amarah Qureshi (2012) conducted a study to investigate the relationship of social support and life satisfaction in older adults from nuclear and joint family systems. It was observed that older adults from joint families were more satisfied and socially supported as compared to older adults from nuclear families. No gender differences were found for having social support and life satisfaction.

Jeffrey Dew (2008) found debt in his study was a serious threat to the marital satisfaction of newlywed couples, but it does not explain the linkage between these two variables. According to his study, marital satisfaction decreases as a result of increase or changes in debt. Resultantly, newlywed couples spend most of the time talking about money instead of having healthy communication and understanding with each other. They also become unable to spend positive time with each other, which they dreamt of before marriage.

Life satisfaction and anxiety among couples is not new in research. The new perspective of this study was that it dealt with life satisfaction and anxiety in couples from different family structures simultaneously. This research also studied the family systems of Pakistan (nuclear and joint family) with variables of life satisfaction and anxiety. This study further considered what gender differences can be found among men and women from each couple who are from two different family systems. The present study uncovered the relationships between anxiety and life satisfaction among couples from different family structures as well as dealt with the gender differences with the two above-mentioned variables. Another important area of conducting this research study was to examine the recent trends of living in society in comparison with past trends. It had been observed that people are now considering and preferring to live separately because of the change in their perceptions, or requirements, of their lives. So the measurements of life satisfaction, anxiety, happiness, anger, and more, also changed. Gender roles and values (among men and women) have also been affected by all that. So the researchers felt the need to measure these gender differences on the variables of life satisfaction and anxiety as well as to uncover the fluctuating patterns of living styles (nuclear and joint).

Hypotheses

- Joint family systems will have higher anxiety and lower life satisfaction levels.
- Nuclear family systems will have lower anxiety and higher life satisfaction levels.

- Life satisfaction and anxiety levels significantly differ among men and women belonging to joint and nuclear family systems.
- Women from nuclear family systems will have significantly higher levels of life satisfaction and lower levels of anxiety.
- Women belonging to joint family systems will have significantly higher levels of anxiety and lower levels of life satisfaction.
- Men from nuclear family systems will have significantly higher levels of anxiety and lower levels of life satisfaction.
- Men belonging to joint family systems will have significantly higher levels of life satisfaction and lower levels of anxiety.

Sample

In the present study, the sample was collected through a purposive sampling technique because there was a selected sample with some specific characteristics. Research subjects in the current study were from newlywed couples up to 15 years of marital status. The sample of this research was comprised of 100 subjects (N = 100), out of which a research sample of 50 (n = 50) was taken from each family structure (joint and nuclear) as 25 men (n = 25) from the nuclear family system, 25 men (n = 25) from the joint family system, 25 women (n = 25) from the nuclear family system, and 25 women (n = 25) from the joint family system.

Instruments

Two instruments were used in this study:

- Life Satisfaction Scale (Diener et al., 1985)
- Beck Anxiety Inventory (Beck et al, 1988)

Procedure

Data was collected through the above-mentioned instruments/scales from the couples of nuclear and joint family systems living in Rawalpindi and Islamabad city. All of the research participants were approached directly as well as through mail and guided properly by applying means for collection of research data. They were briefed about the topic of the study and purpose of the study. Informed consent was secured from the participants individually. Instructions

Table 1. Frequency and percentage of participants.

Demographic Variables	f	%
Age		
Young Adulthood (19–40 years)	95	95.0
Middle Adulthood (40–65 years)	5	5.0
Gender		
Male	50	50.0
Female	50	50.0
Family System		
Nuclear	50	50.0
Joint	50	50.0

about the scales were given to them at every stage and when requested by anyone. These questionnaires were collected after three or four days of distribution in the period of three months.

Results

Descriptive statistics of the scale were checked to determine the alpha coefficients of the scale, and its values of skewness and kurtosis were computed to check the assumptions of normality.

Table 1 shows the frequency and percentage of the married couples with respect to age, gender, and family system. Male participants ($f = 50$, 50.0%) were equal in number to female participants ($f = 50$, 50.0%). Couples belonging to the nuclear family system ($f = 50$, 50.0%) were also equal in number with the joint family system ($f = 50$, 50.0%). Participants belonging to young adulthood ($f = 95$, 95.0%) were greater in number than participants belonging to middle adulthood ($f = 5$, 5.0%).

Participants belonging to young adulthood were more satisfied ($M = 26.4$, $SD = 6.30$) and less anxious ($M = 31.2$, $SD = 8.64$). Participants belonging to middle adulthood were less satisfied ($M = 20.4$, $SD = 5.45$) and more anxious ($M = 32.2$, $SD = 7.27$).

Table 2 shows the psychometric properties of study variables. The reliability analysis indicated that the reliability coefficients of the life satisfaction and anxiety scales were 0.81 and 0.80, respectively, which indicated satisfactory internal consistency. The values of skewness and kurtosis for the life satisfaction

Table 2. Psychometric properties of study variables.

Variables	n	M	SD	α	Range Potential	Range Actual	Skewness	Kurtosis
Satisfaction with Life Scale	100	32.20	7.22	0.81	1–35	21–52	0.90	0.24
Anxiety	100	26.11	6.38	0.80	1–84	8–35	−0.75	0.08

Table 3. Mean, standard deviation, and *t* values for married couples, living in nuclear and joint family systems, on Life Satisfaction and Anxiety scales.

Variables	Nuclear (n = 50) M	Nuclear (n = 50) SD	Joint (n = 50) M	Joint (n = 50) SD	t(98)	p	95% CI LL	95% CI UL	Cohen's d
Satisfaction with Life Scale	33.40	6.40	30.92	7.82	1.73	0.10	0.40	5.31	0.35
Anxiety	24.70	6.80	27.54	5.70	2.30	0.02	5.33	0.40	0.50

Note: CI = Class Interval; M = Mean; SD = Standard Deviation; LL = Lower Limit; UL = Upper Limit

and anxiety scales were less than one, which indicated that univariate normality was not problematic.

Table 3 shows mean standard deviation and *t* values for married couples living in nuclear and joint family systems on the scales of life satisfaction and anxiety. Results indicated significant mean differences on life satisfaction with $t(98) = 1.73, p < 0.1$. The findings show that the couples from the nuclear family system significantly scored higher on life satisfaction ($M = 33.40, p < 0.1$) as compared with the couples from the joint family system ($M = 30.92, p < 0.1$). Results indicated significant mean differences on anxiety with $t(98) = 2.30, p < 0.05$. The findings show that couples of joint family systems ($M = 27.54, p < 0.05$) significantly scored higher on anxiety as compared to couples from nuclear family systems ($M = 24.70, p < 0.05$). The result is statistically significant.

Couples From Nuclear and Joint Family Systems

Table 4 shows mean standard deviation and *t* values for male and female research participants on the scales of life satisfaction and anxiety. Results indicated significant mean differences on life satisfaction with $M = t(98) = -0.55, p > 0.1$. The findings show that the women significantly scored higher

Table 4. Mean, standard deviation, and *t* values for men and women on Life Satisfaction and Anxiety scales.

Variables	Female (Nuclear Family) (n = 25)			Male (Nuclear Family) (n = 25)			Female (Joint Family) (n = 25)			Male (Joint Family) (n = 25)			F	P
		95% CI			95% CI			95% CI			95% CI			
	M(SD)	LL	UL	M(SD)	LL	UL	M(SD)	LL	UL	M(SD)	LL	UL		
Satisfaction with Life Scale	28.2(8.95)	20.3	26.1	26.1(6.38)	23.4	28.7	23.1(3.38)	26.3	29.9	27.9(6.75)	24.1	29.7	2.81	0.04
Anxiety Scale	31.7(6.93)	30.8	36.5	33.0(5.93)	30.6	35.5	35.4(7.77)	28.1	34.6	30.4(8.00)	27.1	33.7	1.09	0.03

Note: CI = Class Interval; M = Mean; SD = Standard Deviation; LL = Lower Limit; UL = Upper Limit

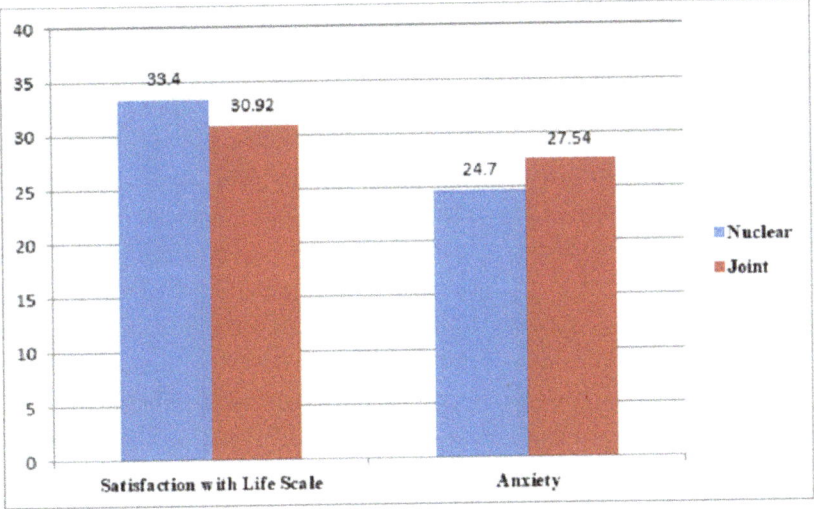

Fig. 1. Graphical representation of mean differences among couples from nuclear and joint family systems on Life Satisfaction and Anxiety scales.

on life satisfaction ($M = 32.60, p > 0.1$) as compared with men ($M = 31.80, p > 0.1$). Results indicated significant mean differences on anxiety with $t(98) = 0.70, p < 0.05$. The findings show that female research participants ($M = 25.70, p > 0.1$) scored significantly lower on anxiety as compared with male research participants ($M = 26.54, p > 0.1$).

Results shown in Table 5 indicated significant differences among men and women belonging to nuclear and joint family systems on life satisfaction and anxiety. Results revealed that women from the nuclear family system scored higher on life satisfaction ($M = 28.2, p > 0.1$) compared to women from the

Table 5. F values and significance of difference between men and women on Life Satisfaction and Anxiety scales (N = 100).

Variables	Female (Nuclear Family) (n = 25)			Male (Nuclear Family) (n = 25)			Female (Joint Family) (n = 25)			Male (Joint Family) (n = 25)			F	P
		95% CI			95% CI			95% CI			95% CI			
	M(SD)	LL	UL	M(SD)	LL	UL	M(SD)	LL	UL	M(SD)	LL	UL		
Satisfaction with Life Scale	28.2(8.95)	20.3	26.1	26.1(6.38)	23.4	28.7	23.1(3.38)	26.3	29.9	27.9(6.75)	24.1	29.7	2.81	0.04
Anxiety Scale	31.7(6.93)	30.8	36.5	33.0(5.93)	30.6	35.5	35.4(7.77)	28.1	34.6	30.4(8.00)	27.1	33.7	1.09	0.03

Note: *CI* = Class Interval; *M* = Mean; *SD* = Standard Deviation; *LL* = Lower Limit; *UL* = Upper Limit

joint family system ($M = 23.1, p > 0.1$). Men belonging to the joint family system came up with the higher levels of life satisfaction ($M = 27.9, p > 0.1$) compared to men from the nuclear family system ($M = 26.1, p > 0.1$). Results indicated that women from the nuclear family system scored lower on anxiety ($M = 31.7, p > 0.1$) compared to women belonging to the joint family system ($M = 35.4, p > 0.1$). Men belonging to the joint family system came up with lower levels of anxiety ($M = 30.4, p > 0.1$) compared to men from the nuclear family system ($M = 33.0, p > 0.1$). It was also observed that women from the nuclear family system scored higher on life satisfaction ($M = 28.2, p > 0.1$), while men from the nuclear family system showed lower signs of life satisfaction ($M = 26.1, p > 0.1$). Women from the joint family system showed higher signs of anxiety ($M = 35.4, p > 0.1$), while men belonging to the joint family system scored vice versa ($M = 30.4, p > 0.1$).

Discussion

The objective of this study was to explore the role of life satisfaction and anxiety in family systems in accordance with gender. In this study the joint family system was observed as having higher levels of anxiety and lower levels of life satisfaction compared with those who were living in the nuclear family system. Different demographics were used in the current study, but three main focused variables were observed: age, gender, and family system. Along with the demographic sheet/consent form, two main questionnaires were used in the present study: Life Satisfaction Scale (Diener et al., 1985) and Anxiety Scale (Beck, 1990). The collection of data from couples was a difficult task due to some reasons like most couples being unwilling or hesitant to share their personal information.

It was hypothesized that the joint family system would have higher anxiety levels and lower life satisfaction levels. It was predicted that the nuclear family system would have lower anxiety and higher life satisfaction levels. It was assumed that life satisfaction and anxiety levels would significantly differ among men and women belonging to joint and nuclear family systems. It was hypothesized also that women from the nuclear family system would have significantly higher levels of life satisfaction and lower levels of anxiety. Results showed that women belonging to the joint family system had significantly higher levels of anxiety and lower levels of life satisfaction. It was predicted that men from the nuclear family system would have significantly higher levels of anxiety and lower levels of life satisfaction. It was also assumed that men belonging to the joint family system would have significantly higher levels of life satisfaction and lower levels of anxiety.

Table 1 shows demographic details of the participants, which include respondents' frequencies and percentages of the couples belonging to joint and nuclear family systems with respect to age, gender, and family systems. Frequency and percentage of the couples were equal on gender and family systems, while couples belonging to the young adulthood stage were greater in number as compared to middle adulthood.

According to the first hypothesis, living in the joint family system results in higher anxiety and lower life satisfaction levels. Results of the present study also supported that those couples who are currently living jointly are not as satisfied in life or have more difficulty in finding happiness and peace. Instead, they have greater levels of anxiety and stress.

Bowen et al's (1957) study focused on living systems and their effects on life satisfaction and anxiety. He supported the idea that living systems/family have great impact on a person's well-being and emotional development. He also argued that healthier lifestyles can enhance positive effects on personality.

Because in the 20th century people had limited access to information, the perceptions about the joint family system as the best living system persisted, but now we have more understanding, information, and perceptions. It also drew attention to some of the negative aspects of the joint family system. It can dampen and restrict a person's capabilities that make them unique. The joint family system makes everyone dependent on each other, but today's world is a world of ambitions for everyone. Individuality is not possible in joint families. Now persons are familiar with their needs, rights, and desires due to education, which makes them ready to live on their own rather than depending on extended families.

According to the second hypothesis, living in the nuclear family system positively results in higher life satisfaction and lowers anxiety levels. Results of the present study also supported that those couples who are currently living separately are much more satisfied with life. They also have lessened anxiety and stress.

According to the rest of hypotheses, men and women from joint and nuclear family systems differ in life satisfaction and anxiety levels. Results showed significant differences among men and women belonging to the nuclear and joint family systems on life satisfaction and anxiety. Results revealed that women from the nuclear family system scored higher on life satisfaction compared to women from the joint family system. Men belonging to the joint family system came up with higher levels of life satisfaction compared to men from the nuclear family system. Results indicated that women from the nuclear family system scored lower on anxiety compared to women belonging to the joint family system. Men belonging to the joint family system came up with lower levels of anxiety compared to men from the nuclear family system. It was also observed that women from the nuclear family system scored higher on life satisfaction, while men from the nuclear family system showed lower signs of life satisfaction. Women from the joint family system showed higher signs of anxiety, while men belonging to the joint family system scored vice versa.

Ashley K. Randall and Guy Bodenmann (2009) derived the idea from their research that stress was the major focus of the last decade in marital research and showed that stress is the measure of understanding the quality of close relationships. They supported the idea that stress is the serious threat to life satisfaction. In this research three major areas were targeted by the American Psychological Association: (1) different theoretical models were assessed, (2) typologies relating to stress models were analyzed and summarized, and (3) findings of stress in couples were summarized, which had some inspirational work.

Limitations

There were some limitations in this study, which leave enough space for future researchers to investigate and refine the findings.

- First, because of the shortage of time and unavailability of the desired couples, it was quite difficult to manage a comprehensive and detailed study because some couples were not willing to participate in the study until they were debriefed. Some participants were not cooperative.

Future studies should investigate the impact of living systems with a more diverse sample.
- Second, the present research studied the impact of family systems on just two types of variables (i.e., life satisfaction and anxiety). Future research should be conducted with more than two types of variables because it is a new aspect of studying comparison between living systems, as results of this study are different from what society perceives about living systems. No other research has been found related to the current study (or may be present but not available to the researchers).
- Third, the age range of couples showed a greater barrier in finding the sample. Thus, an important part of future studies lies in studying diverse samples with a broader age range. Still an effort has been made to make the best possible contribution one could in the given time.
- Fourth, for the acceptance of this research finding, more research is highly needed because these findings are negating the most common perceptions about living styles that have been seen for centuries in much of the whole world.
- Fifth, further research should be conducted on the impact of family systems on couples' life satisfaction and anxiety because with the changing scenario around the globe, the familial patterns of living are also changing significantly. This research negates the idea of happy and satisfied living in joint family structures more than in nuclear family structures. But the sample of the study is much too small to generalize the findings of the study.
- Sixth, the technique of this study was a survey in which questionnaires were distributed in the sample of the study as an instrument. Questionnaires have a drawback in that they do not tell the whole reality and truth about the research topic. So researchers can use other methods for data collection, for a better picture of the reality.

Conclusions

In light of above findings, the following conclusions are drawn:
- Couples from the nuclear family system significantly scored higher in life satisfaction as compared with the couples from the joint family system.

- Couples from the joint family system scored significantly higher in anxiety as compared with the couples from the nuclear family system.
- Female research participants scored significantly higher in life satisfaction as compared with male participants.
- Female research participants scored significantly lower on anxiety as compared with male participants.

REFERENCES

American Psychological Association (APA). (2013). *Diagnostic and statistical manual of mental disorders* (5th ed.). American Psychiatric Publishing.

Arif, N. (2011). Marital satisfaction in relation to the types of marriage. [Unpublished thesis]. University of the Punjab.

Bailey, T., Eng, W., Frisch, M., & Snyder, C. R. (2007). Hope and optimism as related to life satisfaction. *Journal of Positive Psychology, 2*(3), 168–169.

Beck, A. T., Epstein, N., Brown, G,. & Steer, R. (1988). Beck Anxiety Inventory. APA PsycTests.

Bee, H., & Boyd, D. (2009). *The developing child* (12th ed.). Pearson.

Bertalanffy, L. V. (1975). *Perspectives on general systems theory: Scientific-philosophical studies*. George Braziller.

Bowen, M., Dysinger, P. T., Brodney, W., & Basamania, B. (1957). The development of techniques of dealing with five different family units and some patterns observed in the transaction of those families. Murray Bowen papers. Accession 2006-003, Box 4, History.

Caruso, D., & Timmermann, S. (2013, January 25). The disappearing nuclear family and the shift to non-traditional households has serious financial implications for growing numbers of Americans. Huffington Post.

Davison, C., Blankstein, K. R., Flett, G. L., & Neale, J. M. (2008). *Abnormal psychology* (3rd Canadian ed.). Wiley.

D'Cruz, P., & Bharat, S. (2001). Beyond joint and nuclear: The Indian family revisited. *Journal of Comparative Family Studies, 32*(2), 167–194. http://www.jstor.org/stable/41603742

Dew, J. (2008). Debt change and marital satisfaction change in recently married couples. *Family Relations, 57*(1), 60–71. http://www.jstor.org/stable/40005368

Diener, E., & Diener, M. (1995). Cross-cultural correlates of life satisfaction and self-esteem. *Journal of Personality and Social Psychology, 68*(4), 653–663.

Diener, E., Emmons, R. A., Larsen, R. J., & Griffin, S. (1985). The satisfaction with life scale. *Journal of Personality Assessment, 49*, 1–5.

Diener, E., Sandvik, E., Seidlitz L., & Diener, M. (1993). The relationship between income subjective well-being: Relative or absolute? *Social Indicators Research, 28,* 195–223.

Elaine, G., Eugen, L., & Merlin, B. B. (1998). Couple violence and psychological distress. *Canadian Journal of Public Health/Revue Canadienne de Sante'e Publique, 89*(1), 43–47.

Erikson, E. (1956). The problem of ego identity. *Journal of the American Psychoanalytic Association, 56*(4), 121. https://doi.org/10.1177/000306515600400104

Furler, K., Gomez, V., & Alexander, G. (2013). Personality similarity and life satisfaction in couples. *Journal of Research in Personality, 47*(4), 369–375.

Galhardo, A., Cunha, M., & Gouveia, J. (2011). Psychological aspects in couples with infertility. *Sexologies, 20*(4), 255–260. https://doi.org/10.1016/j.sexol.2011.08.005

Heller, D., Watson, D., & Hies, R. (2004). The role of person versus situation in life satisfaction: A critical examination. *Psychological Bulletin, 130*(4), 574–600. https://doi.apa.org/doi/10.1037/0033-2909.130.4.574

Larsen, R. J., Diener, E., & Emmons, R. A. (1985). An evaluation of subjective well-being measures. *Social Indicators Research, 17*(1), 1–7.

Low, N., Lihong, C., & Merikangas, K. R. (2006). Spousal concordance for substance use and anxiety disorders. *Journal of Psychiatric Research, 41*(11), 942–951. https://doi.org/10.1016/j.jpsychires.2006.11.003

Oprisan, E., & Cristea, D. (2012). A few variables of influence in the concept of marital satisfaction. *Procedia—Social and Behavioral Sciences, 33,* 468–472. https://doi.org/10.1016/j.sbspro.2012.01.165

Pavot, W. G., Diener, E., Colvin, C. R., & Sandvik, E. (1991). Further validation of the satisfaction with life scale: Evidence for the cross-method convergence of well-being measures. *Journal of Personality Assessment, 57,* 149–161.

Pimentel, E. (2000). Just how do I love thee? Marital relations in urban China. *Journal of Marriage and the Family, 62*(1), 32–47.

Qureshi, A. (2012). *Social support and life satisfaction among older adults of nuclear and joint family.* [Unpublished thesis]. University of the Punjab.

Randall, A., & Bodenmann, G. (2009). The role of stress on close relationships and marital satisfaction. *Clinical Psychology Review, 29*(2), 105–115. https://doi.org/10.1016/j.cpr.2008.10.004

Rashid, S. (2014). Marital quality and family typology: Effects on Pakistani adolescents' mental health. *European Scientific Journal, ESJ, 10*(10).

Rosario, E. (2005). The emergence of the nuclear family in Mexico. *International Journal of Sociology of the Family, 31*(1), 1–18. http://www.jstor.org/stable/23029707

Sanders, G. F., & Walters, J. (1985). Life satisfaction and family strengths of older couples. *Lifestyles: A Journal of Changing Patterns, 7*(4), 194–206.

Saroj, P., Greenhaus, J., & Granrose, C. (1992). Role stressors, social support, and well-being among two-career couples. *Journal of Organizational Behavior, 13*(4), 339–356.

Solomon, S. C. (1974). Some aspects of extended kinship in a Chinese community. *Journal of Marriage and Family, 36*(3), 628–633. http://www.jstor.org/stable/350736

Suh, E., Diener, E., Oishi, S., & Triandis, H. C. (1998). The shifting basis of life satisfaction judgments across cultures: Emotions versus norms. *Journal of Personality and Social Psychology, 74*(2), 482–493.

Wilder, E. (2003). *The theoretical basis for the life model, Appendix B: research and resources on human development. The Complete Guide to Living with Men.* http://en.wikipedia.org/wiki/Erikson%27s_stages_of_psychosocial_development

SECTION THREE

Pedagogy and Our International, Intercultural Classrooms

CHAPTER FOURTEEN | ANIRBAN RAY

Internationalization of Classrooms Through Cultural Hybridity
Pedagogical Design and Challenges

One of the most visible symptoms of globalization in academics is the emergence of cross-national circular development practices across disciplines. Perhaps nothing has been more endemic to any social institution than the impacts of globalization on higher education (HE) in creating international learning spaces within classrooms. The phenomenon has found traction with institutional administrators insofar as disciplinary initiatives are undertaken to eliminate political and cultural boundaries with integrative learning practices to help leverage institutional images of diversity and inclusivity.

Historically, study abroad programs acted as the main conduit for training students in cross-cultural activities through structured opportunities that involve students learning about the target culture in situ by working on projects under faculty guidance. These short-lived, faculty-led programs are based on the conviction that participating students benefit academically and culturally more than those who do not visit "a foreign culture" under similar circumstances (Santos, 2014). While it is established that study abroad programs integrate immersive learning experience, it is equally true that students in their home country do have immense opportunity to meaningfully engage with international audiences through faculty-initiated curricular participation.

The internationalization of classrooms and curricula can function as a complementary approach to immersive learning, such as through study abroad frameworks, with the sole agenda to encourage students to explore other cultures. The approach underpins cultural hybridity by creating curricular assets in terms of assignments and projects in which students from different cultural backgrounds collaborate with their peers in responding to a common problem. Such a pedagogic approach can help create structures of common engagement that focus not only on developing tools of assessment but also on creating an integrative understanding of cultures through a corpus of shared scholarship.

This essay illustrates two different approaches to the internationalization of classroom experience through two case studies in humanities, at the graduate and ungraduated levels, involving a midsized regional public university in the United States and an international research institution in Pakistan. The main purpose is to discuss the case studies in terms of the background, design, and challenges of making learning experiences truly international. The discussion highlights curriculum designs in two English professional writing (PW) courses: (1) a graduate course, ENG 553: Understanding Intercultural and Global Communication, where American and Pakistani students collaborated on a final project; and (2) an undergraduate course, ENG 312: Writing for Business, in which American students promoted ecotourism in Pakistan by collaborating with students from another undergraduate course in ENG 393: Writing in the Scientific Disciplines, a service course in PW specifically designed for environmental science (EVS) majors. To this end, the essay underlines internationalization as an established concept practiced within HE as a result of global intellectual interdependence and a knowledge-sharing mechanism among scholars, institutions, and the nations. Often, though not always, such mechanisms rely on the institutional ecosystem of information and communication technologies (ICTs).

The Internationalization of Higher Education

Scholars have argued that exposing students to intercultural situations alone does little to improve their understanding of another culture (Kelly, 1963). What is rather more important is to create proper learning opportunities and communicative spaces through education that can facilitate the understanding of complex events and experiences outside a student's own identity (Smith & Mikelonis, 2011, pp. 89–90). A key to providing access to such a framework of learning is to internationalize classrooms through curricular changes.

The traditional approach to teaching intercultural communication in PW courses is largely discursive and hinges on theorizing foundational concepts in intercultural communication (Matveeva, 2008), which are then translated to a series of assignments and readings. With the speedy adoption of the ICTs into writing classrooms, especially in PW and technical communication, curricula are now increasingly focusing more and more on examining cultures in their situated contexts by engaging with audiences who are located in geographically distant contexts. This reconceptualization of pedagogy is facilitated by the internationalization of the entire curriculum that leads to a deeper engagement across identities, attitudes, beliefs, and perceptions.

Benefits of internationalization have been well argued and established mainly as it serves both academic and professional requirements (Qiang, 2003; Altbach & Knight, 2007; Thrush & Thevenot, 2011). First, internationalization addresses the growing demand for creating a global workforce that can interoperate in different cultural contexts. Second, the academic premise is based on creating opportunities for native students to interact with people who are culturally different so that these students are then able to construct more informed perceptions of events with respect to their position in a globalized reality. However, internationalization is sometimes confused with globalization, of which it is an outcome, and therefore clarifying the difference in the two terms is an important first step toward understanding the engagement matrix in the two case studies.

There are two major construals to internationalization. The first is the difference in scope as understood by the terms internationalization and globalization. Second, and more importantly, is the singular distinction of internationalization as applied in HE. Globalization remains a complex phenomenon to define, although for the purposes of the discussion the term can be understood to create a "spatial awareness or to highlight a transformation in the processes of interaction among individuals and groups" (Mitchell & Nielsen, 2012). Globalization reorients our sense of space and time, so much so that geographic distances are framed in terms of the amount of time it requires to access information on and about specific locations (Tomlinson, 1999, cited in Mitchell & Nielsen, 2012) rather than the actual physical gap that separates the distances. At the same time, the process dimension of globalization underscores the importance of social connectivity giving credence to the innovation and subsequent adoption of the ICTs. Importantly, both these conceptualizations reinforce a strong economic ethic of optimization of resources to secure competitive advantage not just over the production of goods and services for global markets, but also over creation of information as an exchangeable commodity.

In the context of HE, the two notions have come to signify a huge flow of global capital into funding both permanent and temporary structures of knowledge creation. Aided by the power of the ICTs, the institutions of HE for the first time are finding themselves in a favorable position to develop and innovate knowledge artifacts with far-reaching consequences involving not just the administrators and faculty, but more importantly students.

Now let's turn to the core notion of internationalization—the term that informs the two case studies in the following section. In the discourse of globalization, internationalization is employed to describe and assess the extent to which the institutions of HE have evolved into global actors. However, for the purpose of the essay, the author is not interested in evaluating the developmental arc of the two institutions—a midsized regional public university in the United States and an international research institution in Pakistan—with respect to the internationalization of these campuses. Thus, the use of the term is restricted to the course-level description where internationalization acts as an instrument of motivation behind the global activities that were made available to undergraduate and graduate students in ENG 312: Writing for Business and ENG 553: Understanding Intercultural and Global Communication, respectively.

There are several key concepts in the definition of internalization. At a broader level, it is understood as campus-based internationalization initiatives to encourage transnational movement of students and faculty personnel leading to four possibilities as noted by Philip G. Altbach and Jane Knight (2007), which serve predefined purposes:

1. "Cross-border supply": constitutes e-learning and distance education through franchising of courses or degrees;
2. "Consumption abroad": underlines the traditional notion of students migrating to the provider country;
3. "Presence of natural persons": involves temporary exchanges and visits of intellectual workers like professors and researchers; and
4. "Commercial presence": comprises service providers establishing branch campuses/joint ventures with local institutions.

At its core, internationalization is conceptualized as a "process of integrating international or inter-cultural dimensions into the teaching, research and service functions of HE institutions" (Knight, 1999, p. 21). Others have defined internationalization as an approach that looks at planning, preparedness, and implementation (Qiang, 2003) rather than on the purpose of adopting the mechanism. The four categories include: (a) activity approach, which is the traditional format that encourages curriculum development and student/faculty exchange; (b) competency approach that centers on orienting students and faculty toward intercultural and intersubjective awareness; (c) ethos approach that encourages the development of an "international dimension" at an institutional level that favors intercultural capacity building; and (d) process approach, which aims to integrate an international dimension within pedagogy and research practices with support coming from the programmatic and institutional level for sustainability purposes (Qiang, 2003, pp. 250–251). It is worth noting that beside the two conceptual frameworks, purpose-driven and approach-driven, a vast majority of the literature (Davis, 2003; Bhalla, 2005; Knight, 2006; Altbach & Knight, 2007) in the field seeks to understand internationalization as a phenomenon predicated on the economic and, by extension, welfare interests of participating institutions.

Evidently, various meanings are attached to the term internationalization that underline the core concept of sharing information, knowledge, and academic training by and for faculty and students. A major potential for a successful internationalization lies with the faculty willingness to design and manage appropriate course content and curriculum to provide a substantive intercultural learning experience (Gill, 2016). To that end, an important assumption driving internationalization stems from the need to create global classrooms that can embrace some complementary aspects of both purpose- and approach-driven frameworks. The convergence helps create a student-centered learning environment in which students explore and negotiate intercultural contexts with adequate curriculum support.

It is worth mentioning that the two case studies discussed in the essay embody features like cross-border supply (purpose-driven) and activity, competency, ethos, and process dimensions (approach-driven) with modifications to suit the pedagogical and student learning objectives. Importantly, both the participating institutions in the United States and in Pakistan have demonstrated evidence to support various categories (from the purpose- and approach-driven frameworks), including cross-border supply, presence of natural persons, and all four elements from the approach-driven model of institutionalization However, this essay seeks to shed light specifically on the internationalization of two English PW courses; a discussion to address institutional internationalization warrants a separate thesis altogether.

Developing Ecotourism in Pakistan: A Case Study

Rationale of the Study

The study is drawn from a PW course in the English department at the public university in the United States. The Pakistani university was directly not part of the action plan as the scope of study encompassed identifying, researching, and developing content of a phenomenon located outside of one's immediate and known contexts; however, Pakistan functioned as the cultural site of the project that students explored for the purpose of the project. The study was premised on building intrapersonal spaces of negotiation between two groups of students that shared common cultural but different educational backgrounds and skillsets. Given that the two courses were in PW, the curricular challenge was to simulate a real working context for ecotourism promotion design from planning to implementation. The students from English 312: Writing for Business were identified as project managers (PMs) and were paired with students from English 393: Writing in the Scientific Disciplines, also identified as subject matter experts (SMEs), in order to propose a viable plan for promoting ecotourism in Pakistan. ENG 393 was taught by a colleague of the author from the PW unit of the English department who volunteered enthusiastically and agreed not only to incorporate the cultural perspective to her own curriculum design, but also shared her invaluable expertise to design the main white paper assignment.

Ecotourism has become an important subject of academic discussion, especially with the United Nations declaration of the year 2002 as the International Year of Ecotourism with the aim to inject public and social awareness in the busy 21st-century lifestyle; the peer-reviewed *Journal of Ecotourism* was also established in the same year to initiate research-based dialogs in academia. According to a report published by the Center for Responsible Travel in conjunction with Stanford University, ecotourism as a concept did not exist within the broader definitions of tourism prior to the late 1970s but emerged as the "fastest growing sector of the tourism industry" by the early 1990s (Honey & Krantz, 2012, p. 11). It has been argued that the impact of ecotourism besides nature and communities can potentially serve as a vehicle for economic development in less developed countries (LCDs) in Southeast Asia in particular (Weaver & Lawton, 2007). Based on such criteria, the project identified Pakistan as a potential site of inquiry where the Ecotourism Society of Pakistan systematically integrates tourism research and economy by working with the underprivileged people living in the mountains of Pakistan. Similarly, the Sustainable Tourism Foundation Pakistan also plays a key role in promoting environmental responsibility and sustainable practices in the region with their efforts to minimize the environmental stress from indiscriminate commercial tourism. Both these organizations strive to improve the social and economic quality of life in Pakistan by foregrounding nature as the fundamental unit of development.

In the backdrop of this growing awareness to connect environmental, economic, and social concerns, the project was developed to introduce facets of the social and cultural heritage of Pakistan to the American audience through the framework of ecotourism. The initiative involved students in ENG 312: Writing for Business, an undergraduate PW course, to promote ecotourism in Pakistan and raise environmental awareness among U.S. audiences by developing white papers and poster presentations. For this purpose, the students in the business writing course collaborated with EVS majors enrolled in another PW course, ENG 393: Writing in the Scientific Disciplines. The structure encouraged both PW and EVS students to share expertise on a project involving interdisciplinary research within a cross-functional environment.

Overview of the Project

The project was part of the partnership between a midsized regional public university in the United States and an international research institution in Pakistan. As an extension of public diplomacy outreach—"Collaborative Model for Enhanced Teaching, Research, and Community Engagement"—a three-year grant was provided by the U.S. Department of State to the U.S. public university to initiate and coordinate research and collaboration. The author was awarded a mini-grant, institutionally disbursed through principal investigators at the U.S. public university, to develop curriculum with the purpose of facilitating intercultural collaboration, research, and learning.

Ecotourism is an inherently interdisciplinary pursuit that presents one approach to the "wicked problem" of humans' roles in the ecosystems they inhabit. Ecotourism strives to provide integrated, sustainable solutions to both economic and ecological problems in a given location. This project thus specifically explored and promoted ecotourism in Pakistan.

The project was divided into three main phases—research, promotion, and presentation. Research included identifying strategic ecotourism locations and collecting secondary data for the purpose of analyzing its economic and cultural impact in those regions. The section was also required to collect primary survey data from the U.S. university community to examine audience awareness on the subject of ecotourism in general and in LCDs such as Pakistan in particular. Because the phase focused on investigations on ecotourism and environmental pacts, it was broadly coordinated by the EVS majors from ENG 393 who were lending expert knowledge on the subject. This phase was instrumental in providing environmental, geographic, social, and, above all else, cultural information on a region that was understood, by an American audience, mainly through political lenses afforded by mainstream media and newspapers.

In the second phase—promotion—the primary task was planning for the promotion of ecotourism sites in Pakistan to American audiences, which mainly involved students, staff, and faculty members in the U.S. university. The promotion was carried at two levels: (1) utilizing social media such as Facebook and Twitter to promote ecotourism to a wider audience in the United States, and (2) developing a white paper for raising environmental awareness for the local, mainly campus-centric audience. Based on the results from the first phase, the PW students, acting as the PMs, were involved in content development, channel selection, and marketing strategy. They took the lead by employing various social media marketing strategies, content branding techniques through paid, earned, and owned social media, concept mapping ideas, and document design techniques. As an added contribution to the project, the teams were asked to consider sharing the content of their research through the EcoTour blog; EcoTour is an organization working for environment conservation that actively invites blog posts for their site on ecotourism and green travel among other issues.

The final phase involved designing a team poster for the end-of semester poster competition. The poster competition was designed by PW students in ENG 312. Students and faculty members from English and other departments were invited to the session. A note on the promotion and presentation merits mention here: the strategy for the marketing and design of posters were carried out with careful attention to cultural sensitivities. For instance, certain areas that were identified as politically "disturbed" were mentioned on the white paper and posters under a disclaimer with sources identified. From a purely ethical and academic integrity standpoint, it was essential to inform the target audience (in the United States) about any perceived security threats reported by sources like the CIA World Fact Book. But at the same time, the information was presented in direct quotes or under disclaimer clauses without any attempts being made to draw further political inferences.

Curricular Challenges

Logistical challenge was the major concern. Differing class schedules and disciplinary orientations were the two main factors that were difficult to resolve given the nature of the two courses. A closed Facebook group was created by the author with shared administrative rights between both instructors to introduce the two classes. It was meant to be used as a forum—an extended virtual classroom space to manage conversations.

The students were put into groups of four, two students from each course, totaling 10 groups (the two sections of ENG 312 and ENG 393 had 20 students each). Regular announcements were posted to the group interface to maintain transparency and equal accessibility to students of both courses. The posts comprised updates from each course in terms of progress, reading materials, and assignment descriptions. Students were also asked to introduce each other and to coordinate through the interface. It was a helpful window for faculty to monitor individual groups' progress without necessarily mandating additional reporting on the part of the groups.

While Facebook was used to coordinate meetings and announcements, Google Doc sites were created as working platforms for sharing content from research, promotion, and white papers. Both instructors had access to all the 10 shared Google Doc sites so they could readily intervene in case of group conflicts. Beside the structural issues, there were also concerns among students about sharing grades. They feared their grades may suffer at the hands of the instructor coordinating the other end of the project. This was easily fixed when each instructor decided to grade for their course only, relieving the students of their speculative anxiety.

Level of Internationalization

The initiative touches the core of the intercultural pedagogic practices by allowing the students to "describe, interpret, and evaluate" the context in order to understand, reflect, and revise ethnocentric biases (Smith & Mikelonis, 2011, p. 95). The study exemplifies both at the process and product levels (i.e., the three stages of the project and the final social media marketing and white paper, respectively) a shift in the cultural assumptions of the students. For instance, at the start of the project only 10% (two out of 20) students in ENG 312 could locate Pakistan on the world map, but by the end not only did everyone know where to point out the country on the world map, but they were also able to articulate names of places, cultural artifacts associated with certain regions, tribal groups living in the areas, economic and social conditions affecting those regions and their inhabitants, and measures undertaken to protect natural resources.

To that extent, the case study demonstrates defined patterns of internationalization as conceptualized in the approach-driven paradigm. The curriculum is premised on the activity approach in that it creates structured "activities" (social media marketing and white papers) targeting a particular cultural context. It shifts the learning paradigm from theorizing about a cultural context to actually engaging with it through conducting research and developing artifacts. Similarly, the curriculum links to the competency approach on levels where students in both ENG 312 and ENG 393 were introduced to the problem from their respective positions of strength acting as PMs and SMEs, respectively. Working as cohorts, the students developed an appreciation of intercultural contexts and factored their shared perspectives from a common outcome.

As noted before, although the scope of the essay sidesteps institutional capacity building at facilitating internationalization, it must be mentioned that the motivation came from a higher level of institutional partnership between the two educational institutions in the United States and Pakistan mentioned in the foregoing sections. This directly speaks to the ethos approach that embraces an "international dimension" in planning and implementation of internationalization in HE. Finally, the curriculum development highlights the relevance of the process-based approach by expanding the learning framework into an international dimension pushing the students to explore cultural contexts outside their known domains. The course and the curriculum received support from the programmatic and the institutional level, providing another level of process-based integration.

Given their disciplinary training the students within a cohort were able to converge on the project with an informed set of ideas. The case study was an opportunity to build a qualitative understanding of an environmental process through a cultural route. The approach paradigm within the internationalization framework transformed business writing and a science writing class into a format of experiential learning that involved revisiting ethnocentric assumptions about a culture that is viewed through media rather than explored through research.

Analyzing Track II Diplomacy Between India and Pakistan: A Case Study

Rationale of the Study

Viewed from a geopolitical standpoint the relationship between India and Pakistan, historically, has been fraught. Once a single nation but riven into two different political entities in 1947, India and Pakistan have tried and tested diplomatic, military, and political measures to coexist peacefully, which for differing reasons have only been partially successful. The Indian subcontinent as such, as observed by policymakers in the region and elsewhere, has remained politically very much charged and competitive. But in the backdrop of such uncertainty, the one instrument of diplomacy that has been strenuously pursued by both sides is the international game of cricket.

Cricket plays an important symbolic function for Indians and Pakistanis alike, and as such, many view cricket as a potential instrument for "track II and track III" level diplomacy, forging a bottom-up, informal channel of communications between the members of the two nations. It is argued that "'[m]odern' diplomacy is no longer only considered in terms of relations between states but must now take account of wider relationships and modes of dialogue" (Wiseman, 1999, p. 36). What is significant therefore is to cultivate a form of soft diplomacy that is accessible both in form and practice. The graduate project therefore revolved around creating a dialog between American and Pakistani students to understand the history, context, and efficacy of using cricket as a diplomatic option. It is particularly important to note that American politics have systematically played and still play an important role in the India–Pakistan relationship. As such, introducing a group of American graduate students to the relevance and the context was not too logically farfetched.

The primary objective was to facilitate a curriculum and cultural partnership between the graduate students at the two institutions in the United States and Pakistan. Admittedly, it was thought that internationalization would enable a creation of an advance-level intercultural graduate course to function as an interactive platform for students from both of these countries to generate and improve intercultural knowledge through cohort-driven experiences.

Overview of the Project

The project involved graduate-level collaboration between the American and Pakistani students from both American and Pakistani institutions. Like the previous case study, this too was made possible due to institutional initiatives undertaken by the U.S. and Pakistani institutions under funding from the U.S. Department of State. The graduate project was similarly funded as a mini-grant to design a curriculum "to promote mutual understanding through educational and cultural exchanges between American citizens and citizens of other countries" (https://www.state.gov/r/). Unlike the previous case study, however, this one actually involved students from two different cultural contexts to join forces on a common purpose. The American students in ENG 553: Studies in Rhetoric and Literacy: Understanding Intercultural and Global Communication partnered with graduate students from Pakistan to analyze the role cricket plays or can play in bridging bilateral cultural gaps between India and Pakistan.

Divided into three phases, the project required students to collaborate with their international cohorts. There were four groups with two students in each group from both institutions totaling four in each group. Given the small size of the participating students, which was 16 in total, including eight students from each institution, it was seen as an opportunity to design a curriculum having short modules with quick deliverables. What followed was an "object-oriented" model (see Table 1) divided into three phases with a defined object of delivery in each phase.

The author coordinated with his counterpart at the university in Pakistan to recruit interested students for the project. Unlike the students on the American campus who worked on the project as part of their graduate course, it was a voluntary participation for Pakistani students. After recruiting the students from the Pakistan campus, the author created a closed Facebook group where students from the two universities met and introduced themselves. Both the instructors had the administrative rights and access to the group page and were able to monitor and coordinate announcements.

The table illustrates the structure and organization of the curriculum development. In the first phase each group set up a virtual project management space such as Google Docs and performed task analysis, assigned role responsibilities, and designed a workflow process factoring in the distributed and temporal nature of the project (time difference factor). Because cricket was not a popular sport in the United States, each cohort pair educated their counterpart on the two most popular sports in the United States and Pakistan, namely, baseball and cricket, respectively. It also acted as an important icebreaker where each pair could open up to their counterpart pair within a given cohort. Each cohort also prepared a brief cultural report about the United States and Pakistan based on the five cultural dimensions of Geert Hofstede (1984)—power distance, individualism, uncertainty avoidance, masculinity, and long-terms orientation—and discussed and cross-validated information based on their cohort's findings.

Table 1. Object-oriented model of the project.

Phases	Process	Goals	Deliverable
Orientation Introduction and task analysis	Team formation	Familiarize with intercultural cohorts and establish rules of cooperation	Brief cultural report
Production Research and analysis	Collect primary and secondary data on India and Pakistan vis-à-vis conflict and track II diplomacy	Explore, theorize, and describe problems	Final project report
Presentation	Present findings before class	Share findings with instructor and other stakeholders	Multimodal presentation using PowerPoint or Prezi

The second phase focused on the history of cricketing ties between India and Pakistan and explored the notions of sports diplomacy in general and cricket diplomacy in particular. The groups collected primary data from campus surveys and secondary data from the existing literature, which included scholarly papers from Indian, American, and Pakistani scholars. The second phase was also exciting as the author promoted cricket by organizing campuswide on-field matches that involved academic and nonacademic communities in the United States and a few Pakistani scholars who were visiting the American campus under the Department of State grant. The phase culminated with a final project report from the four groups with research inputs from all 16 students.

The final phase involved a class presentation, which took place on the U.S. campus by students in ENG 553 who also represented their respective cohorts from the Pakistani institution. Using multimodal presentation techniques, the students reported on their findings on confidence building measures and strategies for rapprochement to improve the bilateral ties between India and Pakistan.

Curricular Challenges

There were a few obvious challenges facing a curriculum design of this complexity. First, it was difficult to coordinate between two international locations. Students were stressed to keep up with the time differences that had negatively impacted their collaboration process. Although Facebook and emails were used as channels of communication, the time lag influenced when and how the channels were used. Second, there were technological issues as some websites and URLs were not accessible in Pakistan, which sometimes made content sharing a huge challenge. For instance, at the time of this course, in the fall of 2015, students at the U.S. campus had to contend with the Pakistan Telecommunication Authority's ban on YouTube. Another technological complication arose from the asynchronous nature of meeting. Given the time differences, real-time Skype sessions were not possible, although students from both campuses managed to hold one single Skype session for the duration of the whole six weeks. Lastly, American students felt that their stakes in the project were much higher than their Pakistani counterparts because of the assessment process involved in the project. While participation was voluntary for Pakistani students and did not influence their academic performance, the project had direct impact on the grades of the American students.

Despite the many manifest and hidden challenges surrounding the curriculum design, the students drew a lot of intellectual and cultural capital out of the project. Some of them went beyond the Facebook group and established personal connections, while others took interest in learning more about cohorts' culture in terms of food and festivals. Given the curricular challenges as they were, the modules developed in small multiplicities with quick turnarounds proved very effective to mitigate some of the challenges of geographic and technological gaps.

Level of Internationalization

Based on the criteria set by the two partnering institutions, the graduate project encapsulated major objectives as part of its learning experience. The project aligned itself with the broader framework of internationalization, which was well defined within the institutional objectives of the Department of State grants.

Toward that end, internationalization involved linking students from both the institutions in the United States and Pakistan on a common platform with an accessible repository of resources in terms of the closed Facebook group. It also involved engaging local community, which of course was comprised of faculty members, students, and staff from across the university, but also drew individuals who were not part of the university as such. Further, the project addressed a major component of institutional requirements in the form of supporting a collaborative research initiative where students participated in the intercultural cohort and shared findings on the project. Finally, the project facilitated public lectures and dialogues by having six Pakistani scholars engaging American students in a face-to-face informal symposium.

Further appraisals reveal that curricular internationalization promoted a reconceptualization of citizenship. Internationalization is a powerful means for students to become consciousness of their entitlement to the idea of global citizenship. As pointed out, rather than characterizing themselves in terms of cultural and regional subgroups, the students started redefining their roles in terms of opportunities and interactions on an "international scale" (Mitchell & Nielsen, 2012). In their final reflection, the American students admitted that the project afforded a great opportunity to convert their fear of performance at a graduate course into an invaluable firsthand cultural experience of working with people who differed in terms of cultural and geographic identity but who shared a lot of common assumptions.

The graduate project further reflected features of process view of internationalization mainly in modified terms: (a) cross-border supply where a component of distance education was involved through the recruitment of international students, creating digital interfaces for communication, and sharing of course materials including syllabi, assignment descriptions, readings, and multimedia presentations, and (b) presence of natural persons comprised face-to-face participation of exchange professors and researchers in a classroom symposium. The symposium organized by the author invited the visiting scholars from the Pakistan university in ENG 553 to take part in an open forum discussion with students on an India–Pakistan bilateral relationship and the role U.S. diplomatic efforts could play in settling some existing disputes. Thus, the project was able to leverage internationalization best practices in providing a crucial learning experience for students located in two diverse cultural backgrounds.

Conclusion

While globalization is a condition, internationalization is a choice. Institutions that are invested in the internationalization of their campuses provide ground-level infrastructure like classroom spaces, robust hardware, appropriate software, internet bandwidth, and disciplinary freedom. At the disciplinary level, the instructor must enjoy a certain level of curricular freedom including course selection, syllabus design, and a flexible schedule. Contours of internationalization may vary, but the process itself expands the scope of intercultural learning experience and promotes mutual understanding, collaboration, and connectivity among students.

The two case studies highlight hybrid teaching and learning practices in conjunction with a supportive disciplinary and institutional ecosystem that inherently believe in the transfer of learning materials, knowledge, and logistics between courses and campuses located outside of political borders. Where in the first case study students developed an appreciation for intercultural differences and sensitivity toward handling cultural information, in the second instance, students explored cultural assets by negotiating real-life cultural contingencies—which helped students understand both the United States and Pakistan in context (i.e., outside their own territorial boundaries).

Ultimately, internationalization gains value from the conviction that the process of shaping a discourse is a social act, constructed intersubjectively, in which meaning takes form outside of the subjective self, somewhere in between the shared spaces.

REFERENCES

Altbach, P. G., & Knight, J. (2007). The internationalization of higher education: Motivations and realities. *Journal of Studies in International Education, 11*(3–4), 290–305. https://doi.org/10.1177/1028315307303542

Bhalla, V. (2005). International students in Indian universities. *International Higher Education, 41*, 8–9.

Davis, T. M. (2003). *Atlas of student mobility*. Institute of International Education.

Gill, S. (2016). Universities as spaces for engaging the other: A pedagogy of encounter for intercultural and interreligious education. *International Review of Education, 62*(4), 483–500.

Hofstede, G. (1984). Cultural dimensions in management and planning. *Asia Pacific Journal of Management, 1*, 81–99. https://doi.org/10.1007/BF01733682

Honey, M., & Krantz, D. (Eds.). (2012). *Alternative models and best practices for sustainable coastal tourism: A framework for decision makers in Mexico*. Center for Responsible Travel.

Kelly, G. A. (1963). *A theory of personality*. W. W. Norton & Co., Inc.

Knight, J. (1999). Internationalisation of higher education. In Organisation for Economic Co-Operation and Development (Ed.), *Quality and internationalisation in higher education* (pp. 13–28). OECD.

Knight, J. (2006). *Internationalization of higher education: New directions, new challenges. The 2005 IAU global survey report*. International Association of Universities.

Matveeva, N. (2008). Teaching intercultural communication in a basic technical writing course: A survey of our current practices and methods. *Journal of Technical Writing and Communication, 38*(4), 387–410. https://doi.org/10.2190/TW.38.4.e

Mitchell, D. E., & Nielsen, S. Y. (2012). Internationalization and globalization in higher education. In H. Cuadra-Montiel (Ed.), *Globalization—education and management agendas* (pp. 3–22). InTech Open. https://doi.org/10.5772/3256

Qiang, Z. (2003). Internationalization of higher education: Towards a conceptual framework. *Policy Futures in Education, 1*(2), 248–270. https://doi.org/10.2304/pfie.2003.1.2.5

Santos, S. D. (2014). A comprehensive model for developing and evaluating study abroad programs in counselor education. *International Journal for the Advancement of Counselling, 36*(3), 332–347. http://dx.doi.org.liblink.uncw.edu/10.1007/s10447-014-9210-7

Smith, S. L., & Mikelonis, V. M. (2011). Incorporating "shock and aha!" into curriculum design: Inter nationalizing technical communication courses. In B. Thatcher & K. St. Amant (Eds.), *Teaching intercultural rhetoric and technical communication: Theories, curriculum, pedagogies, and practices* (pp. 89–112). Baywood Pub. Co.

Thrush, E. A., & Thevenot, A. (2011). Globalizing the technical communication classroom: Killing two birds with one stone. In B. Thatcher & K. St. Amant (Eds.), *Teaching intercultural rhetoric and technical communication: Theories, curriculum, pedagogies, and practices* (pp. 65–86). Baywood Pub. Co.

Weaver, D. B., & Lawton, L. J. (2007). Twenty years on: The state of contemporary ecotourism research. *Tourism Management, 28*(5), 1168–1179. https://doi.org/10.1016/j.tourman.2007.03.004

Wiseman, G. (1999). *Polylateralism and new modes of global dialogue*. Centre for the Study of Diplomacy.

CHAPTER FIFTEEN | MICHELE PARKER

Acculturation, Identity, and Race Relations While Performing Globalization

Around the world, people within institutions of higher education participate in global initiatives, which include exchanges of student, staff, and faculty as well as joint research and teaching activities (e.g., Clark & Wilson, 2017; Cooper & Mitsunaga, 2010; Higgitt et al., 2008; University of North Carolina Wilmington, n.d.). In particular, faculty, students, and staff engage in globalization efforts to "enhance research and knowledge capacity and to increase cultural understanding" (Altbach & Knight, 2007, p. 291) as well as "enhance competitiveness, prestige and strategic alliances" (Altbach & Knight, 2007, p. 293). As society identifies and addresses topics that have worldwide implications, globalization is increasingly salient (Bottery, 2006).

Thus, it is important to consider how the field of *educational development*, known for supporting institutional change and ensuring institutional quality (Sorcinelli et al., 2005), can internally support collaborations resulting from globalization efforts. Thus far, scholars have conducted case studies of international collaborations identifying challenges and successful strategies (Clark & Wilson, 2017; Cooper & Mitsunaga, 2010; Crossley & Holmes, 2001; Hubball & Edwards-Henry, 2011). Specific to educational development, I (in Cruz, Manginelli, Parker, & Strahlman, 2018) discussed how identity shapes our professional work and evolves due to international collaborations in Latin America. To extend this work, the purposes of this essay are (1) to explore how we can use identity, race relations, and acculturation in international collaborations, and (2) to consider how specific strategies can be used in educational development to facilitate this in hopes of strengthening globalization. The definitions used are:

- Acculturation: "the dual process of cultural and psychological change that takes place as a result of contact between two or more cultural groups and their individual members" (Berry, 2005, p. 698).

- Identity: social identifiers such as ability (mental or physical), age, ethnicity, gender, race, and religion (Independent School Diversity Network, n.d.).
- Race relations: relations among and between racial groups (Bobo, 1999).
- Globalization: "increasingly frequent contacts between states, peoples, races, and religions, so that previously separate cultures are moving toward a global village" (Fei, 2005, p. 143).

Relevant Literature

The present essay summarizes theoretical and empirical work on identity, race relations, and acculturation. The essay then relates this literature to international collaborations and argues for examining these topics in our professional work. The essay's final section examines specific strategies from closely related subjects that we can use in educational development to benefit faculty, staff, and students.

Positionality

For transparency, I am writing from an American perspective. My involvement in international collaborations began in 2013. This experience includes coleading five study abroad trips (three times to Belize and twice to Ethiopia) with University of North Carolina Wilmington (UNCW) undergraduate, master's, or doctoral students who apply knowledge and skills in K–12 or postsecondary education settings internationally. My work in educational development extends a decade. It consists of working on diversity issues from various platforms (e.g., as a member of the Task Force on High Impact Practices, the UNCW Diversity Committee, the Black Faculty and Staff Association, and leading the university-wide mentoring program). My identity, not often discussed in professional contexts, is Afro-Latina. More specifically, my heritage is Panamanian. I am a woman in my late 30s with a Ph.D. in educational research, statistics, and evaluation. The latter indirectly pertains to socioeconomic class, one of the eight primary social identifiers (Independent School Diversity Network, n.d.). The social identifiers mentioned are among the salient aspects of my identity.

While leading an undergraduate internship in Belize in March 2016, a European woman approached and asked me for the daily specials in the hotel restaurant. On a different occasion, while greeting interns departing for local schools, I stood outside the hotel. I fully acknowledged that, given my race and ethnicity, I blended in with Belizeans who were cleaning and preparing the hotel rooms for guests. Since then, I have considered acculturation, identity, and race relations in the context of international collaborations in scholarly work and teaching and learning opportunities.

Identity

A plethora of literature exists on identities such as being Jewish, Arab Muslim, female in the Gambia, Latin migrants in rural Spain, or Black immigrants in the United States (e.g., Davidheiser, 2005; Gil-Lacruz et al., 2013; Ramirez-Valles, 1999; Nwadiora, 1995; Worchel, 2005). Consistent themes across the literature on identity are the importance of narratives and facilitating international dialogue and interaction across cultures (e.g., Cushner, 2005; Worchel, 2005). In his work on culture and in- and out-groups, Worchel (2005) expressed that when one group identity (e.g., religion) is salient, individuals will disadvantage the people in the out-group. Both Worchel (2005) and Berry (2005) agreed that acceptance and tolerance of cultural diversity, immigrants, and national minorities in society are embedded in one's identity. Admittedly, an array of social identifiers (e.g., age, religion, race) is multiplied by intersections of identity. Systems of oppression or discrimination affect groups of people differently (Independent School Diversity Network, n.d.). Furthermore, Fiume (2005) eloquently stated that

> rigid boundaries ... both privilege and exclude in categories they circumscribe, affect, in a determining way, everyone's life by influencing understanding of, and attitudes towards, race, class, gender, and ethnicity. Particularly significant are the implications of the attitudinal and social consequences. (p. 52)

Interactions based on in-group and out-group membership (Worchel, 2005) can exist for any social identifier (Independent School Diversity Network, n.d.) or combination of social identifiers.

Race Relations

In specific countries, the historical development and current status of race relations are examined by scholars such as Fei (2005), Anonymous (2014), and Miller (2011). In this essay, attention to race relations is not about understanding how a specific race shaped identity or how racial relations were institutionalized (Bobo, 1999). Instead, the focus on race relations is based on recognizing the interconnection between dimensions of dominance-oppression and inclusion-exclusion (Bobo, 1999). Recently, a course on White racism has garnered widespread attention in the United States. In a news article, Norman (2018) said people "derive, in some measure, material and psychological benefits by being racialized as white" (para. 14). According to Bobo (1999), the racialized social order involves negative stereotypes, feelings, and a commitment to relative status positioning. He said that competition and threat are at the core of racial prejudice and, naturally, racial relations. There is "a bubble of unreality as it concerns racial matters" (Norman, 2018, para. 11).

Acculturation

Indeed, the literature on acculturation reflects human diversity and individual behavior examined and understood as adaptations to ecological and cultural contexts (Berry, 2005). Empirically, scholars have documented the acculturation process for individuals and groups (e.g., Berry, 2005; Stuart & Ward, 2011). More specifically, Zanini (2014) discussed resistance and cultural identity among Italian descendants living in Brazil while dealing with gender and social class. Meanwhile, Berry (2005) examined intercultural relations and acculturation of peoples from the Pacific region spanning hemispheres. In comparison, Afable-Munsuz and colleagues (2009) researched acculturation and health in older Latino adults in the United States. Concurrently, Stuart and Ward (2011) conducted a mixed method study of Muslim youth in New Zealand.

Regarding acculturation, Worchel (2005) iterated that how groups adapt to one another can facilitate interaction. He reminded us that the in-group strongly influences an individual or group's acculturation process. There are preferred versus adopted strategies for acculturation mentioned in the literature. Additionally, seven distinct areas of acculturation, such as work, economic situations social relations, and religious beliefs/customs, are discussed. While an individual or group may assimilate one way, the host culture may have different preferences across these areas (Worchel, 2005). Like Berry (2005), this essay links acculturation and intercultural relations to the concept of differentiation. The more differentiated a person's life, the better they adapt to intercultural living.

Globalization

Our lives are linked to each other through globalization—a source of positive change and potential conflict (Marsella, 2005). Our global village (Fei, 2005) is a web of economic, political, social, technical, and environmental forces. Concomitantly, Bottery (2006) defined six kinds of globalization, namely: (1) environmental, (2) cultural, (3) demographic, (4) political, (5) American, and (6) economic. With globalization, we face challenges (e.g., hegemonic, homogenization, or sociotechnical) that are growing amidst our interdependency (Marsella, 2005). According to Cooper and Mitsunaga (2010), globalization presents challenges for faculty at colleges and universities. Specifically, cross-institutional, cross-national collaborations with faculty involvement are frequently market driven. Through cross-cultural interactions, faculty may encounter unanticipated challenges and may be unprepared to handle these challenges. With international collaborations, another potential challenge is technological (Cooper & Mitsunaga, 2010). Challenges in higher education about globalization may reverberate at the individual, group, classroom, or program level (POD Network, 2016).

Acculturation, Identity, Race Relations, and Globalization

With globalization, the constraints of geography on states, people, races, and religions are receding (e.g., Bottery, 2006; Fei, 2005). This recession has implications for social and cultural arrangements (Bottery, 2006), such as acculturation, identity, and race relations. Thus far, theoretical and empirical work on these topics, examined separately, reveals complexity. When combined and considered with "globalization work," this complexity is magnified. Given identity politics (Cho, 2010), and who experiences what in a specific context, less than positive experiences can hinder efforts while positive experiences can facilitate globalization. As Bobo (1999) remarked, race relations and prejudice are tied to attitude, affect, stereotype, and group identity. An example from an IIUI–UNCW conference session chair illustrates this:

> During a visit to the Tohono o' Odham reservation, I was stopped on my way back to Tucson by the Border Security Patrol. The officer asked for my passport. When I told him that it was with the Canadian High Commission, for visa purposes, he thought I was a Mexican who had crossed the border illegally and had fabricated this story! He appeared to have no idea about

Pakistan and spent 45 minutes doing a background check on me before he would allow me to return to Tucson. (Shaheena Ayub Bhatti, personal communication, January 12, 2018)

In this same conversation, the Pakistani scholar revealed that while standing at the bus stop, Mexicans were upset with her for not knowing Spanish—which they assumed was her native language. The layers to identity and its complexity abound. Either or both experiences could have prompted discontentment and diminished efforts to increase diplomacy between nations (e.g., Fulbright, State Department grant). Not only can melding group identity involve unnecessary racial stratification, but it can also create stressful conflicts of interest and affect real-life situations (Bobo, 1999) such as globalization.

How Are These Topics Connected to Educational Development?

Cushner (2005) dutifully articulated the importance of students and faculty understanding the world and its people. With the focus on teaching and learning communities (Felten et al., 2007), educational developers can play a role in the globalization process. Not only do we need to increase cultural understanding (Altbach & Knight, 2007) of self, this needs to occur among faculty, administrators, and students—worldwide. As faculty, we should think critically about identity, acculturation, and race relations as we participate in globalization (Bottery, 2006; Cooper, & Mitsunaga, 2010; Cushner, 2005). Through educational development initiatives faculty can enhance their skills to interact effectively with people of various identities, positively navigate race relations, and become increasing aware of concerns related to acculturation. According to the Independent School Diversity Network (n.d.), cultural competency involves "awareness of one's own cultural worldview, openness towards cultural differences, knowledge of different cultural practices and world views, as well as cross-cultural skills" (para. 3). This approach may strengthen international collaborations and our ability to affect change positively as globalization ensues.

As faculty, when do we engage in reflective practice or critical reflection for our academic/professional development (and for the benefit of others)? When do we discuss the "complexity, juxtaposition, and intersection of identities" such as gender, age, race, and religion (Romo & Chavez, 2006, p. 142)? As Erickson (1989) relayed, we can shift our reflective awareness of structures and characteristics of culture (and identity). Typically, culture becomes transparent, despite its scope and distribution (e.g., personal, familial, institutional, societal) due to the patterning of routine actions that are habitual. Hence, opportunities to apply tools and knowledge in new domains encourage people to synthesize information in new ways through authentic contexts (Erickson, 1989).

Grounded in literature, Cho (2010) described activities that can be adapted by faculty preparing for and engaging in international collaborations. The strategies can be based on (1) the project of experience, (2) the project of antisystem, and (3) the project of inclusion. Concerning the professional toolkit available to academic developers, Carew and colleagues (2008) discussed three strategies that we can employ to support culturally aware, critically responsive, and adaptive professional work. These are (1) reflective writing, (2) periodic and ongoing collegial discussion about the detail and bases of individual experiences, and (3) cowriting to explain our individual and collective practice.

Notably, preservice teachers are asked about their personal and professional identities. They are asked to clarify privilege (or lack of), reflect on transformative events and contexts surrounding their experiences, and describe their development (Romo & Chavez, 2006). In juxtaposition, as faculty in higher education, would it not benefit our students and us to do the same? These strategies may increase awareness and understanding of acculturation, identity, and race relations and strengthen the ability of faculty to engage in globalization with cultural competence. At the conference session I presented in at the Second IIUI–UNCW Conference, a person said publicly, "Even if you are a Black person, you have a good heart." This quotation reinforces the need to discuss and reflect on our professional interactions.

Forge ahead six months, and I received a two-week late assignment from a distance education student enrolled in a fully online asynchronous graduate course. From last term, I know the student is taking UNCW classes from her native African country. I asked about extenuating circumstances to ensure fair and responsive application of course policies for late work. Her email read:

> I don't often want to talk about this because the circumstances surrounding these extenuating circumstances are my decision and choice only. I have been having issues with the internet. I buy internet on gigabytes monthly. But the monthly internet I buy runs out in 2 to 3 days because of school

work meaning I need to buy another to do my work. This assignment required extensive internet access. I repeatedly searched for articles to use, especially with the age limit imposed, to no avail. After spending a lot of money on the internet last semester, all I wanted to do this time was register for an elective that may not require much, unlike my core courses until I return to the United States. Unfortunately, there was no elective available at the time of registration. Hence I registered for this class. I normally log in, download assignments, and work on them offline. The assignments that I struggle with the most are the ones that involve extensive use of the internet. I try to manage myself the best I can. Most of my late work is due to power outages and internet issues.

At once, I recognized "socioeconomic class" as one of the social identifiers in this real-world situation. In addition, I contemplate the differences in this student's experience compared to mostly White peers taking the online course in America. As a faculty member, I reflect on experiences abroad when I experienced internet issues and had pressing deadlines and the stress this caused. As a faculty member actively engaged in globalization work, how do I respond appropriately to the individual student's needs in this course? Within the classroom, as the immediate teaching and learning community? In the future, scenarios like this will likely become more prevalent.

Does globalization privilege certain groups over others resulting in inclusion or exclusion? How will faculty meet the needs of students and ultimately (and effectively) meet the goals of our institution as globalization continues? As Romo and Chavez (2006, p. 142) articulated, "…learning to think about ourselves in a 'broader' context, making crossings and connections, reflecting on our position and power, and articulating a vision of social justice are necessary civic skills" for globalization. This information applies across key audiences (e.g., faculty, postdoctoral scholars, administrators, graduate students) in educational development (POD Network, 2016).

Conclusion

This essay relates literature on identity, race relations, and acculturation to globalization and argues we should examine these topics in our professional work. Examples from international collaborations and globalization efforts are provided, along with strategies that faculty can use to further this work in educational development. As practicing educators, reflecting on our personal and professional identities seems advantageous. Reflection can positively affect how we relate to one another and strengthen teaching and learning communities as globalization occurs. We need to increase cultural understanding to facilitate working together. Awareness of acculturation, identity, and race relations can prompt changes professionally as we practice the mantra *think globally and act locally*. Globalization provides increased opportunities for us to learn about ourselves, others, and global factors affecting society (Bottery, 2006).

REFERENCES

Afable-Munsuz, A., Liang, S. Y., Ponce, N. A., & Walsh, J. M. (2009). Acculturation and colorectal cancer screening among older Latino adults: Differential associations by national origin. *Journal of General Internal Medicine, 24*(8), 963–970.

Altbach, P. G., & Knight, J. (2007). The internationalization of higher education: Motivations and realities. *Journal of Studies in International Education, 11*(3–4), 290–305.

Anonymous. (2014, December 4). Blacked up: Dutch race relations. *The Economist, 413*(8916). https://www.economist.com/news/europe/21635517-worsening-clash-over-tradition-and-racial-sensitivities-blacked-up

Berry, J. W. (2005). Acculturation: Living successfully in two cultures. *International Journal of Intercultural Relations, 29*(6), 697–712.

Bobo, L. D. (1999). Prejudice as group position: Microfoundations of a sociological approach to racism and race relations. *Journal of Social Issues, 55*(3), 445–472.

Bottery, M. (2006). Education and globalization: Redefining the role of the educational professional. *Educational Review, 58*(1), 95–113.

Carew, A. L., Lefoe, G., Bell, M., & Armour, L. (2008). Elastic practice in academic developers. *International Journal for Academic Development, 13*(1), 51–66.

Cho, S. (2010). Politics of critical pedagogy and new social movements. *Educational Philosophy and Theory, 42*(3), 310–325.

Clark, C. H., & Wilson, B. P. (2017). The potential for university collaboration and online learning to internationalise geography education. *Journal of Geography in Higher Education, 41*(4), 488–505.

Cooper, J., & Mitsunaga, R. (2010). Faculty perspectives on international education: The nested realities of faculty collaborations. *New Directions for Higher Education*, 69–81. https://doi.org/10.1002/he.391

Crossley, M., & Holmes, K. (2001). Challenges for educational research: International development, partnerships and capacity building in small states. *Oxford Review of Education, 27*(3), 395–417.

Cruz, L., Manginelli, A., Parker, M. A., & Strahlman, H. (2018). Historia reimagined: Storytelling and identity in cross-cultural educational development. *Transformative Dialogues: Teaching & Learning Journal, 11*(3), 1-11.

Cushner, K. (2005). Conflict, negotiation, and mediation across cultures: Highlights from the fourth biennial conference of the International Academy for Intercultural Research. *International Journal of Intercultural Relations, 29*, 635–638. https://doi.org/10.1016/j.ijintrel.2005.07.014

Davidheiser, M. (2005). Culture and mediation: A contemporary processual analysis from southwestern Gambia. *International Journal of Intercultural Relations, 29*, 713–738. https://doi.org/10.1016/j.ijintrel.2005.07.010

Erickson, F. (1989). Culture in society and in educational practice. In J. A. Banks & C. A. M. Banks (Eds.), *Multicultural education: Issues and perspectives* (pp. 32–60). Allyn and Bacon.

Fei, X. (2015). *Globalization and cultural self-awareness.* Foreign Language Teaching and Research Publishing Co., Ltd. and Springer.

Felten, P., Kalish, A., Pingree, A., & Plank, K. (2007). Toward a scholarship of teaching and learning in educational development. In D. Robertson & L. Nilson (Eds.), *To improve the academy: Resources for faculty, instructional and organizational development: Vol. 25* (pp. 93–108). Jossey-Bass.

Fiume, P. (2005). Constructivist theory and border pedagogy foster diversity as a resource for learning. *The Community College Enterprise, 11*(2), 51–64.

Gil-Lacruz, M., Hernandez, P. M., Abad, L. C., & Bernat, E. E. (2013). Community integration and participation: The role of the social network in Latin American migrants in a rural province (Teruel, Spain). *Acción Psicológica, 10*(2), 129–142.

Grabinger, R. S., & Dunlap, J. C. (1995). Rich environments for active learning: A definition. *Research in Learning Technology, 3*(2), 5–34.

Higgitt, D., Donert, K., Healey, M., Klein, P., Solem, M., & Vajoczki, S. (2008). Developing and enhancing international collaborative learning. *Journal of Geography in Higher Education, 32*(1), 121–133.

Hubball, H., & Edwards-Henry, A. (2011). International collaboration to align institutional teaching development, learning-centred curricula, and the scholarship of curriculum and pedagogy in higher education. *The Caribbean Teaching Scholar, 1*(1). https://journals.sta.uwi.edu/ojs/index.php/cts/article/view/4

Independent School Diversity Network. (n.d.). *What is diversity?* ISDN. http://www.isdnetwork.org/what-is-diversity.html

Marsella, A. J. (2005). Culture and conflict: Understanding, negotiating, and reconciling conflicting constructions of reality. *International Journal of Intercultural Relations, 29*(6), 651–673. https://doi.org/10.1016/j.ijintrel.2005.07.012

Miller, K. (2011). *Race relations*. Greenhaven Press.

Norman, G. (2018, January 9). *White racism class at Florida university will be guarded by police officers*. Fox News. http://www.foxnews.com/us/2018/01/09/white-racism-class-at-florida-university-will-be-guarded-by-police-officers.html

Nwadiora, E. (1995). Alienation and stress among Black immigrants: An exploratory study. *Western Journal of Black Studies, 19*(1), 60–71.

POD Network. (2016). *What is educational development?* POD Network. https://podnetwork.org/about-us/what-is-educational-development/

Ramirez-Valles, J. (1999). Women in solidarity: Women's community work, the welfare state, and the politics of narrative identity in Mexico. *Critical Public Health, 9*(2), 85–101.

Romo. J. J., & Chavez, C. (2006). Border pedagogy: A study of preservice teacher transformation. *Educational Forum, 70*(2), 142–153.

Sorcinelli, M. D., Austin, A. E., Eddy, P. L., & Beach, A. L. (2005). *Creating the future of faculty development: Learning from the past, understanding the present*. Jossey Bass.

Stuart, J., & Ward, C. (2011). A question of balance: Exploring the acculturation, integration and adaptation of Muslim immigrant youth. *Psychosocial Intervention, 20*(3), 255–267.

University of North Carolina Wilmington. (n.d.). *Partner institutions*. https://uncw.edu/international/partners.html

Worchel, S. (2005). Culture's role in conflict and conflict management: Some suggestions, many questions. *International Journal of Intercultural Relations, 29*(6), 739–757. https://doi.org/10.1016/j.ijintrel.2005.08.011

Zanini, M. C. (2014). Writing, publishing and constructing memories: The literature produced by descendants of Italian immigrants in Rio Grande do Sul State (Brazil). *História Unisinos, 18*(2), 378–391.

CHAPTER SIXTEEN | HADEEQA SARWAR

Implications of Urduization in Pakistani English to Comprehend It as a Second Language

Language is the source of expressing ideas and emotions. In different countries, more than one language is spoken. Pakistan is a multilingual country. There are many languages spoken in Pakistan; Urdu and English are the two most prominent languages used for communication/interaction and education. Urdu is the national language of Pakistan, while English is used as an official as well as a second language. The dialect of English that is spoken in Pakistan is called Pakistani English. Pakistani English basically refers to the dialect in which the effect of Urdu is quite prominent. The interference or transfer of a first language (L_1) in second-language (L_2) learning is a natural phenomenon. Generally speaking, learning a first language is considered easier than learning a second language. Sometimes, this process of transfer of L_1 in L_2 is conscious and sometimes it is unconscious. This concept of interference of a first language in second-language learning is multifaceted.

This essay focuses on whether the first language or mother tongue can be considered a facilitator and contributing factor in second-language learning. An interesting point regarding language is that all human languages share some common characteristics (i.e., all languages have the ability to produce an infinite number of sentences by using the limited set of rules, structures, and words).

Language Learning

Language is the most important gift of God because language is used by humans to convey their inner thoughts and emotions; it helps human beings learn the way of communication with others. Language also fulfills the needs of communication, and it also establishes the rules and aids in maintaining culture. Generally, language and culture are closely related. Culture gives identity to an individual and language gives identity to the culture of a particular area. The words in a language are the reflection of the culture and the people who speak that language and share that culture. When an individual learns a new language, they not only learn a language, but they also learn to think in the way of the new culture. According to Said Ghafoor Ghafoori and Ezzatullah Saghar (2021, p. 4561), "Language can be viewed as a verbal expression of culture. It is used to maintain and convey culture and cultural ties."

An interesting point is that there are different dialects of one language. This means that speakers of one language have several different ways of using the language. For instance, Urdu is the national language of Pakistan; it has different dialects, which are spoken by the community or subgroups. A community's ways of using language reflect the culture of that community, so like other shared practices, language is also a way of displaying group identity. A language both reflects and affects a culture's way of thinking, and changes in a culture influence the development of its language. For example, when some new concept or thing arises in any culture, a specific "word" is needed to define that concept or thing. Urdu is the national language of Pakistan. It reflects Pakistani culture. When Urduization is done in English, it not only reflects the words of Urdu, but it also expresses the culture of that language.

Human beings have natural desires for interaction and socialization. Historically, men used to make sounds to express their thoughts and feelings. Later on, these sounds became words. Language learning is very important to generate and express thoughts. The whole world becomes easily accessible through language learning because if an individual knows different languages, they can communicate in those languages easily. Learning different languages broadens the mind to accept the culture and lifestyle of various societies in the world. Learning a language is an interesting process. It involves a lot of things. The first step in language learning is to develop familiarity with a language by reading and understanding it.

First Language/Native Language

The mother tongue or L1 is a language that a child acquires after birth. The language that a child learns first is known as one's native language or mother tongue. Language is obviously a vital tool. The first language is the main language, which people speak in some specific region or area. The terms first language, second language, and third language are used to indicate various levels of skills in a language, so it can be said that a person knows more than one language at first- or second-language level.

Second Language

Second language is a language that someone learns to achieve some purpose (i.e., when it is difficult to communicate with foreigners in their own language, or when it is necessary to achieve goals in education or a profession). The ability to communicate in a second language is becoming an essential skill in today's world. Second-language learning describes the process of understanding, speaking, and writing another language fluently.

A second language is a language that a person consciously learns to achieve the goal of communication. Learning a second language can be difficult; it takes much time, patience, and practicing. Learning a second language can be affected by the patterns of the first language. This effect of first language on second language is referred to as linguistic interference. Different scholars, researchers, and linguists have different views about the interference or transfer of L_1 in L_2 learning.

L_1 transfer in L_2 can be conscious or unconscious. The positive aspects of language interference are less often discussed, but they can be very important. Generally speaking, the process will be more positive if the learner is aware of the relationship between the two languages. It is most often discussed as a source of errors (negative transfer), although where the relevant feature of both languages is the same, it results in correct language production (positive transfer).

Heidi Dulay et al (1982) defined interference in *Language Two*: "[I]nterference is the automatic transfer, due to habit, of the surface structure of the first language onto the surface of the target language."

Pakistan has an increasing interest in English-language education. There are many English courses offered in Pakistan, such as ELT (English Language Teaching), TEFL (Teaching of English as a Foreign Language), TESOL, and master's courses in English, English diplomas, and spoken English. English has become the language of media, trade, and science. In Pakistan, the importance of English is growing, and now English is compulsory in almost all schools and colleges.

Indigenization

The word "indigenize" refers to the adaptation of things in a local culture from other cultures. Indigenization is an important and interesting process that helps in learning L_2. So indigenization means transformation, or changing, to suit a local culture. In language, indigenization is done to minimize or sometimes to remove the alienating effect. The concept of indigenization is very interesting, and to some extent it is very helpful in the language-learning process. The process of indigenization can be used as one of the tools to learn a language. Another important aspect of indigenization is that it indigenizes the words, which are related to culture, of the native language in the second language. This concept of indigenization minimizes the alienating effects of the second language.

Urduization

Urdu is the national language of Pakistan. Although there is a variety of languages spoken in Pakistan, Urdu has its own distinguished place. The origin of Urdu is quite interesting, and the basic characteristic of Urdu is that it is an amalgamation of many languages. Many words of Urdu are borrowed from different languages. This is one of the reasons for the popularity of Urdu. As English is a global language, Pakistan has growing interest in English as a second language. Tariq Rahman states in "Language Policy, Multilingualism and Language Vitality in Pakistan" (2012), "Pakistan is a multilingual country with six major and over fifty-nine small languages. However, the languages of domains of power-government, corporate sector, media, education etc. are English and Urdu."

"Urduization" is done in Pakistani English very frequently. In Urduization, the words from Urdu are indigenized into English so that the alienating effect of English can be minimized for Pakistani learners. Urduization is an interesting concept. When the words from Urdu are added in English, then English becomes more understandable and the learner feels comfortable communicating and can grasp the idea or context in a better way.

Some examples of Urduization given by R. J. Baumgardner and colleagues (1998) in Pakistani English include:

- Most of the agricultural landholdings in Jhang district are small—with the typical Chaudhry toking on his chillum under a shady tree at his dera while loyal servants massage his shoulders.
- The Bismillah Ceremony of the three-day annual Urs of Hazrat Baba Bullay Shah was performed here by giving ghusal to the Mazar amidst recitation of Darood-o-Salam by devotees in hundreds, says a handout.

The researcher wants to test whether this interesting concept of Urduization will help in learning English as a second language and in minimizing the alienating effect of English for learners. Another important question is whether this concept of Urduization will be helpful for Pakistani learners in particular, because those learners will be more familiar with Pakistani culture and society and their way of thinking.

Population/Sample

The sample of the undertaken research included the students of master's degree in English language and literature (first semester) at the National University of Modern Languages.

Literature Review

Recent research recognizes that L1/L2 influence can be positive as well as negative and operates in both directions because there is cross-linguistic influence. It means that L1 has an effect on L2 acquisition and L2 has an effect on L1. The main focus of this research is to find out whether Urduization in Pakistani English is useful to minimize the alienating effect in teaching/learning English as a second language. A lot of work is done on the negative and positive effects of the first language on second-language learning. The interference of L1 in L2 learning is an interesting and important point to discuss because if it has positive effects, it can enhance and facilitate second-language learning.

Uriel Weinreich (1953) has stated in *Languages in Contact* that there are three areas in which the first language may interfere in the second language: phonological, lexical, and syntactic levels. The first area is phonological, which deals with the pronunciation part of a language; the second area is lexical, which deals with vocabulary or words; and the third part is syntactic, which deals with the word structure. The above-mentioned areas are the main areas of any language. If the first language interferes in these three areas, then it means that first language interference is worth mentioning.

In the book *Linguistics Across Cultures*, Robert Lado (1957, p. 2) claimed that "those elements which are similar to [the learner's] native language will be simple for him, and those elements that are different will be difficult." According to Lado (1957), the first language is quite helpful in second-language learning. As the learner is in the habit of using L1, when they learn L2, it will be easy for them to deal with the similarities of L1 and L2. The common characteristics and similar elements of L1 and L2 will be simple and easy for them, but the elements that are different and dissimilar in these two languages will be difficult and new for the learner.

Martin L. Albert and Loraine K. Obler (1978, p. 246) state in *The Bilingual Brain* that:

> It is clear that words in one language and their translation equivalents in the other (when such exist) are related in the brain in a nonrandom way, much as a word and its synonym in the same language may be connected in an associational network.

Albert and Obler also favored the same idea that words of one language and their translation or equivalents in the other language are in the mind of a learner or speaker and they are connected to an associational network. This connection will be helpful in learning new words or lexical items. For example, if a person wants to learn English as a second language and his native language is Urdu, "kursi" is an Urdu word and its translation equivalent in English is "chair," so he can associate the concept of kursi with chair and he will be able to memorize the word chair in the target language. For both kursi and chair, the associational network will be "furniture." So, in this way, a learner can take help from his first language to learn the vocabulary items of a second language.

Vocabulary is one of the most important parts of any language, and this is also considered an initial step of any language. Lexical items of L1 help the learner understand and memorize the vocabulary items of L2. So, it can be stated that the first language has positive and helpful interference in second-language development.

Hashim H. Noor has mentioned in his case study "Some Implications on the Role of the Mother Tongue in Second Language Acquisition" (1994; p. 98):

> Attention is given mainly to two aspects of the L1–L2 relationship: positive transfer of knowledge from L1 in the process of learning L2, and negative transfer, or interference. It is best to view L1 as a contributing factor in L2 development.

Noor (1994) has studied the interference of L1 on L2 to find out whether L1 is a facilitator or a barrier in L2 learning. Noor states that the first language should be considered as a facilitator in second-language learning because learners of L2 take help from their first language to learn and understand L2 Noor further states that in the L1–L2 relationship, there are both negative and positive aspects of transfer of L1 in L2, but the findings show that, compared to the negative transfer, L1 has more positive and helpful transfer of knowledge in L2. So, it would not be wrong to conclude that L1 is a contributing factor in L2 development.

Jing Liu (2008) concluded that

> L1 use in L2 vocabulary learning or providing translation equivalents have several advantages. They are an easy and efficient way of depicting the core meaning of a word. Knowing the L1 equivalent also gives the learner a sense of certainty about the meaning of the word. (p. 68)

This research deals with the use of L1 vocabulary in learning L2 vocabulary items. Vocabulary items of the first language are considered the facilitator in learning the vocabulary items of the second language because the second-language learners take help from lexical items of the first language to understand the concepts of lexical items of the second language. Again, according to this research, the first language should be seen as an effective tool to learn a second language.

Research Methodology/Data Collection

This research followed a multimethod approach, amalgamating qualitative and quantitative approaches. The present study is exploratory as well as descriptive in nature. In general, the researcher is trying to explore whether L1 interference can be seen as a contributing factor in learning a second language. More specifically, the researcher wants to judge whether Urduization in Pakistani English is useful in comprehending English as a second language.

As this research follows a multimethod approach, descriptive research complements this approach. The researcher has selected survey research because it is useful, and it fulfills the requirements of the present research.

The theoretical framework of the current study is the theory of contrastive analysis. Robert Lado was the person who laid the foundation of this theory. In his book *Linguistics Across Cultures* (1957, p. 45), Lado claimed that "those elements which are similar to [the learner's] native language will be simple for him, and those elements that are different will be difficult."

Contrastive analysis deals with the similarities and the differences between L_1 and L_2 at the same time. Contrastive analysis makes the contrast as well as the comparison to explore the similarities and differences between first language and second language. On the basis of those similarities, the structures and items of target language can be learned easily and effectively. As far as this particular research is concerned, the researcher wants to test whether L_1 can be seen as a facilitator in L_2 learning. So, the theory of contrastive analysis has been adapted to explore the phenomenon.

The basic tool for data collection is a worksheet. The researcher wants to find out whether the transfer of L_1 is a contributing factor in comprehending L_2, so the worksheet is designed to test the comprehension of learners/the selected sample. The worksheet contains the comparison of an article written in Standard English with that of the same article having indigenized words of Urdu in English.

Some articles were added in the worksheet, and the respondents need to summarize those articles. The articles were written in Standard English, and then the same articles with Urduized forms were given and the respondents were asked to summarize those articles as well. In order to collect data, the researcher gave the worksheets to the selected sample of students and the instructions were given to the sample; after giving some time, the researcher took the worksheets from the subjects so that the validity of the research question could be analyzed.

Data Analysis

The researcher has analyzed the data through SPSS.

The researcher has included two passages. Both passages are the same; the only difference is that in one paragraph, Urdu words are used, while in the second paragraph, there is no indigenization of Urdu words. Both paragraphs were given to the respondents, and they were asked to summarize them. The first paragraph is indigenized with Urdu words, while the second passage is completely in Standard English. The purpose of this question is to analyze whether more respondents have correctly analyzed the indigenized paragraph, or if they have better understanding of the Standard English paragraph.

The results are analyzed statistically in the form of frequency tables and graphs. The first paragraph is named "Urduized," while the second passage is titled "English." The first passage in the worksheet is given below, and the Urdu words are in boldface type.

Hallmarks of **thela** food were the taste, the freshness and the price. For a pittance, the **thelawala** tempted you as much with his items as by his call. The mobile ones were prominent at all those places where a snack was most welcome. I remember, from railway stations and from railway crossings, "**bayl aanday garam**" with which, salt came in a little "**puria**." In summer, **rau** and **singharay** were very popular.

The respondents read and summarized the paragraphs, and the researcher has analyzed the passage through SPSS. The researcher has designed three scales to analyze the summary given by the respondents. These three variables are "good description," "average description," and "poor description."

According to the analysis of the Urduized passage, among 56 students, 30 respondents came up with a "good description," 14 students gave an "average description," and four subjects could not describe the article properly, so their description was placed under "poor description." Eight of the respondents did not give any response to this question. Slightly more than 53% of subjects gave a good description, 25% came up with an average description, while 7.1% of the sample gave a poor description. Just over 14% of responses remained passive, so their analysis is missing.

Urduized

The above-mentioned description shows the results of the Urduized passage. The results indicate that most of the respondents have given good descriptions, and the Urdu words seem helpful for developing understanding and comprehension of the given passage. The majority of the respondents analyzed the passage correctly, perhaps because the Urduized words that are indigenized in the passage are frequently used in Pakistani culture and some of the Urdu words used do not have any equivalent in English. For example, in the passage, the expression "bayl aanday garam" has no equivalent in English. This expression is just translated as "hot boiled eggs" in the other passage, which is purely in English. Culture plays an important role in comprehending, analyzing, and understanding the language.

The next passage as mentioned above is completely taken from Standard English. The same instructions were given to the respondents that after reading the passage, they are supposed to summarize it. The passage is given below with the words highlighted that were used as an equivalent of Urdu words.

Table 1. Urduized passage comprehension test results.

	Frequency	Percent
Good	30	53.6
Average	14	25
Poor	4	7.1
Total	48	85.7
Missing response	8	14.3
Grand total (N)	56	100

Hallmarks of **pushcart** food were the taste, the freshness and the price. For a pittance, the **hawker** tempted you as much with his items as by his call. The mobile ones were prominent at all those places where a snack was most welcome. I remember, from railway stations and from railway crossings, "**hot boiled eggs**" with which, salt came in a little "**sachet**." In summer, **sugar cane juice** and **water chestnut** were very popular.

The analyses of the responses show that 10 students gave a "good description," 25 came up with an "average description," while 11 gave a "poor description." The responses of 11 subjects are missing. Proportionally, 17.9% gave a good summary, 42.9% gave an average description, and 19.6% of respondents gave a poor description, while 19.6% of subjects did not suggest any summary.

English

If the results of the passage written in standard English are compared with results of the Urduized passage, it is quite clear that the majority of the respondents have analyzed the Urduized passage appropriately as compared to the passage written in Standard English. One of the reasons can be because the Urdu words added in the article are more common in Pakistani culture, so it was easy for the respondents to identify and understand the Urduized passage

Table 2. English passage comprehension test results.

	Frequency	Percent
Good	10	17.9
Average	24	42.9
Poor	11	19.6
Total	45	80.4
Missing response	11	19.6
Grand total (N)	56	100

more clearly. This analysis indicates that Urduization in English is a facilitator in comprehending English when it is learned as a second language.

The theory of contrastive analysis is also concerned with the comparison and contrast of discursive levels among languages. The analysis indicates that L1 has positive effects on L2 learning, and the contrastive analysis theory is highly concerned with whether the native language has positive or negative effects on L2 learning. The results of discursive levels indicate that L1 can be taken as a contributing factor in L2 learning, so this discursive section of the worksheet is also related to the theory of contrastive analysis.

Conclusion

In the current research, the findings clearly demonstrate that L1 is a facilitator in L2 learning. The theory of contrastive analysis has been helpful in judging the influence of the first language on second-language learning.

Findings

The researcher is able to draw the findings on the basis of collected data. The findings are as follows:

1. The present study highlights that first language can be seen as a contributor and facilitator in second-language learning.
2. The findings indicate that Urduization in Pakistani English is helpful in comprehending English as the second language.
3. The results also highlight that the learners/respondents have shown a positive attitude toward using their L1 in the process of learning a second language.

The concept of Urduization in Pakistani English is very common. It is done because the indigenization of Urdu words in English is helpful in comprehending and understanding English.

In a nutshell, the first language or mother tongue can be considered a helpful factor in second-language learning. The concept of indigenizing Urdu words in Pakistani English is useful and helpful in comprehending English as a second language. A balanced approach is needed that sees a positive role for L1 but also recognizes the importance of maximizing L2 use in the classroom.

REFERENCES

Albert, M. A., & Obler, L. (1978). *The bilingual brain: Neuropsychological and neurolinguistic aspects of bilingualism*. Academic Press.

Baumgardner R. J., Kennedy, A. E. H., & Shamin, F. (1998). *The English language in Pakistan*. Oxford University Press.

Dulay, H. (1982). Language interference: The influence of Indonesian mother tongue on Indonesian learners of English. In H. Dulay, M. Burt, & S. Krashen (Eds.), *Language two*. Oxford University Press.

Ghafoori, S. G., & Saghar, A. E. (2021). The relationship between language and culture. *International Journal of Creative Research Thoughts, 9*(1), 4559–4562.

Noor, H. (1994). Some implications on the role of mother tongue in second language acquisition. *Linguistica Communicatio, 6*(1–2), 97–106.

Lado, R. (1957). *Linguistics across cultures: Applied linguistics for language teachers*. University of Michigan Press.

Liu, J. (2008). L1 used in L2 vocabulary learning: Facilitator or barrier. *International Education Studies, 1*(2), 65–69.

Rahman, T. (2012). *Language policy, multilingualism and language vitality in Pakistan*. Academy of the Punjab in North America. https://apnaorg.com/research-papers/english/paper-21/page-1.shtml

Weinreich, U. (1953). *Languages in contact*. Linguistic Circles of New York.

CHAPTER SEVENTEEN | LANCE CUMMINGS

Rhetorical Listening Across Borders

A Report on Attitudes and Contexts Around English for Academic Purposes at International Islamic University, Islamabad

During my first visit to International Islamic University, Islamabad (IIUI) in Pakistan in November 2015, I remember distinctly one moment while listening to a focus group when a female faculty member asked me directly: "Why are you asking all these questions?" As it turns out, it is much more common for U.S. visitors to do most of the talking. Another faculty member complained that often times talking was oversimplified or simply did not fit Pakistani contexts. As a scholar of rhetoric, focused on how context and audience shape communication and persuasion, I explained that my goal for this first trip was to listen—to learn about contexts that shape Pakistan's scholarly and academic endeavors.

In my field, we call this "rhetorical listening" (Booth, 2004; Ratcliffe, 2005). In his first description of this term, Wayne Booth points out that there is not just one rhetoric—not just one way to communicate, one way to persuade, or one way to create knowledge. The core, then, of any scholarly endeavor must include rhetorical listening:

> What is inescapable is that underlying all our differences about what makes good communication there is one deep standard: agreement that whatever the dispute, whatever the language standards, communication can be improved by *listening to the other side, and then listening even harder to one's own responses.* (Booth, 2004, p. 21; emphasis in original)

Such a principle is even more important when working across what many see as a political divide between Pakistan and the United States, especially considering the colonial legacy of English instruction (Pennycook, 1998; Phillipson, 1992). In short, there is a long history of English and Americans coming into Pakistan to "talk" about language. That's why I came to listen.

In addition to taking a listening stance, this research attempts to take what has been called a "trans lingual" stance that questions static notions of English and seeks to understand the multilingual experience as a positive resource for scholars to use academically (Canagarajah, 2011; Horner & Trimbur, 2002; Pennycook, 1998). In other words, the notion that there is an ideal and static form of English that is most suited to academia is a rarely examined assumption in the knowledge-making processes of the scholarly world. This assumption becomes more questionable as speakers of other Englishes enter disciplinary communities. The resources that multilingual speakers of English bring to academic writing are often concealed by these kinds of notions. So, this research does not seek to identify and solve some "problem" with English for academic purposes (EAP) in Pakistan, but to listen and observe the powerful language practices that drive scholarship in Pakistan ... and ultimately to learn from them.

Though this report only scratches the surface of the important contexts around EAP at IIUI, I hope that these observations will give insight to U.S. scholars who want to work with Pakistan but may not be familiar with these contexts. I also hope that Pakistani readers may learn a bit about themselves by looking through my limited eyes. This is only the beginning of the conversation for me ... and I hope it is read in that way.

Methodology

To focus on listening, I wanted to elicit as much response and description from Pakistani participants as possible. My questions focused less on how English was being used and more on how participants perceived English being used.

Research Questions

What kind of attitudes do faculty and administration have toward academic English in Pakistan? What kind of trans lingual practices, rhetorical patterns, and styles are developing? How are these perceived by different forms of institutional assessment? What opportunities for dialogue exist in the studies of rhetoric and writing?

To answer these questions, I gathered salient and recent research on English in Pakistan. At IIUI, I delivered one online survey and conducted five focus groups with students and faculty in the English departments of both the male and female campuses. I focused on attitudes and approaches to writing in English that might inform further research and collaboration.

Survey Overview

In collaboration with administration at IIUI, a 30-minute survey was distributed at IIUI in English. There were 108 respondents, 72% of which were under age 30. The survey was slightly weighted toward the female campus with 44% respondents being men and 56% women. The overall design of the survey sought to explore different connections between social and linguistic backgrounds of faculty and students with attitudes toward English and academic writing. The survey was divided into six sections: general background, language background, EAP attitudes, questions specific to researchers, questions specific to faculty/instructors, and questions specific to students.

The survey worked to parse out some of these complex contexts by providing several options and/or opportunities to construct a unique response. For example, the first three questions asked what participants considered their first language, what language they heard the most in childhood, and what language they were exposed to the most. Monolingual perceptions on language often assume that all three of these are the same language. Participants could add as many languages as they deemed fit in each of these categories. Informed by trans lingual approaches, this survey hoped to contest this U.S.-centric assumption, while also capturing the complex linguistic backgrounds in Pakistan.

Nationality and Ethnicity

The survey results show not only a diversity of backgrounds, but also diverse approaches to constructing national, cultural, and linguistic identity. All respondents identified their nationality as Pakistani, even though there are students and faculty with other origins at IIUI. This may indicate a need for wider distribution of the survey at some point. Results for ethnicity were much more diverse, which often included descriptors or qualifiers, for example, "Belongs to Pushtun society with their own culture, tradition, and literature. Believe in honesty, brotherhood, humanity, unity, hospitality." Or another example, "I am Baloch, live in Balochistan. We have our own culture and traditions." Table 1 gives an overview of results (without qualifiers or descriptors).

Table 1 is rather simplified, as many respondents combined identities. For example, many responded as Pakistani and Muslim or as another ethnicity

Table 1. Breakdown of self-identified ethnicities.

Ethnicity	Responses
Punjabi	34%
Muslim	21%
Pakistani	11%
Baloch	8%
Asian	7%
Kasmiri	3%
Pashtun	2%
Pathan	2%

and Muslim (for example, Punjabi and Muslim). Likely this represents some response to an effort to find unifying identities across ethnicities. Some respondents even explicitly stated that they "do not believe in ethnic divisions" or that "first I am Pakistani."

At the same time, other respondents focused on highlighting their unique identities or unique conglomeration of identities. For example, Baloch was always mentioned independently of other ethnicities, while others combined identities like, "I am Punjabi Muslim from Pakistan." This may indicate a relationship between class and ethnicity. Those ethnicities with less cultural capital may be less likely to fold their identities into a broader national or religious identity.

When working with our colleagues at IIUI, either in research or in developing effective approaches to academic writing, U.S. scholars will need to be aware of these diverse identities and how they may affect writing at many levels. More research and dialogue that examines these contexts alongside writing can help widen our conceptions of academic writing and provide insights for developing and publishing student and scholarly work.

Table 2. Order of multiple languages.

	L1	L2	L3	L4	L5	L6	L7
Urdu	60%	26%	5%	1%			
Punjabi	15%	10%	8%	4%			
English	12%	20%	14%	3%			
Balochi	4%						
Pushto	2%	5%					
Kasmiri	3%						
Pushtun	2%						
Potohari	2%						
Arabic			5%	2%	1%	2%	
Hindko			1%				
French			2%				
Saraiecki			1%	1%			
Japanese				2%			
Persian					2%		1%

Language and Educational Backgrounds

Educational level was high; almost 80% had an undergraduate degree, which indicates most of the respondents were faculty and graduate students. Responses also varied with regard to primary language, though Urdu was by far the most identified with English and Punjabi coming significantly second.

Half identified as multilingual, two-thirds of which identified more languages up to seven. This is important to note for any kind of collaboration with IIUI. Each individual writer will be influenced by their own set of linguistic knowledge and experiences. This also means that writers at IIUI bring with them diverse rhetorical and linguistic resources for developing academic writing in their field. At the same time, most respondents had extensive experience with English. For example, 75% of respondents started learning English before age 10.

Collaborators should understand that scholars and students at IIUI will also be influenced by a variety of different kinds of English. What U.S. scholars might perceive as "error" may simply be a different kind of English.

Critiques of Survey

Because there were plenty of opportunities for write-ins and text answers, there were some interesting critiques of the survey throughout. For example, when asked what varieties of English they would like their children to learn, one respondent noted that they do not want their children to learn English, pointing out the survey's assumption that all Pakistanis learn or want to learn some form of English. When asked what kind of writing workshops should be offered, another respondent said, "How to get rid of corruption in Pakistan and how to win a scholarship for UNC." Another student asked for workshops related to Pakistan as a nation.

Though these responses are not particularly helpful for identifying topics in writing, they should be noted. Anyone hoping to collaborate and develop writing between the United States and Pakistan should be aware of the complex network of attitudes around English and academic writing. EAP is by no means neutral or apolitical.

Analysis of Contexts Around EAP in Pakistan

Along with most other Southeast Asia countries, Pakistan has a long multilingual history where languages have been in constant contact through cooperation, competition, or conflict. In the mid-20th century, the establishment of sovereign states instituted a "language-education-policy" modeled by colonial approaches to language instruction, largely depending on a monolingual frame of reference (Tickoo, 2006, p. 167). Through this frame, linguistic diversity is often viewed as a threat to nationhood and a single, unified language is necessary for collaborating in education, government, and administration (p. 168). Even though Pakistan is a multilingual country with six major and 58 minor languages, English still maintains the status of an official language, and Urdu is the cultural language contributing to national identity (Rahman, 2005, p. 24). The use of these two languages is generally perceived as necessary for building a cohesive nation-state.

At the time of independence in 1947, none of the five Pakistani provinces could claim any kind of monolingualism or hegemonic linguistic power. For

Table 3. Five-caste system (compiled from Rahman, 2006).

Institution	Language	Class	Funding Source
Madrasahs	Urdu or Indigenous	Poor	Charity
Urdu-Medium	Urdu	Lower Class	Government
Ordinary English medium	English, sometimes Urdu	Middle Class	Family
Elitist English medium	English	Upper Class	Family
Cadet Colleges/Public Schools	English	Powerful Elite	Family and/or Government

this reason, the dynamic roles English plays in Pakistan are interwoven within a web of complex linguistic and cultural relationships. English is not simply the language used to communicate with the world and other nations, but a way of communicating across ethnic groups. English as an official language has been enforced under the assumption that a single language is essential for efficient nation building.

The Three Language Formula

The educational policies developed within these contexts have often been called "The Three Language Formula" (Tickoo, 2006, p. 170). Students are taught languages hierarchically within their "proper" societal function. For example, students usually learn their regional language as a first language, Urdu as a "nation-building" language, and English as the language of science and scholarship. The relationship between these languages can vary greatly according to the kind of education students obtain before entering the university. Often called the five-caste education system (see Table 3), researchers point out that students from higher socioeconomic levels tend to have better access to English language education, which perpetuates many of these class distinctions (Bari, 2016; Mahboob, 2017; Rahman, 2006).

During the course of my interviews, faculty members were more likely to define students by socioeconomic status than ethnic or linguistic background, though these intersect in complex ways. Education is polarized in Pakistan around socioeconomic class, primarily indexed by medium of instruction. For example, "vernacular-medium" schools are often meant for the working class, while English-medium schools are primarily attended by the middle and upper classes (Rahman, 2006, p. 10). Socioeconomic factors also affect instruction in many ways. For example, public schools are more likely to have fewer trained teachers, more outdated material, and fewer resources, as well as larger classes with less technology (Shahbaz & Yongbin, 2015, p. 461). As a result, Pakistani students come to IIUI with a wide variety of backgrounds and resources.

Faculty at IIUI frequently referred to versions of this five-caste system when describing the diverse backgrounds in English of their students. EAP literacy narratives by both students and faculty identified early educational contexts as heavily influencing the difficulty level of entering into EAP discourse.

Though the Three Language Formula does make room for the many other indigenous languages of Pakistan, the underlying teaching ideologies often maintain monolingual principles in the instruction of English. For example, instruction within this model can fail to understand and accept established styles and strategies used by learners in acquiring new languages and rarely accept the strengths that a multilingual learner brings into the classroom. According to Ahmar Mahboob (2017), university teaching of English in Pakistan often disassociates language from content in order to simplify instruction through focus on form alone. As a result, students often have a limited understanding of how disciplinary knowledge and conventions intersect with language and can affect performance in academic and professional writing.

Though it is difficult to make the same conclusion about IIUI specifically from this limited pilot study, there are indications that this disassociation may contribute to difficulties obtaining academic, disciplinary, and professional discourse, particularly when looking to publish in more global venues. When asked what topics their instructors discussed most in class, students overwhelmingly mentioned grammar and "fixing" mistakes:

> In Pakistan, we talk about grammar and sentence structure, first and foremost. At least, this is my main focus. My next step in dealing with writing in English is diagnosing why our students make these mistakes and how they can be avoided.

Organization was a close second, though some students did mention more contextual factors, like society, culture, and disciplinarity. When asked what aspects of EAP were the most difficult, "style" and "translation" ranked the highest with grammar close behind. Academic conventions and cultural contexts ranked quite low. Yet when asked to offer their own topics, many actually added categories that would fall more within these last two. This may indicate some degree of disassociation between languages (grammar/style) and content (academic and cultural contexts).

Applying a rhetorical lens that integrates indigenous ways of seeing can be a key way to develop student and faculty awareness of EAP, while also fostering the unique set of resources Pakistani students and scholars bring to global scholarship.

Pakistani English

Most Western linguists consider Pakistani English (PE) a variety of English or, in Braj Kachru's terms (1990), a "world English." In other words, varieties of English, like those used in Pakistan, exist within "distinct language ecologies" with their own "contexts and usage" (Kachru, 1990, p. 1). English language standards, whether in the United States, England, or Pakistan, do not exist as an abstract or idealized form, but must be understood locally. Kachru famously organizes different varieties of English as they relate to "colonial centers" (see Figure 1). Most scholars place Pakistan in the expanding circle, or on the border with the outer circle, because Pakistani English has not become as institutionalized as Indian English but holds more prestige than Englishes found in China or Russia. It should be noted, though, that Kachru's model does not explicitly take into account the possibility of multiple Pakistani Englishes, which itself may not be as monolithic as often represented by WE proponents.

Unlike Indian English (IE), there are fewer institutional resources that support PE as a standard variety of English. In most cases, the distinctive qualities of PE are recognized by specific linguistic features, for example:

- grammar,
- word formation,
- lexical variations, and
- borrowing. (Baumgartner, 1993, p. xvi)

Because these aspects have not been codified in any significant way, most Pakistanis seem to recognize PE as mostly oral, except when integrated within creative writing texts. This may contribute to a strong focus on grammar and word-level competencies. What some Westerners may call errors are often PE traits that are accepted as common in most contexts and reinforced by English instruction, PE books, and Pakistani literature (Baumgartner, 1993, p. xiv). A strength that Pakistani writers bring to EAP is this creative use of language,

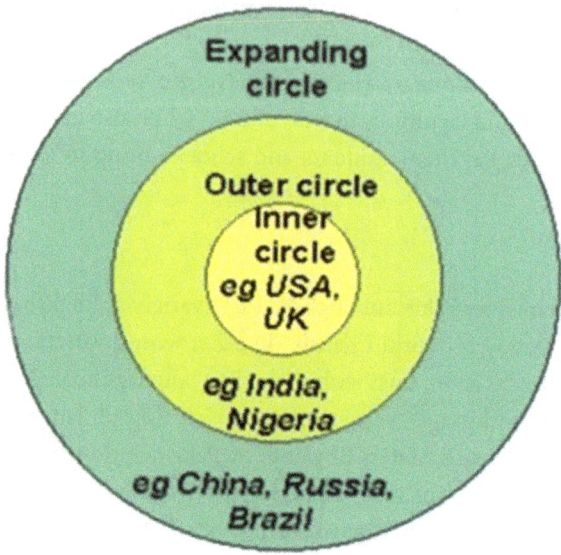

Fig. 1. Kachru's Three Circles (Wikimedia Commons).

though how to transfer these skills is not clear, because academic writing is primarily controlled by notions of British English (BE) standards.

In EAP, the difficulty arises when the contexts around English are not easily discernible as more concrete contexts, like the streets of Pakistan. Most writers and reviewers have some ideal form of English by which they judge research and publications, but that standard is rarely made explicit, though BE is often implicitly at play. In fact, most interviewees pointed to BE as the standard for academic writing, though there seemed to be some confusion as to the nature of BE, particularly among students. During the group interviews, most students categorized kinds of English according to social function: BE for academia, American English (AE) for pop culture, and PE for local and regional use. That said, many stated that they often mix these together and have a hard time identifying and isolating each variety, even within their instruction at IIUI. This may indicate that fluidity and movement between varieties is quite common, especially among young people, and may be at odds with expectations in the university and in publication avenues.

Even so, Pakistan has a strong tradition of elevating PE creatively in both poetry and fiction. In WE terms, deviations from more standard varieties like AE and BE can be seen as innovations rather than errors (Kachru, 1990, p. 28). In fact, Kachru (1990) calls these deviations a "linguistic vehicle for creative

Table 1. Standard varieties of Englishes.

	BE	AE	PE
What variety of English do educated Pakistanis speak?	64%	2%	25%
What variety of English do you write?	70%	3%	2%
Which varieties of English do you want your children to learn?	67%	38%	18%

writing" (p. 19). During the course of my interviews, only a few faculty seemed to have a strong awareness of this WE model, but more explicit reflection on PE seemed most prominent in creative writing contexts, though in sharp distinction with academic writing. Several students asked whether "informal writing" or writing for intentional or creative purposes is a valid form of academic writing from my perspective. From a rhetorical point of view, these creative and intentional uses of language are important resources in academic writing that may be untapped by students and scholars.

Though English instruction in Pakistan has been well studied, research on writing is much more difficult to find. Much of the writing research has been heavily influenced by creative writing and/or linguistics. For example, Mahmood, Batool, Shah, and Parveen (2013) published a corpus-driven analysis of modal verbs by comparing PE fiction with BE fiction. In fact, many of the faculty at IIUI have integrated the study of PE with the study of fiction and poetry. On one hand, creative writing has become a "safe place" for PE to develop, but BE is still seen as a higher standard. In other words, the respectability of PE is mostly restricted to creative writing and does not transfer to academic or professional writing.

As a scholar in rhetoric and composition, I see opportunities for studies in rhetoric to help bridge the gap between creative writing and academic writing, especially because Pakistan already has such a strong and unique tradition of rhetoric. The advantage of rhetoric studies is that the interpretive lenses often applied to literature can also be applied to academic writing of both scholars and students.

Recommendations for Developing Writing Collaborations Between Pakistan and the United States

As part of this grant research, I have made the following recommendations for future collaborations and faculty development.

Develop EAP Initiatives and Collaborations

Faculty focus group interviews revealed very little formal training in EAP until grad school. In fact, several faculty cited their dissertation advisor as the first person to introduce ideas of EAP to them. There is very little systematic training in writing at the undergraduate level. Realizing this, several faculty have been implementing new writing pedagogies into their courses. Having an informal collaborative group can help instructors share ideas about writing and provide a place for small writing seminars.

Explore Professional Writing

Generally, 40% of respondents stated they were comfortable writing for informal, formal, and academic contexts, but only 14% felt comfortable with professional writing in English. Writing scholars in the United States may have opportunities to explore business, science, and medical writing. We can learn more about how different Englishes function rhetorically in these contexts while also operationalizing these findings alongside our colleagues teaching this writing in Pakistan. For example, a Pakistani colleague and I have begun collecting a corpus of business writing that can be used to study how this writing happens in Pakistan in ways that might inform future instruction.

Continue Online Collaborations

When giving their literacy narratives, students with a passion and aptitude for English often referred back to a moment or interaction with an English speaker. This implies that more contact with U.S. students may increase motivation for language learning and writing at IIUI. Though face-to-face interactions can be difficult to manage due to Pakistan's location and political relationship with the United States, classes can collaborate asynchronously online. For example, in my recent comparative rhetoric class, English students in the United States discussed Sufi rhetoric on Yammer, an Enterprise Social Network much like Facebook.

Propose Research Collaborations in Rhetoric

During my visit to IIUI, I gave a lecture on the history of rhetoric in the United States and how that history has shaped our view of rhetoric and writing. Though IIUI's English departments are mostly comprised of linguistics and literary scholars, there are several strong traditions of rhetoric that can inform writing instruction at IIUI and develop our rhetorical theories here in the United States. Specifically, I encourage the exploration of women's rhetoric, Sufist rhetoric, and Urdu rhetoric.

Conclusion

At the time of this writing, it's been three years since I've developed this report ... and I am still listening. That said, I've also begun talking. I continue to explore the richness of Sufi rhetoric, a core religious influence in Pakistan, and my friend (de-identified) and I have begun researching business English in both Pakistan and the United States. I believe we still have a lot to learn from how English is used in Pakistan, and I hope the readers of this essay will join our conversation. From my experience, we've only scratched the surface of what Pakistan can teach the world through its rich culture and tradition.

REFERENCES

Barber, M. (2010). *Education reform in Pakistan: This time it's going to be different.* Pakistan Task Force, Islamabad.

Bari, F. (2016). *In which medium?* Dawn. www.dawn.com

Baumgartner, R. J. (1993). *The English language in Pakistan.* Oxford University Press.

Booth, W. C. (2004). How many rhetorics? In *The Rhetoric of Rhetoric: The Quest for Effective Communication* (pp. 3–22). Blackwell Publishing.

Canagarajah, S. (2011). Translanguaging in the classroom: Emerging issues for research and pedagogy. *Applied Linguistics Review, 2*(1), 1–28.

Horner, B., & Trimbur, J. (2002). English only and US college composition. *College Composition and Communication, 53*(4), 594–630.

Kachru, B. B. (1990). *The alchemy of English: The spread, functions, and models of non-native Englishes.* University of Illinois Press.

Lin, X. (2011). An analysis of English learning agendas: Private college students in China as the new and more pragmatic type of English learners. In *Proceedings of the 16th conference of Pan-Pacific Association of Applied Linguistics.* Pan-Pacific Association of Applied Linguistics.

Mahboob, A. (2017). English medium instruction in higher education in Pakistan: Policies, perceptions, problems, and possibilities. In I. Walkinsah, B. Fenton-Smith, & P. Humphreys (Eds.), *English as a medium of instruction in higher education in Asia-Pacific: Issues and challenges* (pp. 71–91). Springer International.

Mahmood, R., Batool, A., Shah, S. K., & Parveen, S. (2013). A corpus-driven comparative analysis of modal verbs in Pakistani and British English fictions. *Research on Humanities and Social Sciences* 3(11): 28-37.

Mansoor, S. (2003). Language planning in higher education: issues of access and equity. *The Lahore Journal of Economics*, 8(2), 17–42.

Pennycook, A. (1998). *English and the discourses of colonialism*. Routledge.

Phillipson, R. (1992). *Linguistic imperialism*. Oxford University Press.

Rahman, T. (2005). Passports to privilege: The English medium schools in Pakistan. *Peace and Democracy in South Asia*, 1(1), 24–44.

Rahman, T. (2006). The educational caste system: A survey of schooling and polarization in Pakistan. In R. Zia (Ed.), *Globalization, modernization, and education in Muslim countries* (pp. 151-163). Nova Science Publishers.

Ratcliffe, K. (2005). *Rhetorical listening: Identification, gender, whiteness*. Southern Illinois University Press.

Shahbaz, M., & Yongbin, L. (2015). The role of societal and contextual factors in second language learning motivation: A perspective from tertiary students in Pakistan. *Chinese Journal of Applied Linguistics*, 38(4), 451–471.

Tickoo, M. L. (2006). Language in education. *World Englishes*, 25(1), 167–176.

CONTRIBUTORS

Imran Adeel is an MPhil scholar in the Department of English at the International Islamic University, Islamabad. His areas of study include discourse studies, narratology, systemic functional linguistics, English language, applied linguistics, and critical discourse analysis.

Manzoor Khan Afridi earned his PhD in international relations from Jilin University China and completed postdoctoral research at the University of North Carolina Wilmington, United States. His area of research is Pakistan–China relations, Pakistan's foreign policy, and Pakistan's Tribal Areas. He has produced a number of PhD and MS/MPhil scholars. He has published research papers in national and international journals and serves on various journals' editorial and review boards. His book on Pak–China relations is in process of publication. Dr. Afridi has participated in various national and international conferences as a presenter. He is a member of committees at IIUI and other universities. He is a regular commentator on national and international issues on various TV and radio channels. Currently he serves as associate professor in the Department of Politics and International Relations, International Islamic University, Islamabad.

Manzoor Ahmad is assistant professor in the Department of Politics and International Relations at the International Islamic University, Islamabad. He researches and teaches about international relations, regionalism, the politics of South Asia, and international political economy.

Faiza Anum is a lecturer in the Department of English at the University of Lahore, Pakistan. She has published poems in multiple journals and anthologies, and her poetry has been chosen as a finalist for highly selective prizes.

Muhammad Shahbaz Arif is the former dean of the faculty of the arts and sciences, G. C. University, Faisalabad, Pakistan. He is a prominent researcher in linguistics and an esteemed teacher and supervisor.

Diana Ashe is professor of English and director of the Center for Faculty Leadership at the University of North Carolina Wilmington, where she also served for many years as the director of the Center for Teaching Excellence. A member of the UNCW–IIUI partnership grant team, she publishes in faculty development, environmental rhetoric, and professional writing. She teaches courses in professional and technical writing, rhetorical theory, and, now and then, Appalachian literature.

Pascale Barthe A professor of French at the University of North Carolina Wilmington, Pascale Barthe specializes in early modern France. She is the author of *French Encounters With the Ottomans, 1510–1560*. Her new research project examines political, religious, and literary intersections between the kingdom of Louis XIV and the Safavid and Mughal Empires.

Caroline Clements is a professor of psychology at University of North Carolina Wilmington and former director of the Center for Teaching Excellence and the Center for Faculty Leadership there. She was principal investigator in the Department of State's sponsored partnership program between UNCW and International Islamic University, Islamabad, from 2016 until its completion; she served on the grant team before becoming principal investigator. She delivered many lectures in multiple universities in Pakistan during her five years of travel in that country. Her experience in Pakistan was transformative, and she is grateful for the many enduring friendships she developed there. Her current research specialty is in prevention of partner violence, and she is passionate about teaching, research and, most especially, mentoring.

Lance Cummings an associate professor in the Department of English at the University of North Carolina, specializes in professional writing and rhetoric. An active and engaged scholar and teacher, Professor Cummings has received multiple grants for his work in applied learning and international collaboration, especially involving work in Pakistan and Poland.

Sadaf Farooq is assistant professor in the Department of Politics and International Relations at the International Islamic University, Islamabad. She researches and teaches about diplomacy, terrorism, and international relations.

David Graber research focuses on national cultural traditions and cultural prestige across western and eastern Europe. Since 2010, he has taught courses in Russian and German language, international studies, and eastern European civilization at the University of North Carolina Wilmington.

Mahmood ul Hassan is lecturer in the Department of English at International Islamic University, Islamabad. He holds a BA (Hons.), an MA, and an MS in English language and literature. Currently he is pursuing a PhD in English literature from International Islamic University, Islamabad. His interests are diverse, including literary studies, postcolonial literature, and South Asian society and literature.

Nazia Iqbal is assistant professor and acting chairperson of the Department of Psychology, Female Campus, at the International Islamic University, Islamabad. With a

PhD from Quaid-I-Azam University and a postdoctoral fellowship from Michigan State University, she specializes in social, family, and organizational psychology.

Ubaraj Katawal is associate professor of English at Valdosta State University, Valdosta, Georgia. His specializations include contemporary global Anglophone literature, contemporary American multiethnic literature, and contemporary British literature. His academic works have appeared in numerous journals such as *Postcolonial Text*, *boundary 2*, and *Interdisciplinary Literary Studies*.

Aaron S. King is an associate professor of political science within the Department of Public and International Affairs at the University of North Carolina Wilmington, where his teaching and research focus broadly on American politics, institutions, competition, and representation. His research has been published in various outlets including *American Political Science Review, Journal of Political Science Education, Congress & the Presidency, Social Science Computer Review*, and *Politics & Policy* as well as a monograph entitled, *Unfolding Ambition in Senate Primary Elections: Strategic Politicians and the Dynamics of Candidacy Decisions*.

Amna Mahmood is professor and dean of social sciences in the Department of Politics and International Relations at the International Islamic University, Islamabad. She has published dozens of articles and three books, including *Emerging Independence Between China and the US; Government, State, and Society in South Asia*; and *External Relations of Pakistan*. A member of the UNCW–IIUI partnership grant team, she is a regular analyst for television on topics of political and international relations.

Daniel S. Masters is professor and chair of the Department of International Studies at the University of North Carolina Wilmington. A member of the UNCW–IIUI partnership grant team, he studies and teaches on global terrorism, international relations, comparative politics, Russian/post-Soviet politics, and international security.

Muhammad Khalid Masud delivered the Professor Ahmad Al-Assal Memorial Keynote Speech, at the Second IIUI–UNCW Conference on Local Cities, Foreign Capitals: Finding the Local Anchor in the Global Cultures, October 9–11, 2017, at the International Islamic University, Islamabad. He is the director general of the Islamic Research Institute, International Islamic University, Islamabad. He is the author of many influential volumes and articles on Islam and legal issues.

Michele Parker is professor of educational leadership at the University of North Carolina Wilmington, where she specializes in research methods, nontraditional students, mentoring, technology and education, and educational development. An experienced faculty developer both locally and internationally, she teaches in UNCW's college teaching certificate program and the coaching and mentoring certificate program.

Her research includes dozens of articles and book chapters in leading, peer-reviewed publications along with *Taking Flight: Making Your Center for Teaching and Learning Soar*, which she wrote with Laura Cruz, Brian Smentkowski, and Marina Smitherman.

Rahul Bjørn Parson Rahul Bjørn Parson is an assistant professor in the Department of South and Southeast Asian Studies, University of California, Berkeley. His area of specialization is Hindi literature and literary history, with a particular emphasis on Hindi movements in Eastern Gangetic India.

Naeem Qurban is an associate producer of a current affairs program on ARY News, a leading news channel of Pakistan. He received a bachelor's degree in politics and international relations from International Islamic University, Islamabad and a master's degree in international relations from the same university. His thesis was on "US Policy Towards ISIS in the Middle East."

Anirban Ray is an associate professor and chair of the Professional Writing Program in the Department of English at the University of North Carolina Wilmington. He teaches undergraduate and graduate courses in business writing, cyber-activism, digital composing, information design, globalization and intercultural communication, and research methods. His research interests include digital literacy, applied learning pedagogy, and cross-cultural communication.

Hadeeqa Sarwar acquired the MPhil degree in English linguistics from the National University of Modern Languages, Islamabad, Pakistan. She currently works as a lecturer in the English Department at NUML, Islamabad, Pakistan.

Asma Shaheen is a clinical psychologist and teacher of psychology at PACE (Pakistan Academy of Competitive Exam). She was awarded a Gold Medal when she earned her MS in clinical psychology from International Islamic University, Islamabad. She is also an internationally certified drug addiction therapist (ICAP-I).

Muhammad Sheeraz is professor and chair of the Department of English at the International Islamic University, Islamabad. A member of the UNCW–IIUI grant partnership steering committee, he served as conference secretary for the Second IIUI–UNCW Conference. He is the author of several book-length works, including *Hour of Decline*, *Mughal Sara'ey*, and *Nasloon ne Saza Paee*, in addition to many papers in Higher Education Department-recognized journals, translations, stories, and poems in literary journals.

Muhammad Suleman is a research associate at the Centre for Pakistan and Gulf Studies (CPGS) Islamabad working on political Islam, violent extremism and terrorism, Sufi culture of Pakistan, and regional relations and connectivity. He can be reached at shahid.ndu@gmail.com. He tweets at @M_S_Shahid.

J. Benjamin Taylor is assistant professor of political science in the School of Government and International Affairs at Kennesaw State University in Georgia, United States. He researches and teaches about American politics, focusing on political behavior, including political communication and media effects, Latino politics, and public opinion.

www.ingramcontent.com/pod-product-compliance
Lightning Source LLC
Chambersburg PA
CBHW051040160426
43193CB00010B/1018